THE

STRATEGIC SALES LEADER

Iron Duke Publishing
©Derek Wellington Johnson 2024
ISBN 978-1-7335489-1-5

THE
STRATEGIC
SALES
LEADER

MASTERING THE ART OF
VISION, STRATEGY, AND EXECUTION

DEREK WELLINGTON JOHNSON

Contents

Part IV

COLLABORATION, OFFICE POLITICS, POWER, AND LEADERSHIP

Why You Need This Book

"Whoever can handle the quickest rate of
change is the one who survives."

—Legendary strategist and creator of the OODA Loop, Col. John Boyd

"The illiterate of the 21st century will not be
those who cannot read and write, but those
who cannot learn, unlearn, and relearn."

—Alvin Toffler

This book was written for four types of people:

1. CEO/President or leader for ANY organization with a B2B sales team. If you don't know what a great sales leader does, how do you know if your sales leadership are doing their jobs? This book will give you the critical information you need to secure your sales team's success.

2. Current sales leader: Reading this will ensure you're keeping up with the latest and best practices in sales leadership. Even the most seasoned and successful sales leadership veteran will learn many new ways to stay successful.

3. Newly promoted to sales leadership: Most great salespeople promoted into sales leadership roles fail. Reading this book will make sure you don't become another statistic and give you the highest probability of great success.

4. Aspiring sales leader: You eventually want to get promoted into sales leadership and need to fully understand what it takes to succeed.

With few exceptions, if you were in a sales leadership role during the Covid-19 pandemic, you learned how quickly your life and your sales pipeline could change. Supply chains collapsed, lead times exploded, millions became sick and died. Whatever we used to think was normal evaporated and those of us who adapted rapidly to the new "normal" not only survived, we thrived.

When the economy imploded in 2008, many of us lost our homes, our jobs and in some cases our careers. Despite the skyrocketing unemployment and global instability that sealed the fate of many, some of our fellow sales professionals with an eye for opportunity and a nose for money flourished.

If you were in sales when the Twin Towers came down on 9/11, you remember the abject horror of wondering what was going to happen next. The collective panic we felt first as humans and then as sales professionals. Yet some amongst us managed to find a path out of the dark cave of despair into the light of success.

The question is why? Why did some sales teams surpass their quotas while others imploded under the pressure? The answer to that question (and many others you may have not even thought to ask yet) is the premise of this book.

If the Covid-19 pandemic taught us anything, it's that our sales plans and strategies, no matter how well thought out, can be irreparably damaged or destroyed at a moment's notice.[1] The subsequent supply chain issues that followed added another level of pain to the equation.

We were awash in a sea of uncertainty. Will we be able to hit our quotas? Will we be able to meet in person with our key clients and partners? Which variant of Covid is going to disrupt us this month? Will the components for our products be available? Will our team remain healthy enough to meet critical deadlines?

As if that wasn't enough, the very painful human toll beat us down even further. Many of us lost family members and friends, colleagues, and co-workers. The relentlessness of it all was enough to pummel any optimism we had. Yet we continued, not necessarily because of our inner strength (though it certainly helped) we carried on because we had no choice. Stopping wasn't an option. As sales leaders, our team, and our family looked to us for answers, whether we could provide them. As Winston Churchill once said, "If you're going through hell, keep going."

Add in the passive and active saboteurs within your organization such as the head of marketing who doesn't know how to get you good leads, or create good messaging for your team, or the head of products who is convinced they think they know more about selling than you do and never misses a chance to remind you. We won't even get into new product launches that

---

1   Fairlie, R., & Fossen, F. M. (2021, March 31). The early impacts of the COVID-19 pandemic on business sales. National Center for Biotechnology Information. https://www.ncbi.nlm.nih.gov/pmc/articles/PMC8009687/

don't get launched on time (vapor ware), or products that are buggy and don't work as advertised, yet your team is expected to sell them.

So, why this book and why now? Because we learned in the most painful of ways that what we're doing as leaders simply wasn't good enough. The world we thought we lived in had been torn from underneath us and a new way of leading and thinking about the future was and is required.

Get comfortable being uncomfortable. Know that uncertainty will be and forever remain a fundamental part of our reality. You don't have to like it. Just acknowledge it and act appropriately.

If your organization viewed sales strategy formulation as an annual event, you now know that this simply won't do in our new world. So, what then? We need to create a fast moving, real time, strategic mechanism that responds as each new threat rears its fearsome head.

This is not just about strategic sales theory, it's about application. This is not just about sales leadership motivation; it's about instilling a leadership mindset within your entire organization. To do anything less is to doom your organization to permanent obsolescence.

I don't trivialize the extreme pain, suffering and agony that millions feel when the world is in a state of upheaval. Quite the contrary, however, those of us in sales will always have a responsibility to make a sale no matter what is occurring on this planet. Don't expect that to change anytime soon.

I make a promise to you that if you invest in this book, and faithfully apply the concepts I share with you, YOU WILL

SUCCEED. If you don't, donate the book to your local library, email me and I will send you a full refund. You can find my contact info at the end of the book.

Read on, learn and apply.

Overview of Vision, Strategy, and Execution

This book is structured around three fundamental pillars:

1. **Vision**: The foundation of any successful sales strategy is a clear and compelling vision. This section will help you develop a profound understanding of your market, recognize emerging opportunities, and envision the future you aim to create. Through practical checklists and real-world examples, you will learn how to craft a vision that inspires and aligns your team to accomplish more than they ever thought possible.

2. **Strategy**: Strategy is where your vision begins to take shape. This section delves into the mechanics of strategic planning, from understanding competitive dynamics to setting actionable goals. You'll discover how to formulate strategies that are not only ambitious but also achievable, ensuring that your sales efforts are focused and impactful.

3. **Execution**: The best strategies are only as good as their implementation. This final pillar focuses on the execution of your sales strategies, covering everything from recruiting, hiring, training team alignment and leadership to performance monitoring and adaptation. Practical tips and strategic insights will equip you to turn plans into actions and results.

How This Book Will Transform Your Approach

By the end of this book, you will not only have a thorough understanding of the principles of strategic sales leadership but also possess the tools and confidence to apply them. Whether you're a CEO, a seasoned VP of Sales aiming to refine your approach or a new Director of Sales looking to make your mark, this book will change how you think about sales leadership. With detailed frameworks, interactive elements, and actionable advice, "The Strategic Sales Leader" is not just a guide but a roadmap to achieving exceptional leadership and sales excellence in your organization.

This book promises to be an indispensable resource in your journey to becoming a strategic sales leader who not only meets but exceeds expectations in today's demanding business environment.

Part I

VISION

"Leadership is the capacity to translate vision into reality."

—Warren Bennis

"A team aligned behind a vision will move mountains."

—Kevin Rose

"If you want to build a ship, don't drum up the men to gather wood, divide the work, and give orders. Instead, teach them to yearn for the vast and endless sea."

—Antoine de Saint-Exupéry

"When Aeschines spoke, they said, 'How well he speaks.' But when Demosthenes spoke, they said, 'Let us march!"

—Plutarch

Throughout this section, we will delve into the key elements that contribute to the development of a compelling sales vision. We will discuss the process of understanding market dynamics, client needs, and competitive landscape to gain valuable insights that inform your vision. We will also explore the art of envisioning the future, thinking beyond the present, and setting ambitious but achievable goals that align with your organization's broader strategic objectives.

Furthermore, we will examine the importance of effective communication in articulating and cascading the sales vision throughout the organization. By communicating the vision in an exciting and relatable manner, sales leaders can ignite enthusiasm, build buy-in, and foster a shared sense of purpose among team members.

By the end of this section, you will have a clear understanding of the critical role that a strategic sales vision plays in driving success. Armed with this knowledge, you will be equipped to craft a vision that inspires and motivates your sales teams, sets a clear direction for action, and propels your organization towards achieving remarkable results. So, let us embark on this journey of vision-building and unlock your potential as a strategic sales leader.

CHAPTER 1

Becoming a Visionary Leader People Want to Follow

"If you command wisely, you'll be obeyed cheerfully."

- Thomas Fuller

"The very essence of leadership is that you have to have vision. You can't blow an uncertain trumpet."

- Theodore M. Hesburgh

"Vision without action is just a dream, action without vision just passes the time, and vision with action can change the world."

- Nelson Mandela

According to numerous research studies conducted and published over the past decade, fifty percent of all leaders and managers are failures. More specifically, most people in leadership positions are "estimated to be ineffective (that is, a disappointment, incompetent, a mis-hire, or a complete failure) in their current roles." [2]

---

2   Elaine Biech, The ASTD Leadership Handbook (Alexandria, VA: Association for Talent Development, 2010)

The Corporate Executive Board (CEB) estimates that 50 percent to 70 percent of executives fail within 18 months of taking on their role, whether they were hired externally or promoted from within.[3]

This failure rate is not just limited to the initial months; even two years after executive transitions, between 27 percent and 46 percent of them are considered failures or disappointments. A similar study by CEB Global suggests that 60 percent of new managers fail within the first 24 months of their new role.[4]

The challenge in leadership success is further underscored by a Fortune survey, which reveals that only 7 percent of CEOs believe their companies are building effective global leaders, and a mere 10 percent affirm that their leadership development initiatives have a clear business impact.[5]

Despite significant investments in leadership development, with U.S. companies spending nearly $14 billion annually, there appears to be a gap between the resources devoted to nurturing new leaders and the actual effectiveness of these efforts.[6]

These findings highlight the critical need for more

---

3   Ettore, M. (2020, March 13). Why Most New Executives Fail -- And Four Things Companies Can Do About It. Forbes. https://www.forbes.com/councils/forbescoachescouncil/2020/03/13/why-most-new-executives-fail-and-four-things-companies-can-do-about-it/

4   Arruda, W. (2023, February 15). Why Most New Managers Fail And How To Prevent It. Forbes. https://www.forbes.com/sites/williamarruda/2023/02/15/why-most-new-managers-fail-and-how-to-prevent-it/

5   Feser, C., Nielsen, N., & Rennie, M. (2017, August). What's missing in leadership development? McKinsey Quarterly. https://www.mckinsey.com/~/media/mckinsey/featured%20insights/leadership/whats%20missing%20in%20leadership%20development/whats-missing-in-leadership-development.pdf

6   Gurdjian, P., Halbeisen, T., & Lane, K. (2014, January 1). Why leadership-development programs fail. McKinsey Quarterly. https://www.mckinsey.com/featured-insights/leadership/why-leadership-development-programs-fail

effective leadership development programs and the importance of addressing the high failure rates among leaders and managers. If your goal is to beat the odds and not be amongst the statistics above, read, learn, and apply what you're going to read in this book.

If you're an aspiring leader or already in a leadership role, you need to be aware of the high failure rate of leaders and commit to becoming the best leader you can be.

No one cares how great your vision is until they realize they want to follow you. The challenge is in getting people to willingly follow you. General George S. Patton once said, "Always do everything you ask of those you command."

Over 2,300 years ago, Xenophon the Greek military leader, mercenary, philosopher, and historian advised us that "Leaders must always set the highest standard. In a summer campaign, leaders must always endure their share of the sun and the heat and, in winter, the cold and the frost. In all labors, leaders must prove tireless if they want to enjoy the trust of their followers." It goes without saying that you must lead by example. Anything less and your team will not respect you.

Xenophon was a student of Socrates, the ancient Greek philosopher who lived in Athens during the 5th century BCE. While his fellow student Plato went in one direction, Xenophon went in another. By the time he was 26, he would become Commander-in-Chief of the Greek Army.

Socrates had a lot to say on leadership and how leaders earned respect. In the book Memorabilia, Xenophon[7] wrote

---

7   Xenophon. Memorabilia. Translated by Amy L. Bonnette. Agora Editions, 2001

about this. One day, Socrates is engaged in a conversation with a new promoted cavalry commander. As Xenophon at one time was also a cavalry commander, some experts believe the story he wrote about is autobiographical. When Socrates asked why the young cavalry commander wanted to be a leader despite the inherent risks, he responded with a few different answers, but Socrates kept digging until finally the young officer responded it was because he wanted to leave the Athenian cavalry better than he found it. If your team knows you're trying to make them better than you found them, you will quickly be on your path to becoming respected.

Then Socrates began to question how exactly he would leave them better than he found them? The young officer responded with all the diverse ways he would help them to become better such as improve the cavalry mounts, train the horses and men on equestrian skills, and then train them on various cavalry tactics. Socrates paused and then said, 'And have you considered how to make the men obey you? Because without that, horses and men, however good and gallant, are of no use.'

'True but what is the best way of encouraging them to obey Socrates?' asked the young officer.

To which Socrates responded, 'Well, I suppose you know that under all conditions, human beings are most willing to obey those they believe are the best. Thus in sickness they most readily obey the doctor, on board ship, the pilot, on a farm, the farmer, whom they think to be the most skilled in his business.'

'Yes, certainly,' agreed his student.

Socrates: "Then in this matter of cavalry also we may reasonably suppose that he who is looked upon as knowing his business best will command the readiest obedience."

Student: "If then, I can prove to my troopers that I am better than all of them, will that suffice to win their obedience?"

Socrates: "Yes, if along with that you can teach them that obedience to you brings greater glory and surer safety to themselves."

People will readily follow individuals they believe possess superior qualifications or greater expertise in a specific domain.

To command respect and eager obedience, you must KNOW your job inside and out and know it better than anyone on your team. Which is one of the reasons (hopefully) that you're reading this book.

Once you've established this, then you can move on towards creating an inspiring vision for the team. But first we need to define what leadership and management are, and how they differ.

What Is the Difference Between Leadership and Management?

> "Management is doing things right; leadership is doing the right things."
>
> —Peter Drucker

> "Management is about coping with complexity. Leadership, by contrast, is about coping with change."
>
> —John Kotter

Before we dive into the differences between sales leadership and sales management, we need to understand what leadership is versus management. Leaders do the right things; managers do things right. Leaders focus on the complexity of change; managers focus on the complexity of routine. Leadership and management are two distinct ways of organizing and motivating people. Leadership is about inspiring and guiding individuals or teams towards a goal, while management is about establishing systems and processes to ensure that work is completed efficiently and effectively. In general, leadership focuses on vision and direction, while management focuses on execution and implementation. Leaders create value, while managers count value. Leaders focus on change and growth, managers focus on stability and maintaining the status quo. In order to succeed you'll need to be able to lead or manage depending on the circumstances. And remember, some managers do not lead, and some leaders do not manage.

Now that we have defined the difference between leadership and management let's talk about the difference between sales management and sales leadership. Unfortunately, the traditional sales management role is simply a person who manages the sales team and pressures them relentlessly to make sure they achieve their quota. Think of them more of a punitive group of people than a supportive group of people. Managers in most organizations lead from a fear-based perspective saying things like, "You better get your numbers up or else you're going to be put on a PIP (Productivity Improvement Plan) and walked out the door."

If you ask salespeople what they think about their sales leadership or sales management, many will tell you, "All they do is hammer me all day for my quota and ask me about my pipeline. They don't do anything to support me and to help me succeed."

That right there is a difference between sales leadership and sales management. The sales leader will actively help their team succeed. They will create a strategic framework and once they have the framework in place they will be able use strategic execution to carry out that strategy. They'll give them the tools they need to succeed, whether that means sales and marketing collateral, help with lead generation, the ability to attend the right trade shows, and the crucial time to focus on sales tasks as opposed to administrative tasks.

The other thing that a sales leader does is create a cohesive team in which the efforts of one salesperson help build on the efforts of another salesperson in a different territory. Why is that important? because most salespeople are like islands on their own in the middle of nowhere. They're completely independent silos. If one salesperson has a great quarter, or a great year, none of their success helps the other members of the team in terms of building credibility for the organization. This is especially important if you're trying to enter a new vertical or maybe expand into an existing vertical or help launch a new product.

Yes, most companies will add new logos to their corporate PowerPoint presentation that salespeople can point to during a sales meeting, however doing so doesn't create a cohesive strategy and tactical plan to unify your team's forces and efforts. Most sales organizations just have separate people flailing away, painfully crawling their way towards quota attainment.

The sales leader also needs to motivate and inspire their team. Not the kind of motivation or inspiration that comes from a sales commission or SPIFF. You have to understand the inner psychology of each of your respective salespeople to help them get the most out of themselves. There is an old saying that says you can either light a fire underneath someone or you can light a fire within someone. Which do you think gets better results? Is it the individual who is internally motivated to work smarter, work harder and work longer than the person who is driven by the fire underneath them, meaning the fear of being fired, or of being pressured and brow beaten?

Strategic Leadership and How to Earn Your Team's Respect

To earn your team's respect, you have to lead by example. When it makes sense, travel with your team. Do it to help them position themselves to win more opportunities and do it so they know that you're talking to talk and walking the walk. They need to know that you're not sitting in some ivory castle while they slug it out in the trenches. If you also have to deal with flights being repeatedly canceled, being stuck in traffic while heading to see a prospective new client, sleeping in hotels with bad beds that leave your back feeling like someone took a bat to it, and eating fast food on the run between meetings, your team will see that you are one of them. It will also give a clear perspective of what they regularly must endure.

This concept of leading by example isn't new. Alexander The Great was deeply respected by his soldiers despite being young. A prime example was when he said this to his troops: "Perhaps you will say that, in my position as your commander, I had none of the labors and distress which you had to endure to win for me what I have won. But does any man among you honestly feel that he has suffered more for me than I have suffered for him? Come now, if you are wounded, strip and show your wounds, and I will show mine. There is no part of my body but my back which has not a scar; not a weapon a man may grasp or fling the mark of which I do not carry upon me. I have sword-cuts from close fight; arrows have pierced me, missiles from catapults bruised my flesh; again, and again I have been struck by stones or clubs—and all for your sakes: for your glory and your gain."[8]

Let's take a moment to break down the significance of his speech and what it means if you wish to be respected by your team.

This quote from Alexander the Great speaks to his perceived shared hardships and experiences with his soldiers and is an appeal to solidarity and mutual respect. He seeks to remind them that, despite his position as a commander, he does not shy away from the front lines and does not put his soldiers through anything he wouldn't face himself. This is a crucial part of being respected and followed. Your team must see you as an example to be emulated.

The first part, "Perhaps you will say that, in my position as your commander, I had none of the labors and distress which you had to endure to win for me what I have won," presents a possible accusation that Alexander might have had an easier time due to his high status. He was responding to rumors or grumblings from some of his soldiers.

He then retorts, "But does any man among you honestly feel

---

8   Arrian. The Landmark Arrian: The Campaigns of Alexander. Edited by James Romm, translated by Pamela Mensch, series edited by Robert B. Strassler. (New York: Anchor, 2012)

that he has suffered more for me than I have suffered for him?" implying that he, too, has faced great hardships—perhaps even more than those faced by his soldiers.

His invitation to compare wounds is a master class in showing that he not only talks the talk, and he walks the walk. "Come now, if you are wounded, strip and show your wounds, and I will show mine," is both literal and symbolic. It's a gesture that underscores his personal bravery and involvement in the battles, his willingness to be injured for the cause.

"There is no part of my body but my back which has not a scar," Alexander emphasizes his participation in the heat of the battle, his scars serving as evidence that he never turned his back to the enemy.

"Not a weapon a man may grasp or fling the mark of which I do not carry upon me. I have sword-cuts from close fight; arrows have pierced me, missiles from catapults bruised my flesh; again and again I have been struck by stones or clubs," these lines reiterate his engagement in combat and his determination to lead from the front. Do you lead from the front, or watch safely from behind?

His concluding lines, "and all for your sakes: for your glory and your gain," assert that his sacrifices and sufferings were not solely for his personal gain, but for the benefit of his men, their glory, and their prosperity. Your team MUST know that you are fighting WITH them and FOR them.

Overall, the quote reflects Alexander's leadership style and philosophy of leading by example. It also shows how he sought to inspire loyalty, respect, and trust among his soldiers by demonstrating his personal commitment to their shared cause.

Thankfully, we don't have to go through actual combat to earn the respect of our team, but it's important to remember that by earning your team's respect, it makes it significantly easier for them to buy into your vision and to follow it passionately.

As Peter Drucker once said, "Leadership is lifting a person's vision to high sights. The raising of a person's performance to a higher standard, the building of a personality beyond its normal limitations."[9]

Commander's Intent and Developing a Strategic Sales Vision

> "It doesn't make sense to hire smart people and tell them what to do; we hire smart people so they can tell us what to do."
>
> —Steve Jobs

Developing a strategic sales vision is an integral part of sales leadership that will help keep your team on track. However, for a strategic vision to be impactful, effective, and achieve results it only works within an organization that's focused on Commander's Intent versus Command and Control.

We need to define Command and Control versus Commander's Intent. Command and Control[10] is the standard hierarchical structure for most companies' organizations. It's a top-down structure in which the boss pushes orders down to

---

9   Peter F. Drucker, The Practice of Management (New York: Harper Business, 2006)

10   U.S. Marine Corps. Command and Control (Washington, D.C.: Department of the Navy, 2018). https://www.marines.mil/Portals/1/Publications/MCDP%206.pdf

their subordinates all the way down through however many layers there are in the organization. One of the problems with Command and Control is that nothing gets done until the order comes from way above and that slows things down. Whereas Commander's Intent[11] simply means that the one main objective or mission that your team is tasked with accomplishing is given to the team. How they achieve the goal or mission is up to the subordinates. Legendary General George S. Patton was a Commander's Intent type of leader.[12] He once said, "Never tell people how to do things. Tell them what to do and they will surprise you with their ingenuity."

By creating a strategic vision along with a Commander's Intent style of leadership you're empowering your team to move quickly, to make good decisions, and because they are closest to the action, they will impress you with the decisions that they make. This is why crafting a vision that inspires and resonates within your team and drives meaningful results is tied to Commander's Intent. If or when anyone in your organization is at a loss as to what they need to do at any given point, they know that they have your strategic sales vision to refer to and guide them. This will reduce the amount of calls and emails to you and upper management, which will help shorten the sales cycle on your organization's end.

You may be asking, "What if I don't trust my team to make their own decisions?" You have two choices, either train them

11   Patterson, J. S. (1995). COMMANDER'S INTENT: Its Evolution in the United States Army. Washington, D.C.: U.S. Department of the Army. https://apps.dtic.mil/sti/pdfs/ADA301158.pdf

12   Alan Axelrod, Patton on Leadership: Strategic Lessons for Corporate Warfare (Englewood Cliffs, NJ: Prentice Hall, 1999)

to gradually make more of their own decisions or cut them loose.[13] Making good decisions is a skill that can be taught. You may need to begin by allowing them to make small and less consequential decisions. As they experience success, this helps to build inner confidence and then you can expand the decision-making boundaries. If certain members on your team don't get better at making their own decisions, you'll have to take a long hard look at firing them and replacing them with someone else. The assumption being that they're not hitting or surpassing their quota.

13   David Horsager, The Trust Edge: How Top Leaders Gain Faster Results, Deeper Relationships, and a Stronger Bottom Line (New York: Free Press, 2012)

CHAPTER 2

Crafting Your Strategic Sales Vision

"The problems of the world cannot possibly be solved
by skeptics or cynics whose horizons are limited by
the obvious realities. We need men who can dream
of things that never were and ask 'why not?'."

—John F. Kennedy[14]

"Action without vision is only passing time,
vision without action is merely daydreaming, but
vision with action can change the world."

—Nelson Mandela

As you may have noticed already, I'm going to be using many military and battlefield analogies. The business world and the battlefield have many similarities. Sales is a zero-sum game, you either win the deal or you lose it. Like in combat, there is no prize for second place. Thankfully, in the sales world, no one is shooting at us. Just like many battles have been lost to poor planning, so companies can be severely damaged. Mistakes in combat

---

14   Kennedy, J. F. (1963, June 28). Address Before the Irish Parliament. John F. Kennedy Presidential Library and Museum. https://www.jfklibrary.org/archives/other-resources/john-f-kennedy-speeches/irish-parliament-19630628

get people killed, mistakes in the business world can cause the loss of market share, jobs and in some cases, bankruptcy.

The main reason for using military analogies is to help train your mind to think both strategically and tactically. It's commonplace to see someone mistake strategy for tactics or vice versa. Every time you read a military metaphor, stop a moment, and reflect on how the central premise can help you with your strategy and tactics.

Whether you and your sales team have been tasked to fight for increased market share or introduce a new product, you're going to feel like you're going to war. Your success or failure will be dictated by many variables. The ones you can control (leadership, strategy, and tactics) will be the foundation upon which generals have also depended on for thousands of years. So, it is these similarities that we will use to guide us.

Vision and the Importance of Having a BHAG: Big Hairy Audacious Goal

"I will never forget when [Franklin D.] Roosevelt announced that we would build thirty thousand fighter planes. I was on the task force that worked on our economic strength, and we had just reached the conclusion that we could build at most four thousand. We thought, "For goodness' sake- he's senile!" Two years later we built fifty thousand. I don't know whether he knew, or if he just realized unless you set objectives very high, you don't achieve anything at all."

– Peter Drucker in an interview with Bill Moyers in 1988.[15]

---

15   Peter Drucker: Father of Modern Management, November 17, 1988 https://billmoyers. com/content/peter-drucker/

"If your dreams don't scare you, they are too small."

- Richard Branson

When President John F. Kennedy said, "This nation should commit itself to achieving the goal, before this decade is out, of landing a man on the moon and returning him safely to earth,"[16] he introduced BHAG to the world. BHAG, or a Big Hairy Audacious Goal is a way to add a higher level of motivation, inspiration and enthusiasm to your team.[17]

The United States' Apollo program, specifically the BHAG set by President John F. Kennedy in 1961 was a goal set during the Cold War and was as much a political statement and demonstration of technological superiority as it was a feat of exploration and science.

The Apollo program[18] required significant advancements in technology, massive financial investment, and intense human effort. At the time, the goal seemed almost unachievable given the state of space technology. However, it served as a powerful motivator for the National Aeronautics and Space Administration (NASA) and its partners. The successful Apollo 11 moon landing in 1969, just eight years after the goal was set, marked a historic achievement in human space exploration and is a classic example of a BHAG being successfully realized.

---

16   John F. Kennedy moon landing speech, May 25, 1961 http://earthsky.org/human-world/this-date-in-science-kennedy-speech-ignites-dreams-of-moon-landing/

17   Jim Collins and Jerry I. Porras, Built to Last: Successful Habits of Visionary Companies (New York: HarperBusiness, 1994)

18   Andrew Chaikin, A Man on the Moon: The Voyages of the Apollo Astronauts, Illustrated ed. (New York: Penguin Books, 2007

In the annals of history and the battlefield, audacious goals have played a pivotal role in rallying troops, achieving victory, and shaping destinies. The term "Big Hairy Audacious Goal" was popularized by Jim Collins and Jerry Porras in their book "Built to Last." A BHAG is akin to a mission that is so audacious, so daring, that it becomes the driving force, the very soul, of an organization's existence. For a sales team, having a BHAG can help give them that extra fuel to get to the next level.

At its essence, a BHAG is a strategic business statement similar to a vision statement, which is created to focus an organization on a single medium-to-long-term organization-wide goal, which is audacious, likely to be externally questionable, but not internally regarded as impossible. Yes, some people may think you or it are insane, but that's a normal response some will have. BHAGs are meant to be clear and compelling, serving as a unifying focal point of effort and acting as a powerful motivator for team spirit.

While we might not realize it, we encounter BHAG's in our day-to-day world. For example:

Google's AI Advancements: Google, now under Alphabet Inc., set a BHAG to organize the world's information and make it universally accessible and useful. Part of this goal includes pioneering in artificial intelligence and machine learning.

Amazon's Global Marketplace: Amazon's BHAG was to build a place where people can buy anything online. This goal has expanded to not just being the largest e-commerce platform but also venturing into cloud computing, digital streaming, artificial intelligence, and more.

Apple's Innovation in Personal Technology: Apple set a

BHAG around reinventing mobile phones with the iPhone. This goal has led to a series of innovations in personal technology devices.

Microsoft's Computing Accessibility: Microsoft's BHAG was to have a computer on every desk and in every home. Over the years, this goal has evolved with the company's growth and the changing technology landscape.

Determining Your Organizational BHAG: Big Hairy Audacious Goal

It's crucial for every organization, regardless of its size or industry, to establish a clear and compelling vision for the future. One of the most powerful tools in your strategic arsenal is defining your BHAG. In this section, we'll explore what a BHAG is, why it's essential, and how to determine the right one for your organization.

Why Having a BHAG Matters

1. **Fosters Alignment:** On the battlefield, as in the boardroom, a well-defined BHAG acts as a rallying point. It aligns troops, or in our case, a sales team towards a common objective. It instills discipline and direction, minimizing distractions and divisions.

2. **Motivates and Engages:** In the heat of battle, a clear and audacious goal motivates troops to move mountains. In sales, a BHAG ignites the fire within your people, turning ordinary individuals into extraordinary achievers.

3. **Attracts Talent:** Just as soldiers flock to a charismatic leader, top talent is drawn to organizations with bold visions. A compelling BHAG acts as a beacon, attracting individuals who relish the challenge of making the impossible possible.

4. **Drives Innovation:** In warfare, adapting and innovating are often the keys to survival. In the sales arena, a BHAG compels us to push boundaries, to innovate relentlessly in pursuit of the extraordinary.

5. **Measures Progress:** On the battlefield, progress is measured in ground gained. In sales, a BHAG provides a yardstick, enabling us to measure how far we've come and how far we have yet to go.

Determining Your Organizational BHAG: A Strategic Maneuver

As General Patton would say, "A good plan, violently executed now, is better than a perfect plan next week."[19] Let's outline the strategic maneuvers required to determine your BHAG. I have a special place in my heart for General Patton because my father served with him in World War II, in Patton's 3rd Army. When you analyze Patton's audacity, speed and ferocity in battle, you quickly realize that we in sales can apply that same mindset.

---

19   George S. Patton, War As I Knew It, edited by Paul D. Harkins (New York: Houghton Mifflin Harcourt, 1995)

The 22 Steps On How to Apply BHAG in Your Sales Organization

Step 1: Reflect on Your Core Purpose and Values

In battle, understanding the purpose of your mission is paramount. Know why you exist, what values you uphold, and let them guide you. Your BHAG should embody these core tenets.

In the chaos of battle, or the challenges of sales, a steadfast adherence to core principles is paramount. Before defining a BHAG, it is essential to have a deep understanding of your organization's core purpose and values. What is the essence of your existence? How do you wish to impact the world? Your BHAG should resonate harmoniously with these foundational pillars, ensuring that it is not just an ambitious aspiration but a genuine reflection of your organizational identity.

Step 2: Conduct a SWOT Analysis

General Patton would advise that before entering the battlefield, one must assess the lay of the land.[18] In business, conduct a SWOT analysis to identify your strengths, weaknesses, opportunities, and threats. Your BHAG should leverage your strengths, address weaknesses, exploit opportunities, and counter threats. We will discuss doing a SWOT analysis later in the book.

Patton once said, "Success is how high you bounce when you hit the bottom." In both warfare and sales, understanding your strengths, weaknesses, opportunities, and threats is akin to knowing the lay of the land before a battle. Your BHAG should leverage your strengths, address your weaknesses, exploit opportunities, and counter potential threats.

Step 3: Define the Timeframe

In both warfare and sales, timing is everything. A BHAG should have a period that synchronizes with your industry's evolution and your organization's capabilities. It should be ambitious but achievable within this timeframe.

In the fluidity of battle or the ever-evolving landscape of business, timing is of the essence. A BHAG is a long-term vision, typically spanning two to five years into the future. It should be both ambitious and realistic within this timeframe. Consider how your industry and market are likely to evolve during this period, and how your BHAG can position your organization as a pioneer or disruptor.

Step 4: Make It Specific and Measurable

In both military operations and sales strategies, ambiguity is the enemy. Your BHAG should be precise and measurable, leaving no room for misinterpretation. Rather than vague aspirations, it should be a meticulously crafted statement with clear objectives and quantifiable criteria for success.

Step 5: Keep It Audacious

As General Patton would say, "Audacity, audacity, always audacity." Your BHAG should be audacious, daring, and bold. It should stretch your sales team beyond its comfort zone, just as Patton's tactics pushed the boundaries of conventional warfare.

Step 6: Seek Input and Feedback

Great leaders, whether on the battlefield or in the boardroom, value the insights of their teams. Gather input and feedback from a spectrum of stakeholders, including your leadership team, employees, clients, and external partners. This collaborative approach not only enriches your BHAG but also fosters commitment and enthusiasm among those entrusted with its realization.

Step 7: Test for Resonance

In the chaos of war or the complexities of business, resonance is the key to unwavering commitment. Your BHAG should evoke emotions, inspire unwavering passion, and ignite a deep sense of purpose among your workforce.

Step 8: Assess Feasibility

A sales plan without the means to execute is futile. Assess the feasibility of your BHAG. Do you have the resources, capabilities, and determination to accomplish it?

Even the boldest battle plans must be grounded in reality. Assess whether your organization possesses the capabilities, resources, and viable pathways to achieve your BHAG. Unrealistic goals can lead to frustration and demotivation, much like charging headlong into an unwinnable battle.

Step 9: Communicate and Iterate

Communication is the linchpin of effective leadership. Once

your BHAG is defined, communicate it extensively throughout your organization. Make it an integral part of your culture, and consistently reinforce its importance. However, be prepared to iterate and adapt as circumstances change. A BHAG is not set in stone; it's a guiding star that can be adjusted if necessary.

Step 10: Create Milestones and Roadmaps

In the fluidity of battle or the complexities of sales, a comprehensive strategy is essential. Break down your BHAG into manageable milestones and create roadmaps outlining the specific steps, resources, and timelines required for each milestone. Much like military campaigns, these tactical plans are essential for guiding your troops toward the overarching strategic goal.

Step 11: Foster a Culture of Innovation

In the battle for innovation, pioneers emerge victorious. Encourage your teams to think creatively and take calculated risks. Invest in research and development efforts to stay at the front of technological advancements.

Step 12: Invest in Talent Development

Just as a general train their soldiers, invest in the development of your sales team. Identify skill gaps within your organization and provide training and development programs to upskill your employees. Additionally, consider strategic hiring to bring in sales rainmakers, and experts who can accelerate progress.

Step 13: Build Strategic Partnerships

Even the most renowned generals form alliances when necessary. Seek strategic partnerships with other companies, educational institutions, or organizations that share your vision. These partnerships can provide access to complementary expertise and resources. Doing so will bolster your capabilities and expand your reach.

Step 14: Monitor Key Performance Indicators (KPIs)

On the battlefield, generals watch the frontlines. In sales, establish and monitor KPIs that keep you apprised of your progress.[20] Establish and regularly monitor Key Performance Indicators (KPIs) that align with your BHAG. KPIs provide a quantifiable means of tracking progress and ensuring that your efforts remain on course. Examples could include market share gains, revenue growth rates, or new logos (new clients).

Step 15: Embrace Agile Project Management

In the fluidity of battle or the dynamic world of sales, adaptability is paramount. Embrace agile project management methodologies to adjust quickly to changing circumstances. Agile principles facilitate rapid adaptation, a crucial trait when working towards a long-term goal.[21]

---

20   Bernie Smith, KPI Checklists (Practical guide to implementing KPIs and performance measurement, Metric Press, 2016).

21   Belinda Waldock, Being Agile in Business: Discover Faster, Smarter, Leaner Ways to Work (Pearson, 2015)

Step 16: Review and Revise the BHAG as Needed

A visionary leader, whether in a military campaign or sales strategy, knows when to adapt. Regularly review and, if necessary, revise your BHAG to ensure it remains relevant and attainable. Flexibility and adaptability are essential characteristics of a dynamic organization.

Step 17: Build Resilience and Adaptability

In the chaos of war or the turbulence of sales, resilience and adaptability are vital. Implement vigorous risk management and scenario planning to prepare for unforeseen challenges. Be prepared to pivot if market conditions or technological advancements require it.

Step 18: Engage clients and Stakeholders

On the sales battleground, clients and stakeholders are your allies. Involve them in the pursuit of your BHAG. Seek their feedback and input to ensure that your goals align with their needs and expectations. Engaged clients can become strong advocates and supporters of your vision.

Step 19: Foster Cross-Functional Collaboration

In warfare, divisions spell disaster. In business, break down silos, and foster cross-functional collaboration to ensure unity and constructive collaboration

Breaking down silos and fostering cross-functional collaboration is essential when working towards an audacious goal.

Encourage teams from different departments to work together, share insights, and pool resources for maximum impact. Just as in a military operation, synergy is often the key to victory.

Step 20: Measure and Communicate Impact

Just as a general reports to superiors, measure and communicate the impact of your efforts to our bosses. On the field of battle or the realm of sales, impact speaks volumes. Regularly measure and communicate the impact of your organization's efforts toward the BHAG. Share success stories, milestones achieved, and the positive changes your organization is making in your industry and the world. Effective communication reinforces commitment and inspires confidence in your vision.

Step 21: Stay Informed and Anticipate Disruptions

In both war and sales, staying ahead requires intelligence and foresight. Stay informed about emerging trends and potential disruptions and be prepared to adapt your strategies accordingly.

Step 22: Celebrate Achievements Along the Way

Acknowledgment and celebration are crucial elements of motivation and morale. Celebrate your achievements, both big and small, along the journey toward your BHAG. Recognition reinforces the significance of your audacious goal and inspires continued dedication.

Your Vision

We've talked about the importance of having a BHAG. Now we'll discuss how to build upon this to create your sales vision. You can't be a great leader without the capacity to inspire and move others. The same holds true for great sales leadership. Yes, salespeople are "coin operated," but if you want to mold your sales team from a loose group of mercenaries to a cohesive unit hell bent on fighting and winning no matter what the cost, you must have a vision and be able to share that vision in a compelling way.

Small visions don't inspire people, massive ones do. As a sales leader, your job is to create a massive vision that is both audacious and frightening. Why frightening? Because if the vision isn't so massive and intimidating, it means you're playing it safe.

Vision creates the 30,000-foot level of what you want to achieve as a sales leader. By creating a worthy vision, inspiration will follow. Once your team is inspired, you can then collaborate with them to create a powerful strategy. Once the strategy has been given life, you can create a structure that will help ensure that the execution will be successful. Everything that happens after that is action.

Strategy without vision will lead to failure. Action without structure will lead to failure. Action without vision will lead to stagnation. Why? Because you lack the inspiration and motivation that will help the team move forward when they inevitably will hit obstacles.

If you're with an organization whose CEO, President or division leader has a grand vision, then this will be easier to accomplish. If that's not the case, that's okay, because you can still create your own vision for the team to aspire to. Remember, creating a vision is not a one-time event. It requires ongoing effort to keep it alive and relevant. Be flexible. Course correction is a normal part of striving for greatness.

Any sales vision you create leading towards your goal achievement must also overlap and benefit with each person and your team as a whole.[22] If you have a vision that neglects the desires of your team and each person on that team, you will have a hard time getting buy-in for your vision.

The "circles" of the Person, the Team and your organization's Goal must overlap. Any goal you aspire towards must also be a win for the organization, the team and each person on your team.

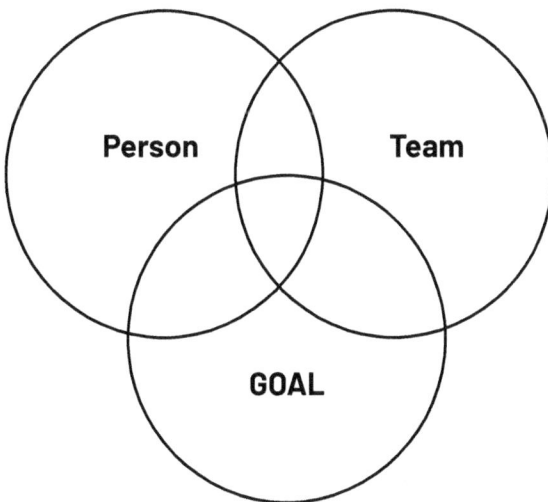

Person   **Team**

GOAL

---

22 John Adair, Strategic Leadership: How to Think and Plan Strategically and Provide Direction. The John Adair Leadership Library (Philadelphia, PA: Kogan Page, 2010)

CHAPTER 3

Communicating Your Vision

"Good business leaders create a vision, articulate the vision, passionately own the vision,
and relentlessly drive it to completion.

—Jack Welch[23]

It doesn't matter how amazing your vision is if it's not communicated in a compelling and powerful way. That's why leaders
like Dr. Martin Luther King Jr, Winston Churchill, Steve Jobs
and others were so successful, they spoke in a way that almost
mesmerized people.

Techniques for Effective Communication

Communicating your vision is crucial for rallying your team
and stakeholders around shared goals and strategies. Effective
communication ensures that your vision is not only understood
but also embraced and acted upon by everyone involved. Let's

---

23   Tichy, N., & Charan, R. (1989, September-October). Speed, Simplicity, Self-Confidence:
An Interview with Jack Welch. Harvard Business Review. Updated March 2, 2020. https://hbr.
org/1989/09/speed-simplicity-self-confidence-an-interview-with-jack-welch

explore some techniques to enhance how you communicate your sales vision, ensuring it resonates clearly and compellingly with your target audience.

1. Clarity and Simplicity

Your vision should be articulated in a way that is easy to understand and free from jargon. This means distilling complex ideas into clear, concise statements. When your vision is simple and direct, it is more likely to stick.[24]

Start with a concise message that you can build upon. Here are some examples to help you generate ideas:

Nike: "Bring inspiration and innovation to every athlete* in the world. *If you have a body, you are an athlete."

- This vision extends beyond just selling products; it's about empowering and inspiring every individual to engage in sports and fitness.

Apple: "To make the best products on earth, and to leave the world better than we found it."

- Apple's vision not only focuses on product excellence but also includes a commitment to sustainability and positive impact.

Disney: "To entertain, inform and inspire people around the globe through the power of unparalleled storytelling, reflecting the iconic brands, creative minds, and innovative technologies that make ours the world's premier entertainment company."

---

24   Chip Heath and Dan Heath, Made to Stick: Why Some Ideas Survive and Others Die (New York: Random House, 2007).

- Disney's vision is about crafting stories that entertain and inspire on a global scale, utilizing their unique capabilities.

Google: "To organize the world's information and make it universally accessible and useful."

- Google aims to empower people by providing access to information, a vision that extends beyond simple search capabilities to a broader mission of information accessibility.

- **Technique**: Use the "Elevator Pitch" method to refine the articulation of your vision to its essence. If you can't explain your vision in 30 seconds, it might be too complex.

2. Consistency

Consistency in messaging is key to reinforcing your vision across all levels of the organization. Regular repetition and reinforcement of core ideas help embed them into the organization's culture.

- **Technique**: Integrate your vision statement into all major communication tools — meetings, emails, internal newsletters, and presentations. Use consistent language and themes whenever discussing plans and strategies.

3. Storytelling

Humans are naturally drawn to stories because they engage us emotionally and memorably. Framing your vision within a narrative that connects your team's everyday efforts to the bigger picture can be powerful.

- **Technique**: Develop a narrative that illustrates where the organization has come from, where it is now, and the future you envision. Include real-life examples of challenges overcome and milestones achieved that align with the vision.

TOMS Shoes used the simple "One for One," to communicate a feel-good story. TOMS tells a compelling story of its origins, starting with founder Blake Mycoskie's trip to Argentina where he saw children without shoes. The narrative then connects this experience to the company's mission of donating a pair of shoes for every pair sold, illustrating the impact of customer purchases.

4. Visual Aids

Visual representations can make abstract ideas more tangible and easier to grasp. Diagrams, charts, and infographics can help illustrate how various elements of your vision connect and support one another. Remember, humans are visual creatures. If you can match your message with strong visuals, it will help your message stick.

- **Technique**: Use flow charts to show the cause and effect of following the vision or create infographics that outline the steps towards achieving the vision. Visual project timelines can also be effective.

5. Interactive Communication

Engagement increases retention of information. Encouraging dialogue about your vision allows for better understanding and alignment, as it enables your team members to ask questions and express concerns.

- **Technique**: Host interactive sessions such as Q&A rounds, workshops, or town hall meetings where your team members can discuss what the vision means to them and how it impacts their roles.

6. Empathy and Emotional Intelligence

Understanding and addressing the emotions and concerns of your team can make your communication more effective. It shows that you value and consider the perspectives and feelings of others, which can foster stronger buy-in and loyalty.

Under Satya Nadella's leadership, Microsoft has placed a strong emphasis on empathy, listening to employees and customers to guide the company's direction.[25] He often tailors his communications to address the diverse concerns and needs of different employee groups, showing that their feedback is valued and considered.

- **Technique**: Tailor your communication to address the specific needs and concerns of distinct groups within

25   Cardenas, B. (2024, January 30). Transformative Leadership: Unveiling Satya Nadella's Three Revolutionary Strategies at Microsoft. Leadership Worth Following. https://worthyleadership.com/transformative-leadership-unveiling-satya-nadellas-three-revolutionary-strategies-at-microsoft/

your organization. Listen actively to their feedback and incorporate it into your discussions about the vision.

7. Digital Tools

In today's digital age, leveraging online platforms can enhance the reach and frequency of your communications. Digital tools can provide innovative ways to share, discuss, and reinforce the vision.

A tool such as Slack is a wonderful way to communicate your vision and updates with employees, leveraging channels for different teams and projects to ensure everyone is aligned and informed.

- **Technique**: Use internal social media platforms, webinars, and video messages to communicate your vision. These platforms can offer informal yet impactful ways to reinforce messages and engage employees.

8. Follow-Up and Feedback

Communication is a two-way street. Providing opportunities for feedback and demonstrating that you act on that feedback is crucial for maintaining trust and commitment.

Salesforce is one of the best organizations when it comes to regularly conducting employee surveys and feedback sessions to gather input on the company's direction and culture.[26]

26   Psico-smart Editorial Team. (2024, August 28). What role does employee feedback play in enhancing workplace satisfaction? Psico-smart. https://psico-smart.com/en/blogs/blog-what-role-does-employee-feedback-play-in-enhancing-workplace-satisfaction-151993

- **Technique**: Implement regular feedback mechanisms through surveys, suggestion boxes, or feedback sessions. Show responsiveness by acting on the feedback and communicating what changes or decisions have been made as a result.

By employing these techniques, you can ensure that your vision for the sales team is communicated effectively, fostering alignment, enthusiasm, and a shared sense of purpose across your organization. This creates a potent foundation for implementing strategic initiatives and achieving long-term goals.

Building Buy-in Across the Organization

As the poet John Donne once wrote, "No man is an island, entire of itself; every man is a piece of the continent, a part of the main." Gaining buy-in for your vision across the organization is crucial for the successful implementation of strategic initiatives. It's about more than just agreement; it's about inspiring commitment and action from all levels of the organization. Let's look at some strategies for building buy-in, ensuring that your vision is not only supported but actively championed by others.[27] Office politics will inevitably determine how much buy-in you get (or don't) from your colleagues, so be sure to factor that into everything you do.[28]

---

27   Joseph Grenny, Kerry Patterson, Ron McMillan, and Al Switzler, Crucial Conversations: Tools for Talking When Stakes are High, 3rd ed. (New York: McGraw-Hill Education, 2021)

28   Barb Grant, Change Management that Sticks: A Practical, People-centered Approach, for High Buy-in, and Meaningful Results (New Zealand: Barb Grant, 2023)

1. Involve Stakeholders Early

Involvement leads to commitment. Engage key stakeholders in the vision development process early on. This not only provides you with diverse perspectives and insights but also makes stakeholders feel valued and part of the process.

- Conduct brainstorming sessions and strategic planning workshops with representatives from different departments. Use these forums to gather input and collaboratively shape the vision.

2. Communicate the 'Why'

People are more likely to buy into a vision if they understand why it matters. Clearly articulate the reasons behind the vision and how it connects to the broader goals of the organization.

- Use storytelling to communicate the origins and importance of your vision. Explain how your vision aligns with the organization's values and how it will benefit everyone in the long term.

3. Highlight Individual Benefits

People want to know what's in it for them. Explicitly outline how your vision will benefit each part of the organization, from senior management to entry-level employees.

- Tailor your communication to address the specific benefits for diverse groups. For instance, show how the vision will open new professional opportunities, enhance job security, get them a raise and maybe even a promotion if your efforts are successful.

4. Create Champions

In sales we strive to find a champion within an organization we're selling to, we must also identify and cultivate champions of the vision within our own organization. These individuals should be influential, respected, and enthusiastic about the new direction. The more you have on your side, the better.

- Equip champions with in-depth knowledge and insights about your vision so they can effectively persuade others. Encourage them to share their positive perspectives in meetings, informal discussions, and through internal communications.

5. Provide Clear Roles and Responsibilities

People support what they can act on. Make it clear how individuals and departments can contribute to the vision. Assign roles and responsibilities that align with achieving specific aspects of the vision.

- Develop clear action plans that outline specific tasks and timelines. Regularly review these plans in team meetings to reinforce roles and show how each contributes to the bigger picture.

6. Demonstrate Quick Wins

Show progress early and often. Quick sales wins boost morale and validate the worthiness of your vision. They serve as tangible proof that the direction chosen is beneficial and that the efforts being made are yielding results.

- Set initial, achievable sales objectives that are linked to the vision. Celebrate these accomplishments broadly across the organization to increase visibility and support.

7. Reinforce with Training and Resources

Support the vision with necessary training and resources. Ensure that everyone has what they need to contribute effectively, reducing barriers to implementation. Always assume that some sort of extra training will be needed to ensure success.

- Identify skill gaps within your sales team and provide training programs. Allocate resources like budget, time, and tools that enable teams to execute their part of the vision successfully.

8. Maintain Open Communication

Keep the lines of communication open with other groups in your organization. Regular updates about the progress, challenges, and successes related to your vision help maintain engagement and interest.

- Use regular newsletters, intranet updates, and town hall meetings to keep everyone informed. Be transparent about both successes and areas of improvement. There's always going to be a "Negative Nancy" or "Danny Downer" in an organization. Be prepared for them.

9. Foster a Feedback Culture

Encourage and value feedback. Regular feedback loops allow for adjustments and show that the leadership is responsive and adaptive to the needs and concerns of the organization.

- Implement a structured feedback system where employees can share their thoughts and suggestions about the vision implementation. Respond to this feedback constructively. As mentioned above, be prepared for negative feedback. Set your ego aside and use the feedback to your advantage. You can't pay your bills with your ego, so leave it at home.

By following these strategies, you can effectively build buy-in across your organization, turning your vision into a shared goal that motivates and unites everyone towards common success.

Reflection Points: Evaluating Your Communication Style

Sometimes, how you say something can be as important as what you say. Effective communication is a cornerstone of leadership, particularly when it comes to articulating and driving forward a strategic vision. To ensure your communication style is resonating with and motivating your team, it's crucial to periodically evaluate and refine your approach. Let's discuss some points to help you assess and improve your communication style.[29]

1. Clarity

- **Reflection**: Do people understand what you're saying the first time you say it, or do you often need to re-explain your points?

- **Improvement Tip**: Practice distilling complex ideas into simple, clear messages. Use analogies or stories if that helps clarify the concepts.

2. Consistency

- **Reflection**: Are you consistent in your messaging across different mediums and over time?

- **Improvement Tip**: Develop key message points and stick to them across all communications. Regularly revisit core messages to ensure they remain relevant and aligned with current objectives.

3. Receptiveness

- **Reflection**: How well do you listen to others during interactions? Do you acknowledge different viewpoints? Be honest here. As Stephen Covey said, "Most people do

---

29   Jay Sullivan, Simply Said: Communicating Better at Work and Beyond (Hoboken, NJ: John Wiley & Sons, 2016)

not listen with the intent to understand; they listen with the intent to reply."[30]

- **Improvement Tip**: Enhance your listening skills by practicing active listening—focus entirely on the speaker, make eye contact, and repeat back what you've heard to ensure understanding.

4. Adaptability

- **Reflection**: Can you adjust your communication style to fit different audiences or situations? Chances are, the way you speak to the warehouse team won't be the same way you speak to your product management team.

- **Improvement Tip**: Pay attention to the reactions of your audience and be ready to adjust your tone, language, or even your message to ensure it is appropriate for the context.

5. Engagement

- **Reflection**: Do you engage your audience effectively when you communicate? Are they attentive, responsive, and motivated? Their body language will reveal everything you need to know.

- **Improvement Tip**: Use questions to engage your audience, invite feedback, and show genuine interest in their

---

30   Stephen R. Covey, The 7 Habits of Highly Effective People: Powerful Lessons in Personal Change (New York: Free Press, 1989)

input. Incorporate storytelling to make your communication more relatable and engaging.

6. Body Language

- **Reflection**: What non-verbal messages are you sending during your communications? Your body language can show a range of emotions from confidence, apprehension, fear, boldness, or doubt.

- **Improvement Tip**: Be aware of your body language. Maintain an open posture, use gestures to emphasize points, and ensure your facial expressions match your message.

7. Empathy

- **Reflection**: Do you consider and address the emotions and concerns of your audience when you communicate? You cannot do this alone!

- **Improvement Tip**: Try to understand the perspectives and feelings of your audience. Tailor your messages to address their concerns and aspirations, showing that you value and understand them.

8. Feedback

- **Reflection**: How effectively do you solicit and respond to feedback?

■ **Improvement Tip**: Regularly ask for feedback on your communication style and openness. When you receive feedback, show appreciation, and take actionable steps to incorporate useful insights.

9. Impact

■ **Reflection**: Do your communications lead to the desired actions or outcomes?

■ **Improvement Tip**: Monitor the outcomes of your communications. If the impact is not as expected, revisit your approach, seeking to understand where disconnects might be occurring.

10. Confidence

■ **Reflection**: Do you communicate with confidence and authority? Re-read #6 above.

■ **Improvement Tip**: Prepare thoroughly before any communication. Practice your delivery and familiarize yourself with the content to boost your confidence. Abraham Lincoln was known to put significant effort into preparing his speeches. He was known to spend hours, even days, writing and revising his addresses to ensure they were impactful.[31]

31　James C. Humes, Speak Like Churchill, Stand Like Lincoln: 21 Powerful Secrets of History's Greatest Speakers (New York: Three Rivers Press, 2002)

By regularly reflecting on these aspects of your communication style, you can continue to refine your ability to convey your vision effectively, inspire your team, and drive your organization towards its strategic goals. Don't think you can just wing it. Very few people have the gift of speaking well spontaneously. If you put in the work, your payoff will be massive.

Communicating Your Vision: Julius Caesar's Commentaries on the Gallic War[32]

Julius Caesar was not only a brilliant general but also a master communicator. His Commentaries on the Gallic War were written to keep the Roman public and Senate informed of his campaigns. By clearly documenting his strategic vision and the successes of his legions, Caesar built a narrative of competence and inevitability. This communication not only ensured support from Rome but also kept his troops motivated, knowing that their achievements were being recognized and celebrated. Caesar's ability to communicate his vision effectively played a crucial role in maintaining morale and securing political backing. It's a tool you can also use.

Once You're Clear on Your Vision

If creating your compelling BHAG and sales vision seems like a lot of work, you're right. Achieving remarkable things in

---

32   Julius Caesar, The Gallic War: Seven Commentaries on The Gallic War with an Eighth Commentary by Aulus Hirtius, 1st ed., Oxford World's Classics (Oxford: Oxford University Press, 2008)

any endeavor means doing more than the next person. By definition, if you're just doing what everyone else is doing, you're going to get mediocre results. You don't want to be mediocre, do you?

The next pillar is strategy.

Part II

STRATEGY

"There is, first, the task of thinking through the mission of the business, that is, of asking the question "What is our business and what should it be?" This leads to the setting of objectives, the development of strategies and plans, and the making of today's decisions for tomorrow's results."

– Peter Drucker [9]

"Now the general who wins a battle makes many calculations in his temple before the battle is fought. The general who loses a battle makes but few calculations beforehand. Thus do many calculations lead to victory, and few calculations to defeat: how much more no calculation at all! It is by attention to this point that I can foresee who is likely to win or lose."

– Sun Tzu, The Art of War [35]

" I believe that you have to understand the economics of a business before you have a strategy, and you have to understand your strategy before you have a structure. if you get these in the wrong order you will probably fail."

– Michael Dell, founder of Dell Computers

"Respecting your opponent is the key to winning any bout. Hold your enemy in contempt and you may miss the strategy behind his moves."

– Col. David Hackworth [33]

33   David H. Hackworth and Julie Sherman, About Face: The Odyssey of an American Warrior (New York: Simon & Schuster, 1989)

T oo often, we hear people confuse strategy with planning and vice versa. Before we dive into the topic of strategy, let's understand it and how it differs from planning.

Strategy

Definition: Strategy is a high-level roadmap designed to achieve long-term objectives. It involves setting goals and determining the best course of action to achieve these goals.

Focus: Strategy is about setting directions, making choices on where to compete, how to differentiate, and how to allocate resources to achieve these goals.

Scope: Broader and more abstract; it's about understanding the competitive landscape, identifying opportunities and threats, and deciding on a general course of action.

Flexibility: Strategies are more adaptable to changes in the external environment. They provide a framework but allow for adjustments as situations evolve.

Planning

Definition: Planning is a more specific, detailed organization of actions and resources to implement a strategy. It involves setting more immediate goals, timelines, and assigning responsibilities.

Focus: Planning is about execution. It's concerned with the "how" - how to operationalize the strategy, how to achieve short-term objectives that lead to the strategic goals.

Scope: Narrower and more concrete; it's about the tactical steps required to move towards the strategic objectives.

Rigidity: Plans are typically more rigid and specific. They outline specific steps and allocate resources in a more fixed manner.

Strategy is about setting the right course and direction for an organization, while planning is about organizing resources and actions in a structured way to execute that strategy. Strategy is the "what" and "why," and planning is the "how" and "when."

Simply put, strategy is about doing the right things. Planning is doing things right.

Perhaps one of the most useful business definitions of the word came from Willie Petersen in his insightful book, "Strategic Learning: How to Be Smarter Than Your Competition And Turn Key Insights Into Competitive Advantage."[34] Pietersen wrote: "Strategy is simply the sum of an organization's choices about where it will compete, how it will create superior value for its clients, and how it will create superior returns to its investors."

Pietersen breaks business strategy into four components/ questions.

1) Where will we compete?
   - In which market segments will we compete?
   - Which clients will we serve?
   - What will we offer our chosen clients?

2) What do we want to achieve?
   - What is our aim?
   - What will be our measure of success?

---

34   Willie Pietersen, Strategic Learning: How to Be Smarter Than Your Competition and Turn Key Insights into Competitive Advantage, Illustrated ed. (Hoboken, NJ: John Wiley & Sons, 2010

3) How will we win?
- How will we win the competition for the value creation for our clients and investors?

4) What will be our key priorities?
- How will we concentrate our scarce resources to achieve success?

As you make your way through this book, think of this strategic framework as the "skeleton" upon which you will add the "flesh" to help guide you as you create your strategy and then put into place a methodology for successful execution.

Perhaps no one captured the strategic mindset better than Sun Tzu, famed author of the Art of War. [35] While the book's exact date of creation and the actual author are still being debated, scholars agree that it was written sometime between 400 BCE and 320 BCE. The name Sun Tzu translates to "Master Sun."

A strategic mindset begins with knowledge. Sun Tzu wrote:

"If you know the enemy and know yourself, you need not fear the result of a hundred battles. If you know yourself but not the enemy, for every victory gained you will also suffer a defeat. If you know neither the enemy nor yourself, you will succumb in every battle."

Having a deep understanding of your competition and your own team is a key part to achieving success. Too many organizations go into a sales situation lacking the necessary competitive intelligence to be successful, and then they wonder why their

---

35   Sun Tzu, The Art of War, translated by Ralph D. Sawyer (New York: Barnes & Noble Books, 1994)

efforts don't yield the results they expected. It's not enough to just know your own team, you also have to know who you're competing against. You should have a deep knowledge base of at least your top three to five competitors. We will go deeper into competitive intelligence later.

The next part of being a good strategic leader is being able to adapt quickly as circumstances change. Sun Tzu wrote this:

"The skillful tactician may be likened to the Shuai-jan. Now the Shuai-jan is a snake that is found in the Chung mountains. Strike at its head, and you will be attacked by its tail; strike at its tail, and you will be attacked by its head; strike at its middle, and you will be attacked by head and tail both."

Most sales organizations rely on one key strength, or perceived current advantage. When the economy inevitably changes, or when your marketplace changes, they get blindsided by something they didn't foresee, and their revenues flounder. A strategic leader prepares their organization for the most probable challenges they foresee and has some backup plans for low probability/high impactful events that are also known as Black Swans.[36]

In Sun Tzu's The Art of War he breaks down the crucial factors behind a winning strategy. They are:

- **Moral Influence:** Do you show that you have integrity, and you inspire your team to act in the right way in the myriad of situations you will find yourself in?

---

36   Nassim Nicholas Taleb, The Black Swan: The Impact of the Highly Improbable (New York: Random House, 2008

- **Generalship:** How good of a leader are you? Your ability to lead, inspire and direct your team is a critical part of being a good "General" as Sun Tzu called it.

- **Climate:** For us in sales, the issue of climate is both literal and metaphorical. Just like the climate can tip the scales of a battle in one direction or another, the economic climate will too. Are we in a recession or is the economy booming? With weather extremes hitting us more frequently, keeping aware of how extreme heat, rain, flooding, drought, and such affect our ability to sell and deliver on those sales is going to be an increasingly important part of how we do business for the foreseeable future.

- **Terrain:** For us terrain involves things such as supply chain issues. Is it flowing or is it congested? As we learned from Covid-19, it's one thing to be able to sell a product, and it's a whole other thing to actually be able to deliver it. Terrain can also be new legislation that impedes our ability to sell whether it be a specific product, or in a specific geography.

- **Doctrine:** This is where you stipulate exactly what it is that you, your team, and your organization stand for. It can't be nebulous. it must be something your team can refer back to.

- **Strengths:** Do you understand your strengths and how and where they can help you win? Are you clear on if those strengths are no longer as relevant as they used to be? Most advantages we have in sales are normally not long-lasting, so we must continually adjust.

■ **Training:** How often do you train your team? And to what level of expertise? With the world changing as quickly as it does, limiting training to just the onboarding process will preclude your team from achieving the highest levels of excellence.

■ **Discipline:** You can't be a good leader without expecting your team to be disciplined. Salespeople are notoriously hard to discipline, however by integrating disciplinary protocols within your sales methodology you will have a better team as a result.

Remember that as a leader there are factors that you can control, and factors you can't control such as terrain and climate. The human versus nonhuman issues is also a factor in your potential success or failure.

Human:

■ **Office politics:** Everyone has an agenda. Are you aware of the agenda of the people in other divisions who may either help you or sabotage your efforts? Are you aware of the office politics between members of your sales team and members of other units in your organization? You will need to factor them to create a cohesive strategy.

■ **Motivation of your team:** While most salespeople are coin operated, they still benefit immensely from having something to keep them motivated other than just money. The challenge for you is to determine what motivates your team as a unit and what motivates your team individually.

- **Discipline of your team:** We already mentioned this above, however it's worth reiterating that an undisciplined sales team is not an effective sales team.

- **Leadership capabilities of your organization's leaders:** We don't function in a vacuum, the leadership capabilities of other people within your organization will impact your efforts and your success or failures. Do you work with an organization with good leaders who have the requisite skill set to lead their teams with excellence so that you can do the same with yours?

- **Personnel capabilities:** With regards to your sales team, every person has their unique strengths and weaknesses in terms of how competently they sell including but not limited to, their energy levels, their charisma, their technical/product literacy and how they're perceived by their clients. The goal isn't to create clones on your sales team. The goal is to understand each of your sales teams' individual capabilities and position them in a way that maximizes their ability to succeed.

Strategy primarily is about focusing on a few things and doing them exceptionally well. There will be tradeoffs that must be made. You can't be all things to all clients. The tradeoffs you make must be based on situational realities. Do you have the time, resources (financial and personnel wise) and wherewithal to proceed down a certain path? Too often companies choose strategies based on hot trends, or just what they think would be cool to pursue, as opposed to taking a good long hard look at their organization, its talent and what is realistic.

The role of a sales leader has evolved significantly over time. For most of sales leadership history, the overarching command was, "Go sell as much as you can!" Then a quota was given to you and your team. If you were lucky, the quota was based on some semblance of reality, and if you weren't lucky, and the number was based on some arbitrary number given to you by either the Board of Directors, the VC's, the private equity firm that had acquired you or the C level executives, you had to figure it out. Most of the time, your quota was arbitrary, "Let's just add 20% to last year." You and your team would have to claw, fight, and practically kill themselves to get there. Most of the time they didn't though.

According to research by the Forrester Group, the average quota attainment for B2B sales organizations is only 47 percent.[37] That's down from 63 percent attainment back in 2011.[38] And if those numbers don't send a trickle of nervous sweat down the center of your back, maybe this will. The average tenure for a VP of Sales is now just 19 months.[39] You may be a

---

37   Marrs, S. (2023, March 14). Your Company's Quota Attainment Is Probably Around 50%, And That's Not A Bad Thing. Forrester Blog. https://www.forrester.com/blogs/your-companys-quota-attainment-is-probably-around-50-and-thats-not-a-bad-thing/

38   Glickel, H. (n.d.). 3 Reasons It May Just Be Harder Than Ever To Hire. Sales Recruiters Inc. Retrieved from https://www.salesrecruiters.com/blog-3-reasons-it-may-just-be-harder-than-ever-to-hire-9.php

39   Orlob, C. (2018, January 29). The average VP of Sales tenure has shrunk — here's why. Gong.io. https://www.gong.io/blog/vp-sales-average-tenure/

sales manager, or sales director, but even if you're not a VP of Sales, those numbers should make you very anxious. That is, if you're not already.

So where does strategy come into play? We are no longer simply focused on closing deals, today's sales leaders are expected to be visionaries, strategic thinkers, and effective communicators who can guide our teams to achieve exceptional results, no matter what the prevailing headwinds may be. In this endlessly morphing business landscape, it is crucial to understand the fundamental principles that underpin strategic sales leadership and establish a strong foothold from which to navigate the minefield of challenges and opportunities that lie ahead. With most sales leaders getting an average of only 19 months to make an impact, if you forge a strategy that turns out to be wrong, you won't have time to course correct.

We will begin by exploring the concept of strategic sales leadership itself. What does it mean to be a strategic sales leader? How does it differ from traditional sales management? We will delve into the key characteristics and qualities that set strategic sales leaders apart, from their ability to think beyond short-term goals to their aptitude for inspiring and motivating teams.

Furthermore, we will examine the importance of aligning your sales vision with the larger organizational goals. By establishing a strong connection between sales and the overarching business strategy, sales leaders can position their teams as strategic partners within the organization and leverage resources more effectively. You can't do this alone. And if you try to, expect to fail in a spectacular way. We will also discuss what to do if your sales strategy is at odds with the organizational strategy.

As you may know, C-level executives don't always understand how best to utilize a sales team, nor what is realistic in terms of sales achievement.

Throughout this chapter, we will draw insights from both business and military history, highlighting exemplary leaders and their approaches to strategic thinking. By examining the successes and lessons learned from renowned figures such as Steve Jobs and General George Washington, we will uncover valuable principles and perspectives that can be applied to the realm of strategic sales leadership.

As we embark on this journey into the foundations of strategic sales leadership, get ready to expand your mindset, challenge conventional thinking, and lay the groundwork for becoming a truly exceptional sales leader.

CHAPTER 4

Unveiling Misconceptions: Core Principles of Effective Strategy

"The essence of strategy is choosing what not to do."

- Michael Porter[40]

"Good strategy is unexpected. How many competitors have already thought of what you are thinking? How many can quickly copy it?"

- Richard Rumelt[41]

"Strategy is about making choices, trade-offs; it's about deliberately choosing to be different."

- Michael Porter[40]

Strategic thinking is often shrouded in misconceptions that can lead organizations astray or stifle innovation. This chapter aims to dispel common myths about strategy and reinforce the core principles that underpin effective strategic planning.

---

40   Michael E. Porter, "What Is Strategy?" Harvard Business Review 74, no. 6 (1996): 61-78.

41   Richard Rumelt, Good Strategy Bad Strategy: The Difference and Why It Matters (New York: Crown Business, 2011)

By redefining strategy through a clear and practical lens, sales leaders can better position their teams for sustained success in competitive markets.

The True Definition of Strategy

The Cambridge dictionary defines strategy as:

> "a detailed plan for achieving success in situations such as war, politics, business, industry, or sports, or the skill of planning for such situations:
>
> *"The president held an emergency meeting to discuss military strategy with the Pentagon yesterday."*
>
> *"Their marketing strategy for the product involves obtaining as much free publicity as possible."*
>
> *"We're working on new strategies to improve our share of the market."*

The term "strategy" is frequently misunderstood and misapplied, leading to confusion and ineffective planning. Strategy, at its core, is not merely about planning or a set of operational decisions. It's about making integrated choices that position an organization uniquely in its market to sustain competitive advantage and achieve long-term success.

1. Strategy is about Choice:

- At its heart, strategy involves making deliberate choices—choosing what not to do just as much as choosing what to do. It's about selecting the paths that will offer the most significant potential to enhance your position relative to your competitors.

2. Strategy is about Future Orientation:

- A strategic approach is inherently forward-looking. It's about anticipating market trends, potential disruptions, and evolving customer needs. Effective strategy prepares your organization not just to navigate the present but to shape the future.

3. Strategy is Integrative:

- Effective strategy integrates various aspects of an organization—from operations and marketing to finance and HR—ensuring that all parts are aligned and working towards the same goals. This integration is crucial for coherent action and resource allocation. We will dive deeper into this in a later chapter.

4. Strategy Focuses on Competitive Advantage:

- The ultimate goal of any strategy is to achieve and maintain a competitive advantage. This involves understanding what your organization can do better than any other and making this the centerpiece of your strategic efforts.

5. Strategy is about Creating Value:

■ Beyond competition, strategy is fundamentally about creating value for customers and stakeholders. It entails understanding deeply the value drivers in your business and industry and continuously finding ways to maximize that value.

6. Strategy Requires Trade-offs:

■ A good strategy often requires making tough choices and trade-offs. You might have to sacrifice short-term gains for long-term success or choose between equally attractive alternative paths. You may need to abandon a geographic area or product because there is no path to success.

7. Strategy is Dynamic:

■ A strategy isn't a one-time plan but a dynamic process that requires ongoing assessment and adaptation. As external conditions change, so too must your strategy if it is to remain relevant and effective. Too many sales leaders write a one time "strategy document" and let it collect dust. Your strategy must be forever changing and evolving as your market ecosystem and economy at large dictate.

Understanding these aspects of strategy is crucial for sales leaders, as it allows them to steer their teams with a clear, strategic direction that is proactive rather than reactive. This understanding also equips leaders to dismantle ineffective practices that are often mistaken for strategy, such as mere goal-setting or short-term planning. In the following sections, we will delve deeper into each of these principles, exploring how they can be applied effectively in the context of sales leadership. This foundational knowledge will help you build a strategic framework that not only drives sales but also contributes to the sustainable growth of your organization.

Common Misconceptions and Strategic Pitfalls

In the realm of strategic planning, several common misconceptions can lead to ineffective strategies and hinder your sales growth. Understanding these pitfalls is essential for sales leaders aiming to develop potent and impactful strategies. Here, we address some of the most prevalent misunderstandings about strategy and outline the pitfalls to avoid.

1. Misconception: Strategy is Primarily About Planning

Misconception: Many sales leaders believe that strategy is primarily about detailed planning and creating comprehensive sales plans that outline every possible scenario. While planning is a vital component, it is not the essence of a successful sales strategy.

Reality: Strategy is about doing the right things. Planning is about doing things right. Most of your competitors will confuse the two. Don't be like your competitors. The true essence lies in understanding the market, anticipating changes, and being agile enough to adapt to new opportunities and challenges.

Things to Remember:

1. **Market Insight Over Rigid Plans**: Instead of focusing solely on creating extensive sales plans, concentrate on gaining deep market insights. Understand your customers' evolving needs, track competitor's moves, and stay informed about industry trends. This market intelligence should inform your strategy and allow for flexibility in execution.

2. **Agility and Adaptation**: In sales, conditions can and will change rapidly. New competitors can emerge, customer preferences can shift, and economic conditions can fluctuate. An effective sales strategy must be adaptable. While a plan provides a roadmap, being able to pivot and adjust tactics in response to real-time data and market feedback is crucial.

3. **Strategic Prioritization**: Rather than trying to plan for every eventuality, focus on strategic prioritization. Identify your key markets, high-potential leads, and critical sales activities. Allocate resources strategically to areas that offer the highest returns and align with your business objectives. Be comfortable walking away from low margin or unprofitable areas, products, and territories.

4. **Execution Excellence**: Strategy works in conjunction with execution and planning. Ensure that your sales team has the skills, tools, and support needed to execute the strategy effectively. Regularly review performance, provide coaching, and adjust based on what's working and

what isn't. Be brutally honest here. There's no room for rose colored glasses, and "happy ears."

5. **Continuous Learning and Improvement**: Treat your sales strategy as a living document. Regularly revisit and revise your strategy based on new insights and feedback from the field. Encourage a culture of continuous learning where the sales team is empowered to share insights and suggest improvements. If you only do this one thing, you will immediately be ahead of your competition.

Example:

Consider a tech company launching a new software product. Instead of creating a rigid 12-month sales plan, the sales leader focuses on understanding the needs of different customer segments, tracking competitor offerings, and staying updated on technological advancements. The sales strategy involves setting clear priorities, such as targeting early adopters in specific industries, and being ready to pivot based on customer feedback and market reactions. Regular team meetings are held to review progress, share insights, and adjust tactics as necessary. This approach ensures that the strategy remains relevant and effective in a dynamic market.

Internalize This:

Effective sales strategy goes beyond detailed planning. It requires a deep understanding of the market, the ability to adapt to changing conditions, strategic prioritization of resources, and a focus on execution excellence. By shifting the focus from rigid planning to agile, informed decision-making, sales leaders can create strategies that drive sustained success and competitive advantage.

2) Misconception: Strategy Must Be Complex

Misconception: There is a common belief among sales leaders that a powerful sales strategy must be overly complex, involving intricate plans and numerous detailed steps. Complexity is often mistaken for thoroughness and effectiveness. As E.F. Schumacher once said, "Any intelligent fool can make things bigger, more complex, and more violent. It takes a touch of genius — and a lot of courage to move in the opposite direction."

Reality: An effective sales strategy does not have to be complex. In fact, simplicity and clarity can often lead to better execution and more successful outcomes. A strategy should be straightforward enough for the sales team to understand, embrace, and execute efficiently.

Things to Remember:

1. **Clarity and Focus Over Complexity**: A complex strategy can be overwhelming and difficult to implement. Focus on clarity and simplicity, ensuring that every member of the sales team understands the core objectives and their role in achieving them. A clear and focused strategy is more likely to be executed effectively.

2. **Prioritization of Key Actions**: Instead of trying to cover every scenario with detailed plans, prioritize key

actions that will have the most significant impact on your sales goals. Identify the critical few activities that drive the majority of your results and focus your efforts there. Focus on the vital few over the trivial many.

3. **Scalability and Flexibility**: Simple strategies are easier to scale and adapt. In a dynamic sales environment, you need the ability to quickly adjust your approach based on market feedback and new opportunities. A streamlined strategy allows for faster pivots and more agile responses.

4. **Effective Communication**: A simple strategy makes it easier to communicate across the sales team. When everyone understands the strategy clearly, alignment and coordination improve, leading to more cohesive and efficient execution.

5. **Measurable and Achievable Goals**: Set clear, measurable, and achievable goals. Avoid overcomplicating your strategy with too many metrics or overly ambitious targets. Focus on key performance indicators (KPIs) that truly matter and are aligned with your strategic objectives.

Example:

Consider a company entering a new market with a flagship product. Instead of developing an overly complex strategy with multiple layers and contingencies, the sales leader creates a straightforward plan: identify the top fifty potential customers, assign dedicated account managers, and set clear goals for initial meetings and product demonstrations. The strategy includes regular check-ins to assess progress and gather feed-back, allowing for quick adjustments. This simple yet focused approach enables the sales team to execute efficiently, stay aligned, and achieve rapid market penetration.

Internalize This:

An effective sales strategy does not need to be complex. By focusing on clarity, prioritization, scalability, effective com-munication, and measurable goals, sales leaders can develop strategies that are easy to understand and implement. Simplifying your strategy ensures better execution, allows for greater flexibility, and ultimately drives better results. Embrace simplicity and focus on the essential elements that will propel your sales organization toward success.

3) Misconception: Strategy is Fixed

Misconception: Many sales leaders believe that once a strat-egy is developed, it should remain unchanged throughout its implementation. They view strategy as a static plan that guides all actions without room for modification.

Reality: An effective sales strategy is dynamic and flexible. It should evolve in response to changing market conditions, customer feedback, and internal performance data. Adapting your strategy ensures that it remains relevant and effective over time.

Things to Remember:

1. **Continuous Improvement Over Static Plans**: A fixed strategy can quickly become obsolete in a fast-paced sales environment. The Covid-19 pandemic forced almost everyone to alter their strategy. Embrace a mindset of continuous improvement, where strategies are regularly reviewed and refined based on new insights and data.

2. **Responsive to Market Changes**: The sales landscape is constantly changing due to factors such as economic shifts, competitive actions, and technological advancements. A flexible strategy allows you to respond promptly to these changes, ensuring that your sales efforts remain aligned with current market realities.

3. **Feedback-Driven Adjustments**: Feedback from your sales team and customers along with internal performance metrics provide valuable information on the effectiveness of your strategy. Use this feedback to make necessary adjustments. Strategies should be living documents that evolve based on real-world experiences and outcomes. Don't let your strategy become calcified.

4. **Agile Methodologies**: Implement agile methodologies[42] in your sales strategy development. This involves setting short-term goals, regularly reviewing progress, and making iterative changes. Agile strategies enable quick pivots and continuous alignment with strategic

---

42   Brad Jeavons, Agile Sales: Delivering Customer Journeys of Value and Delight, 1st ed. (New York, Routledge, 2020)

objectives. Initially, this will take more work, but eventually it will become intuitive.

5. **Empowering the Sales Team**: Encourage your sales team to provide input and feedback on the strategy. When the team feels empowered to suggest improvements and adapt their approaches, they become more invested in the success of the strategy. Be prepared to hear things you may not like. It's important that you don't lash out or your team will stop giving you real feedback.

Example:

Consider a company launching a new product. Initially, the strategy focuses on targeting small to mid-sized businesses in a specific region. However, after a few months, customer feedback reveals that the product is gaining significant interest from larger enterprises and in other regions. Instead of rigidly sticking to the original plan, the sales leader adjusts the strategy to include a dedicated team for large accounts and expands the geographical focus. This flexibility allows the company to capitalize on emerging opportunities and achieve better results.

Internalize This:

An effective sales strategy is not fixed but dynamic and adaptable. By embracing continuous improvement, responding to market changes, leveraging feedback, adopting agile methodologies, and empowering your sales team, you can ensure that your strategy remains relevant and effective. Flexibility in strategy allows you to navigate the complexities of the sales environment and seize new opportunities, driving sustained success and growth.

4) Misconception: Strategy is Only About the Competition

Misconception: A common belief is that a sales strategy should primarily focus on outmaneuvering competitors. While understanding and responding to the competition is important, it should not be the sole focus of your strategy.

Reality: An effective sales strategy encompasses much more than just competition. It involves an integrated approach that includes understanding customer needs, leveraging internal strengths, the economy, and aligning with broader business objectives. While competitive analysis is a critical component, it is only one part of a comprehensive strategy.

Things to Remember:

1. **Client-Centric Approach Over Competitor Obsession:** Prioritizing your customers' needs and preferences should be at the heart of your sales strategy. Understanding what drives your clients' purchasing decisions and how your product or service can best meet their needs is more important than just focusing on what your competitors are doing.

2. **Leveraging Internal Strengths:** Identify and capitalize on your unique strengths and capabilities. These could include proprietary technologies, exceptional customer service, strong brand reputation, or a highly skilled sales team.

Leveraging these strengths can differentiate your offering in ways that are independent of competitive actions.

3. **Aligning with Business Objectives:** Ensure that your sales strategy aligns with the overall goals and objectives of your organization. This alignment helps in ensuring that all efforts contribute to the broader success of the company and fosters a more cohesive and focused approach.

4. **Creating Unique Value Propositions (UVP's):** Focus on creating a unique value proposition that sets your product or service apart. This involves clearly articulating the unique benefits and value that your offering provides to customers, which may not necessarily be a direct response to what competitors are doing. You do have a UVP, right?

5. **Innovative Thinking:** Encourage innovative thinking within your sales team. Rather than always reacting to competitors, foster a culture of proactive innovation where new ideas and approaches are developed to meet customer needs and create new market opportunities. As legendary General George S. Patton once said, "Never tell people how to do things. Tell them what to do and they will surprise you with their ingenuity".

Example:

A software company initially develops a strategy heavily focused on undercutting the prices of its main competitor. However, this approach does not lead to significant market gains. The sales leader then shifts focus to deeply understanding client pain points and developing features that specifically address these needs. By leveraging the company's strong development team and creating a unique value proposition centered around client-centric innovation, the company starts to gain market share and customer loyalty. This approach proves more effective than merely trying to compete on price alone.

Remember This:

An effective sales strategy is multifaceted and extends beyond just focusing on the competition. By adopting a client-centric approach, leveraging internal strengths, aligning with business objectives, creating unique value propositions, and fostering innovative thinking, sales leaders can develop a comprehensive and powerful strategy. This integrated approach ensures that your sales efforts are more strategic, sustainable, and ultimately successful in delivering value to your customers and achieving long-term business goals.

5) Misconception: More Data Guarantees Better Strategy

Misconception: Many sales leaders believe that accumulating vast amounts of data will automatically lead to better strategies. They assume that the more data they collect, the clearer their strategic direction will become.

Reality: While data is crucial for informed decision-making, having more data does not inherently guarantee a better strategy.[43] The true value lies in how you analyze, interpret, and apply

---

43   Richardson, M. (2020, January 8). Sales Metrics: When Are You Measuring Too Much? https://brooksgroup.com/sales-training-blog/sales-metrics-are-you-measuring-too-much/

the data to inform your strategic decisions. It's about quality over quantity and the ability to extract actionable insights from the data you have. As Nassim Nicholas Taleb, the creator of the term "Black Swan" once wrote, "More data, such as paying attention to the eye colors of the people around when crossing the street, can make you miss the big truck."[36]

Things to Remember:

1. **Focus on Relevant Data Over Sheer Volume:** Rather than collecting as much data as possible, focus on gathering relevant data that directly impacts your sales strategy. This includes client behavior, market trends, sales performance metrics, and competitive intelligence.

2. **Data Analysis and Interpretation:** The ability to analyze and interpret data is more important than the volume of data collected. Use advanced analytics tools and techniques to identify strategies, correlations, and insights that can inform your strategy. Training your team in data literacy is crucial for effective analysis.

3. **Actionable Insights:** Prioritize actionable insights that can drive strategic decisions. Not all data points are equally valuable. Focus on data that helps you understand your customers better, refine your sales processes, and identify growth opportunities.

4. **Integrating Qualitative Data:** Quantitative data is essential, but qualitative data, such as client feedback, sales team input, and market observations, also provides critical insights. Combining both types of data gives a

more comprehensive view and leads to more nuanced strategies.

5. **Agility in Data Utilization:** Use data to stay agile and responsive. Regularly review your data and be prepared to adjust your strategy based on new insights. This dynamic approach ensures that your strategy evolves with changing market conditions and client needs.

Example:

A telecommunications company collects vast amounts of data from various sources, including client interactions, network usage, and market trends. Initially, the overwhelming volume of data leads to analysis paralysis, with no clear strategic direction emerging. The sales leader then shifts focus to identifying key performance indicators (KPIs) and critical data points that directly impact client satisfaction and sales performance. By prioritizing relevant data and using advanced analytics to derive actionable insights, the company refines its sales strategy, improves client targeting, and enhances service offerings, leading to increased sales and client retention.

Things to Remember:

More data does not automatically equate to a better strategy. The effectiveness of your sales strategy depends on the relevance, analysis, and application of the data you collect. By focusing on relevant data, developing strong analytical capabilities, prioritizing actionable insights, integrating qualitative data, and maintaining agility in data utilization, sales leaders can create more informed and effective strategies. This approach ensures that data serves as a powerful tool for strategic decision-making rather than an overwhelming burden.

6) Misconception: Immediate Results Indicate Success

Misconception: Many sales leaders equate immediate results with the success of a strategy. They often expect rapid gains in sales or market share as a direct indicator that their strategy is effective.

Reality: While immediate results can be a positive sign, they do not necessarily indicate long-term success. A strategy that delivers quick wins may not be sustainable or scalable over time. True strategic success is measured by consistent, long-term performance improvements and sustainable growth.

Things to Remember:

1. **Long-Term Goals Over Short-Term Wins:** Focus on setting and achieving long-term strategic goals rather than just chasing short-term wins. A successful sales strategy should aim for sustained growth, client loyalty, and market leadership. Too often, sales leaders are so focused on each quarter (especially if you're a publicly traded company) that they forget the long term to their detriment.

2. **Sustainability and Scalability:** Evaluate the sustainability and scalability of your strategy. A tactic that boosts sales temporarily may not be viable in the long run.

Ensure that your strategy can be scaled and sustained as your business grows and market conditions change. Avoid sales gimmicks. Gimmicks are for the desperate and usually destroy your margins in the long run.

3. **Customer Lifetime Value:** Prioritize metrics like customer lifetime value (CLV) over immediate sales figures. Building long-term relationships with customers and maximizing their lifetime value is more indicative of a successful strategy than short-term sales spikes.

4. **Continuous Monitoring and Adaptation:** Implement a system for continuous monitoring and adaptation of your strategy. Use both short-term and long-term performance metrics to assess the effectiveness of your strategy and make necessary adjustments.

5. **Holistic Performance Evaluation:** Evaluate your strategy based on a holistic set of performance indicators, including customer satisfaction, brand reputation, employee engagement, and market position. These broader metrics provide a more comprehensive view of strategic success.

Example:

A software company launches an aggressive sales campaign offering significant discounts to drive immediate sales. While the campaign results in a short-term spike in sales, it also attracts price-sensitive clients who do not stay loyal. The initial success fades as clients move on to other discounted offers.

The sales leader then shifts focus to a strategy that emphasizes value creation, client education, and long-term relationships. By developing a vigorous client onboarding program and providing ongoing support, the company increases client satisfaction and loyalty, leading to steady, sustainable growth.

Internalize This:

Immediate results are not always a reliable indicator of strategic success. A truly effective sales strategy focuses on long-term goals, sustainability, scalability, and customer lifetime value. By prioritizing these elements and continuously monitoring and adapting your strategy, sales leaders can achieve sustained success and growth. Evaluating your strategy through a holistic set of performance indicators ensures that it delivers lasting value and positions your organization for continued success in a dynamic market environment.

7) Misconception: Strategy is Solely the Leadership's Responsibility

Misconception: There is a widespread belief that developing and executing strategy is solely the responsibility of the leadership team. Many assume that only senior leaders have the insights and authority needed to create and implement effective strategies.

Reality: While leadership plays a crucial role in setting the strategic direction, successful strategy development and execution require the involvement and buy-in of the entire organization. Engaging the sales team and other stakeholders in the strategic process ensures better alignment, more innovative ideas, and greater commitment to achieving strategic goals. We all have cognitive blind spots, and by getting that involvement from every aspect of your organization, you'll get insight that would have missed otherwise.

Things to Remember:

1. **Inclusive Strategy Development:** Involve your sales team in the strategy development process. Their firsthand knowledge of client interactions, market conditions, and operational challenges can provide valuable insights that shape a more effective strategy.

2. **Empowerment and Ownership**: Empower your sales team to take ownership of the strategy. When team members feel that they have a stake in the strategy, they are more motivated to execute it effectively. Encourage them to contribute ideas and solutions that align with strategic goals.

3. **Clear Communication and Alignment:** Ensure that the strategic vision and objectives are clearly communicated across the organization. Alignment between leadership and the sales team is critical for cohesive and coordinated execution. Regular updates and open communication channels help maintain this alignment.

4. **Collaborative Implementation:** Strategy implementation should be a collaborative effort. Foster a culture where cross-functional teams work together to execute strategic initiatives. This collaboration ensures that

different perspectives are considered and that resources are optimally utilized.

5. **Feedback and Continuous Improvement:** Establish mechanisms for collecting feedback from the sales team and other stakeholders on the strategy's execution. Use this feedback to make continuous improvements. A dynamic strategy that evolves based on input from the field is more likely to succeed.

Example:

A manufacturing company decides to enter a new market segment. Instead of the leadership team developing the strategy in isolation, they involve key sales representatives, product managers, and customer service teams in the planning process. These team members provide insights into customer needs, competitive landscape, and operational capabilities. By involving the sales team in developing and refining the strategy, the company ensures better alignment and buy-in. The collaborative approach leads to a well-rounded strategy that leverages the strengths and knowledge of the entire organization, resulting in a successful market entry.

Internalize This:

Strategy is not solely the responsibility of the leadership team; it is a collective effort that requires the input, engagement, and ownership of the entire organization. By involving the sales team in strategy development, empowering them to take ownership, ensuring clear communication and alignment, fostering collaborative implementation, and continuously improving based on feedback, sales leaders can create and execute more effective strategies. This inclusive approach not only enhances the strategy's quality but also drives greater commitment and performance across the organization.

Final Thoughts:

By understanding and addressing these misconceptions and strategic pitfalls, you and your sales leaders can develop more effective, adaptable, and aligned strategies that drive your organization forward in a competitive landscape. This clarity and insight into what strategy truly entails are essential for fostering a culture of strategic thinking and execution within your team.

CHAPTER 5

Developing a Winning Sales Strategy

"The sales department isn't the whole company, but the whole company better be the sales department."

—Philip Kotler

"Rowing harder doesn't help if the boat is headed in the wrong direction."

—Kenichi Ohmae[44]

We start this chapter by looking at military history, Sun Tzu (The Art of War) and the Battle of Boju. Understanding this story will help you to better understand how to put the strategic pieces of the puzzle together.

---

[44] William J. Brown, Hays W. McCormick III, and Scott W. Thomas, AntiPatterns in Project Management (New York: Wiley, 2000)

Winning Strategy and The Battle of Boju[45]

In the annals of history, there are moments when the improbable happens, when the forces of the unexpected clash with the tides of inevitability, and the world is left to marvel at the outcome. The Battle of Boju, fought in 506 BCE during the tumultuous Spring and Autumn period of Chinese history, is one such moment. It is a story not just of warfare, but of the cunning that lies at the heart of all human endeavor. And at the center of this tale stands a figure whose name has become synonymous with strategy itself: Sun Tzu. The lessons within this story are ones that will benefit any strategically minded sales leader.

To understand the significance of the Battle of Boju, we must first understand the context in which it occurred. This was a time when China was not a unified nation, but a patchwork of warring states, each vying for dominance in a landscape of shifting alliances and constant conflict. This metaphor fits nicely into our world of sales. The state of Chu, vast and powerful, was one of the giants of this period, its territory sprawling across the fertile lands of the Yangtze River basin. Think of them as the proverbial "800-pound gorilla" of your industry. Chu's power was unquestioned, its army a formidable force that had crushed many opponents.

On the other side was Wu, a smaller state located to the east of Chu. Perhaps you can relate to Wu. While Wu was prosperous,

---

45   Zuo Tradition / Zuozhuan: Commentary on the "Spring and Autumn Annals". Edited by Andrew Plaks, translated by Stephen Durrant, Wai-yee Li, and David Schaberg, University of Washington Press, 2016

it was nowhere near the size or strength of its neighbor. Yet, in the early years of the fifth century BCE, Wu found itself in a bitter rivalry with Chu, a rivalry that would soon ignite into open war. The odds were against Wu from the start; its army was smaller, its resources more limited, and its enemy far more experienced in the art of war.

Enter Sun Tzu, a man whose origins are shrouded in mystery, but whose intellect and insight would soon alter the course of history. As a general in the service of the King of Wu, Sun Tzu was tasked with a seemingly impossible mission: to defeat Chu and secure Wu's future. It was a challenge that would have daunted even the most seasoned commanders, but Sun Tzu was no ordinary leader. He was a strategist of the highest order, a thinker who understood that the true essence of war lay not in brute force, but in the subtle manipulation of the mind.

The Battle of Boju is often remembered as a masterclass in strategy, a demonstration of how a smaller, weaker force can triumph over a larger, stronger one through the use of cunning and deception. Sun Tzu knew that to face Chu head-on would be suicidal; instead, he sought to outmaneuver his enemy, to draw them into a trap of their own making.

Sun Tzu's plan was bold and audacious. He began by feigning weakness, retreating in the face of Chu's advances, and allowing them to believe that they were on the brink of victory. Chu's generals, overconfident and eager to crush their foe, took the bait. They pursued the Wu forces with reckless abandon, stretching their supply lines and exhausting their troops in the process. It was precisely what Sun Tzu had hoped for.

With Chu's forces overextended and their morale waning,

Sun Tzu struck. In a series of lightning-fast maneuvers, the Wu army turned and attacked, catching the Chu soldiers off guard and throwing them into disarray. The battlefield, which had once seemed to favor Chu, now became a killing ground for their troops. Sun Tzu's forces, disciplined and well-coordinated, cut through the Chu ranks with deadly efficiency. What had begun as a seemingly inevitable Chu victory turned into a rout, with the Wu army decisively defeating their much larger opponent.

The implications of the Battle of Boju were profound. It was a victory that secured Wu's place as a major power in the region and dealt a humiliating blow to Chu's prestige. But more than that, it was a moment that cemented Sun Tzu's reputation as one of history's greatest military minds. His success at Boju was not merely a testament to his tactical brilliance, but to his deep understanding of human psychology and the nature of conflict.

Sun Tzu's approach to warfare, as exemplified by the Battle of Boju, was revolutionary. He recognized that the battlefield was as much a mental space as it was a physical one, and that victory often belonged not to the strongest, but to the most perceptive. His strategies, later immortalized in his treatise *The Art of War*, would go on to influence generations of leaders, from emperors to generals to business executives.

In the end, the Battle of Boju was not just a clash of armies, but a clash of minds. It was a moment when the power of strategy was revealed in its purest form, when the improbable became reality, and when a small state dared to challenge a giant—and won. The lessons of Boju, like those of all great battles, extend far beyond the battlefield. They remind us that in the game of life, it is not always the strongest who prevail, but those who can think, adapt, and outwit their opponents. And that is the most enduring legacy of Sun Tzu and his victory at Boju.

Sales Perspective: Lessons from the Battle of Boju

1. Understanding the Market (Know Your Enemy)

- **Sun Tzu's Approach:** Before the battle, Sun Tzu deeply studied the Chu army, understanding their strengths, weaknesses, and tendencies. He knew the terrain, the disposition of the enemy forces, and the mindset of their leaders.

- **Sales Application:** In sales, knowing your competition is crucial. Just as Sun Tzu analyzed his enemy, a sales team should understand the competitive landscape, including competitors' strengths, weaknesses, and strategies. This enables you to position your product or service more effectively.

2. Preparation and Planning (Strategic Thinking)

- **Sun Tzu's Approach:** Sun Tzu meticulously planned his campaign, choosing the timing, location, and methods of engagement that would maximize his army's strengths while exploiting the enemy's weaknesses. He prepared his troops thoroughly, ensuring they were ready for the challenges ahead.

- **Sales Application:** Success in sales often comes from thorough preparation and strategic planning.

Understanding client needs, crafting tailored pitches, and planning how to handle objections are all crucial. Just as Sun Tzu prepared his troops, sales teams should be well-prepared with product knowledge, market insights, and strategic sales plans.

3. Leverage Your Strengths (Focus on What You Do Best)

- **Sun Tzu's Approach:** Despite being outnumbered, Sun Tzu leveraged the mobility, discipline, and morale of his troops. He focused on quick, decisive actions that capitalized on his army's strengths, rather than trying to match the Chu forces in areas where they were stronger.

- **Sales Application:** In sales, it's important to focus on what your company does best. Identify the unique strengths of your product or service and leverage those in your pitch. Don't try to compete directly in areas where the competition is stronger; instead, focus on your unique value propositions.

4. Adaptability and Innovation (Creative Problem-Solving)

- **Sun Tzu's Approach:** Sun Tzu was highly adaptable, responding to changes in the battlefield with innovative tactics. He used deception, surprise, and psychological warfare to disrupt the larger Chu forces, leading them into traps and exploiting their overconfidence.

- **Sales Application:** The sales landscape is constantly changing, and being adaptable is key to success. Just as

Sun Tzu adapted his strategies on the battlefield, sales teams must be flexible and creative in their approach. This could mean adjusting sales pitches based on client feedback, exploring new markets, or finding innovative ways to demonstrate value.

5. Execution (Follow Through with Precision)

- **Sun Tzu's Approach:** Execution was key to Sun Tzu's victory. He didn't just have a good plan; he executed it with precision, ensuring that every part of his strategy was carried out effectively by his troops.

- **Sales Application:** In sales, having a strong strategy is important, but execution is where success is truly determined. This means following through on every step of the sales process, from initial contact to closing the deal, with precision and consistency.

6. Psychological Tactics (Influence and Persuasion)

- **Sun Tzu's Approach:** Sun Tzu used psychological tactics to demoralize the Chu forces, spreading misinformation and creating confusion among the enemy ranks. This weakened their resolve and made them more susceptible to defeat.

- **Sales Application:** In sales, understanding the psychology of your clients can give you a significant advantage. Use persuasive techniques, build strong relationships, and create a narrative that resonates emotionally with your clients. By influencing how clients perceive value, you can make your product the obvious choice.

Conclusion

The Battle of Boju, as interpreted through a sales lens, teaches us that success in sales, much like in warfare, is not just about having the biggest or most resources. It's about strategy, preparation, understanding your market, leveraging your strengths, and executing with precision. By applying these lessons, you and your sales leaders can achieve victory in even the most competitive markets.

Foundations of a Successful Sales Strategy

Creating a successful sales strategy begins with a solid foundation that considers multiple dimensions of the business environment, as well as internal capabilities and objectives. The following elements are essential in laying the groundwork for a successful sales strategy:[46]

1. Clear Objectives:

Your sales strategy should start with clear, measurable objectives. These objectives should align with the broader goals of the organization and be specific enough to guide action and

---

46   Steve W. Martin, Sales Strategy Playbook: The Ultimate Reference Guide to Solve Your Toughest Sales Challenges (California: Tilis Publishers, 2018)

measure progress. Examples include increasing market share, improving client retention, or entering new markets. Yes, obviously you need a defined sales revenue goal, but where do you plan on getting it?

2. Understanding Client Needs:

A deep understanding of your clients' needs, preferences, and purchasing behaviors is crucial. This involves segmenting the market and developing buyer personas to tailor your approach to different client groups effectively. This can't be overemphasized. Your clients have hopes, fears, dreams, and ambitions. Part of your job is to know them inside and out.

3. Competitive Analysis:

Analyze your competitors to understand their strengths, weaknesses, strategies, and client base. This analysis will help you identify opportunities to differentiate your offerings and find niches where you can achieve competitive advantage. Be brutally honest here. Most organizations do a frighteningly good job of lying to themselves. It's the sales equivalent of saying to yourself, "I just need to drop a few pounds," when in reality you're 50 pounds overweight.

4. Market Trends and Dynamics:

Stay abreast of broader market trends and dynamics. This includes technological changes, regulatory developments, and economic factors that can affect your business. Understanding these elements helps you anticipate market shifts and adapt your strategy accordingly. There's no excuse for getting blind-sided by the macroeconomics of the industry you sell in.

5. Value Proposition:

Define a clear value proposition that communicates why clients should choose your products or services over competitors.' This should highlight the unique benefits and features that meet clients' specific needs and desires. It's shocking how most competing sales team's "value proposition" sound exactly the same.

6. Sales Channels:

Identify the most effective sales channels to reach your target clients. This may include direct sales, online sales, distributors, or retail partners. Each channel should be optimized to deliver the best client experience and cost efficiency. Like everything else in sales, these will change over time. Change before you're forced to.

7. Resource Allocation:

Determine the resources required to implement your strategy effectively. This includes budgeting for marketing, sales personnel, training, and technological tools. Allocating resources strategically ensures that you can execute the strategy without spreading your efforts too thinly. Be comfortable either ignoring certain parts of your marketplace so you can bring more forces to bear on others that will prove more profitable over time.

8. Key Performance Indicators (KPIs):

Establish clear KPIs to monitor the effectiveness of your sales strategy. These should directly relate to your objectives and provide insight into what's working and what needs adjustment. Typical KPIs include sales growth, customer acquisition costs, customer lifetime value, and lead conversion rates. Know which KPI's matter and just as importantly which ones don't. As the saying goes, "Not everything that can be counted counts. Not everything that counts can be counted."

9. Risk Management:

Identify potential risks associated with your sales strategy and develop contingency plans. Risks could include competitive responses, changes in client preferences, or supply chain disruptions. Effective risk management allows you to respond quickly and maintain strategic direction even in adverse conditions. Go in with an understanding of how you'll respond if your assumptions are wrong. It's okay to be wrong from time to time, it's not okay to tenaciously keep trying to make something work that isn't and won't.

10. Continuous Improvement:

Finally, incorporate mechanisms for continuous feedback and improvement. Regularly review the strategy's performance and make necessary adjustments. This iterative process ensures that your sales strategy remains relevant and aligned with changing market conditions and business objectives.

By building on these foundational elements, sales leaders can develop a winning sales strategy that not only drives short-term sales results but also contributes to the long-term success and resilience of the organization. The subsequent sections and chapters will delve deeper into each of these elements, providing strategies and tools for effective implementation and management.

Analyzing Competitors and Disrupting Market Norms

To stay ahead in a competitive landscape, you as the sales leader must not only understand your competitors, but also find innovative ways to disrupt market norms.

Analyzing Competitors

Competitor analysis is a critical component of strategic sales planning. It provides insights into your competitors' strengths and weaknesses and helps identify opportunities where your business can gain a competitive edge. This is much more than just doing a SWOT (Strengths, Weaknesses, Opportunities, and Threat) analysis. While a SWOT is good to do and necessary, it is merely one of many tools that you can use.

1. **Identify Key Competitors**: Start by identifying both direct and indirect competitors. Use industry reports, market research, and client feedback to create a comprehensive list. The indirect competitors are the ones that will blindside you. Think in terms of what Airbnb did to Hotels, or Uber did to taxi companies.

2. **Gather Intelligence**: Collect information on competitors' products, pricing, sales tactics, and market reputation. Leverage public sources like their websites, press releases, and financial reports. Additionally, consider purchasing market research reports for detailed analysis.

3. **Analyze Strategies**: Understand the strategies your competitors use to attract and retain clients. This includes their marketing approaches, distribution channels, and customer service practices.

4. **Benchmark Performance**: Compare your products and services against those of your competitors in terms of quality, price, technology, and client experience. This can help highlight areas for improvement or differentiation. You're going to need help from your product team with this.

5. **Monitor Changes and Trends**: Regularly keep tab on competitors' activities. This includes tracking any new product launches, changes in marketing strategies, or shifts in their target markets.

Disrupting Market Norms

With a thorough understanding of the competitive landscape, you can now identify opportunities to disrupt market norms and innovate.

1. **Challenge Industry Assumptions**: Every industry operates on a set of assumptions that define how

companies behave. Identify these assumptions and challenge them by offering fresh solutions that change the way clients think about the products or services.

2. **Innovate Product Offerings**: Consider how you can add unique features or services that set your offerings apart from the competition. This could be through technology, design, or customer service enhancements.

3. **Revise Pricing Models**: Look for opportunities to innovate your pricing strategy to offer more value or flexibility than your competitors. This could involve subscription models, bundling products, or performance-based pricing.

4. **Redefine Customer Engagement**: Develop new ways to engage with clients that create a more personalized or satisfying experience. This could involve using advanced CRM tools, creating interactive online platforms, or providing exceptional post-sale support.

5. **Capitalize on Niches**: Identify niche markets that are underserved by competitors. Tailoring products or services to meet the specific needs of these smaller segments can help you build a loyal client base and reduce competitive pressures.

6. **Leverage Emerging Technologies**: Use technology to disrupt traditional business models. This could include adopting AI, blockchain, or IoT solutions to enhance product capabilities or streamline operations.

Executing Disruption

Successfully disrupting market norms requires careful planning and execution:

- **Pilot New Ideas**: Test new concepts in controlled environments or selected markets to evaluate their effectiveness before a full rollout.

- **Gather Feedback**: Continuously collect client feedback on new initiatives and be prepared to make quick adjustments based on their responses.

- **Build Internal Capabilities**: Ensure your team has the right skills and resources to implement and support new strategies. This may involve training staff or hiring new talent with specialized expertise.

By effectively analyzing competitors and courageously disrupting market norms, you can position your organization to lead rather than follow, driving growth and innovation in your industry. This proactive approach not only differentiates your company but also establishes it as a market leader that shapes industry standards.

Case Studies: Successful Strategy Implementations

You don't need to reinvent the wheel when it comes to creating successful sales strategies. Taking the time to look at different industries can offer actionable insights for you and your sales leaders looking to enhance your strategic approaches. These case studies highlight how distinct companies have implemented innovative sales strategies to drive growth and secure competitive advantages. Focus on the principles behind the case studies below. They may not all be applicable to you and your industry, but they should get your imagination going.

Case Study 1: HubSpot – Mastering Inbound Sales[47]

Background: As the market for digital marketing tools became increasingly saturated, HubSpot recognized the need to differentiate itself from traditional marketing service providers.

   Strategy: HubSpot pioneered the inbound marketing methodology, which focuses on attracting clients through content and interactions that are helpful and not disruptive.

Implementation:

- **Content-Driven Sales Strategy**: HubSpot invested heavily in creating valuable content to attract potential clients, including blogs, white papers, and webinars that addressed common marketing challenges.

- **Educational Approach to Selling**: They positioned their sales team to act as consultants, advising prospects on inbound marketing strategies, thereby nurturing leads through the sales funnel.

- **CRM and Sales Enablement Tools**: HubSpot developed

47   Bartolacci, G. (2018, December 11). HubSpot's Growth Story: Mastering SaaS Marketing Strategy. New Breed. https://www.newbreedrevenue.com/blog/the-evolution-of-hubspot-and-how-you-can-mimic-their-saas-marketing-strategy

a suite of sales and marketing tools that integrated with their platform, making it easier for businesses to manage their inbound strategies and measure results effectively.

Results: HubSpot's strategy transformed how businesses approach marketing and sales, leading to substantial revenue growth and establishing the company as a leader in inbound marketing services.

Case Study 2: Cisco – Customized Solutions in Networking Technology[48]

Background: Cisco faced intense competition in the networking technology market, where products can become commoditized quickly, and differentiation is challenging.

Strategy: Cisco adopted a strategy focused on developing customized solutions and fostering deep partnerships with enterprise clients.

Implementation:

- **Solution-Based Selling**: Instead of selling generic hardware, Cisco worked closely with its clients to develop solutions that addressed specific business challenges, integrating hardware, software, and services.

- **Strategic Account Management**: Cisco implemented a strategic account management approach, assigning

---

48   Pereira, D. (2024, August 22). Cisco Business Model. Business Model Analyst. https://businessmodelanalyst.com/cisco-business-model/

teams to key accounts to build strong, ongoing relationships with major clients.

- **Training and Certification Programs**: Cisco offered comprehensive training and certification programs for its systems, which helped to embed its technology within client operations and lock in long-term client loyalty.

Results: This approach allowed Cisco to maintain its leadership position in the highly competitive tech industry by deepening client engagement and increasing the barriers to switch to competitors. Even though Cisco is still dealing with fierce competitors slowly eroding their market share, they have managed to fight them off better than most.

Case Study 3: Salesforce – Driving Growth with a Customer Success-Centric Model[49]

Background: As competition intensified in the CRM space, Salesforce needed to differentiate itself and deepen client engagement.

Strategy: Salesforce invested heavily in client success initiatives, ensuring that clients could maximize the value from Salesforce products.

Implementation:

- **Dedicated Customer Success Teams**: Salesforce developed customer success teams focused on helping

---

49   Shah, H. (n.d.). How Salesforce Built a $13 Billion Empire from a CRM. Nira. Retrieved from https://nira.com/salesforce-history/

customers achieve their desired outcomes using Salesforce products.

- **Proactive Engagement and Upselling**: Through continuous engagement and by monitoring usage strategies, Salesforce could identify upselling opportunities and provide tailored solutions before customers even recognized the need.

- **Community Building**: Salesforce encouraged user communities and annual conferences like Dreamforce, enhancing user engagement and loyalty.

Results: This strategy not only helped Salesforce retain clients but also drove expansions and upsells, significantly increasing its customer lifetime value and market share.

These case studies exemplify how a well-crafted sales strategy, tailored to the specific strengths and market conditions of a business, can lead to predictable growth and a sustainable competitive edge. Each company used innovative tactics to address their unique market challenges and client needs, providing valuable lessons for sales leaders across industries.

The 10 Strategies of Sales

> "If you find yourself in a fair fight, you didn't plan your mission properly."
> —**David Hackworth**[33]

In the ferociously competitive landscape of sales, having a complete strategic toolkit is essential for any sales leader aiming to drive success. If you do a Google search for "strategy" or "strategic leadership," you will be overwhelmed with the results.

From Alexander the Great, Sun Tzu, General George S. Patton, Steve Jobs, to Jim Collins, Andy Groves, John Chambers, Jeff Bezos, Michael Porter, and Larry Ellison, each of them either used or influenced the strategies we're going to discuss below.

I have incorporated key concepts from the brilliant strategists listed above and tested their ideas in the sales marketplace over several decades and different economic environments. From those ideas and concepts, a strategic sales framework was created that will benefit you tremendously. I have distilled these key concepts into ten sales strategies.

For a sales leader, understanding and applying these ten categories can significantly enhance your ability to adapt to changing market conditions, outmaneuver competitors, and achieve sustained growth. The categories—Attack, Defense, Influence, Movement, Repositioning, Escalation, Deterrence, Integration, Leverage, and Deception—provide a versatile set of strategies that can be tailored to the specific challenges and opportunities faced by your team.[50]

Each category encompasses a range of strategies that can be deployed depending on your strategic objectives. Whether you aim to aggressively capture market share, protect your existing position, or influence the behavior of competitors and clients, these strategies offer actionable strategies to guide your decision-making and execution.

---

50   Patrick Hoverstadt and Lucy Loh, Patterns of Strategy, 1st ed. (Abingdon, UK: Routledge, 2017)

Understanding these ten categories allows you to not only react to the market but also to proactively shape it, positioning your organization for long-term success. Take your time to review them, decide which one(s) would benefit your sales team and organization the most and create a plan to roll out the strategy.

Keep in mind that you will need buy-in from other departments to make all of these work. However, even if you can partially execute on whichever of the strategies you feel your organization will benefit the most, you're still going to be doing more than many of your competitors. We will discuss how to get buy-in later in the book.

The ten categories are:

1. **Attack Strategies** - These focus on aggressive moves to challenge competitors, seize opportunities, or disrupt the market.

2. **Defense Strategies** - Strategies aimed at protecting and sustaining an organization's position, fending off threats, and maintaining stability.

3. **Influence Strategies** - Strategies that involve shaping the behavior of others, including competitors, partners, or even regulators, often through indirect means.

4. **Movement Strategies** - These focus on positioning, either by moving into new markets or adjusting positioning within a market to gain an advantage.

5. **Repositioning Strategies** - Strategies designed to change an organization's position in relation to competitors, often through shifts in perception, branding, or market focus.

6. **Escalation Strategies** - Strategies that involve ramping up actions or responses to outmaneuver competitors or increase market share.

7. **Deterrence Strategies** - Focus on discouraging competitors from taking specific actions, often through demonstrating strength or creating potential costs for the competitor.

8. **Integration Strategies** - These involve strategies that combine or integrate resources, capabilities, or operations, often aimed at creating synergies or increasing efficiency.

9. **Leverage Strategies** - Strategies that maximize the impact of available resources or capabilities, often by focusing them in key areas to create disproportionate effects.

10. **Deception Strategies** - These involve strategies that mislead competitors or other actors, creating advantages through misinformation or strategic ambiguity.

As we go through each of them, reflect on which ones can benefit you the most depending on your current situation.

Attack Strategies

> "Never let the fire choose the spot where it hits you."
>
> —Old US Forest Service Adage

Using *Attack Strategies* involves adopting aggressive tactics to gain market share, outmaneuver competitors, and drive growth. Here's how you can apply some of these Strategies:

1. Market Penetration

- **Focus on High-Potential Segments:** Identify specific segments within your target market that are either underserved or demonstrate high growth potential. Concentrate your sales efforts on these areas by offering tailored solutions that meet the unique needs of these clients.

- **Intensify Sales Efforts:** Ramp up your engagement with prospects and existing clients in these segments. This could involve increasing the number of sales calls, offering targeted promotions, or enhancing your presence at industry events and trade shows to establish a stronger market footprint.

2. Competitive Displacement

- **Target Competitor's Clients:** Actively pursue the clients of your competitors by demonstrating the superior value and benefits of your offerings. Develop and promote special incentives, such as discounts or enhanced service packages, to encourage them to switch to your products or services.

- **Highlight Competitor Weaknesses:** Use competitive intelligence to identify and exploit gaps in your competitors' offerings or service levels. Position your solutions as the better alternative, focusing on areas where your competitors fall short.

3. Product Innovation and Differentiation

- **Leverage Unique Selling Points (USPs):** Emphasize the unique features, benefits, or innovations that set your products apart from the competition. Ensure that your sales team is equipped to clearly communicate these differentiators to potential clients.

- **Introduce New Offerings:** Collaborate with your product development team to bring new solutions or features to the market that address unmet client needs, positioning your company as an industry leader and making your offerings more attractive.

4. Aggressive Pricing Strategies

- **Offer Strategic Discounts:** Implement targeted discounting strategies to quickly gain market share or to win over key accounts. Use pricing as a competitive weapon, particularly in markets where cost is a critical factor in purchasing decisions. Use this sparingly.

- **Emphasize Value:** Focus on value-based selling by highlighting the long-term benefits and ROI that your products or services provide. This approach can help justify your pricing, even at a premium, and can be especially effective in securing high-value clients.

5. Expanding Sales Channels

- **Broaden Distribution Networks:** Explore and develop new sales channels or partnerships that can help you reach additional client segments or geographic markets. Consider expanding into digital channels or forming alliances with complementary businesses to increase your market reach.

- **Leverage Digital Platforms:**[51] Invest in digital sales tools and platforms that can enhance client engagement, streamline the buying process, and provide your sales team with valuable insights to close deals more effectively.

6. Strategic Alliances

- **Form Partnerships:** Establish strategic alliances with other companies that offer complementary products or services. These partnerships can help you access new client bases, enhance your product offerings, or enter new markets more effectively.

- **Collaborative Ventures:** Consider joint ventures or co-marketing initiatives with partners that can amplify your market presence and create new revenue streams, while also providing your clients with more comprehensive solutions.

---

51 Gibson, K. (2024, May 8). Digital Platforms: What They Are & How They Create Value. Harvard Business School Online. https://online.hbs.edu/blog/post/what-is-a-digital-platform

7. Sales Force Expansion

■ **Grow Your Sales Team:** Expand your sales team to increase market coverage and drive more sales opportunities. Consider adding specialized roles focused on particular products, industries, or client segments to better serve specific markets.

■ **Enhance Training and Development:** Invest in advanced sales training programs to ensure your team has the skills and knowledge to aggressively pursue and close deals. Continuous development can also help your team adapt to changing market conditions and client needs.

8. Aggressive Marketing Support

■ **Coordinate with Marketing:** Work closely with your marketing team to launch targeted campaigns that directly support your sales initiatives. These could include lead generation activities, product promotions, and competitive benchmarking that help drive more qualified leads into your pipeline.

■ **Use Data-Driven Strategies:** Leverage analytics and client data to fine-tune your marketing and sales strategies, ensuring that efforts are focused on the most promising opportunities and that resources are allocated effectively.

Defense Strategies

"Generally, defense does not win personal or collective battles."[52]

– Legendary Special Forces/Delta Operator MSG Paul R. Howe of Black Hawk Down renown.

Using *Defense Strategies* involves implementing strategies to protect your market position, retain clients, and fend off competitive threats. Here's how you could apply these strategies:

1. Customer Retention

- **Strengthen Relationships:** Focus on deepening relationships with your existing clients through regular check-ins, personalized service, and proactive problem-solving. Ensure your key accounts receive the attention and support needed to keep them satisfied and loyal.

- **Loyalty Programs:** Develop loyalty or client appreciation programs that reward repeat business and long-term partnerships. This could include offering exclusive discounts, early access to new products, or premium support services to your most valued clients.

2. Contractual Lock-In

- **Long-Term Contracts:** Encourage clients to sign long-term contracts by offering benefits such as price stability,

---

52   Paul R. Howe, *Leadership and Training for the Fight: Using Special Operations Principles to Succeed in Law Enforcement, Business, and War* (New York: Skyhorse Publishing, 2011)

bundled services, or guaranteed service levels. These contracts make it more challenging for competitors to lure your clients away.

■ **Renewal Incentives:** Offer incentives for early renewals or extended contract terms, such as discounts or added features, to secure ongoing business and reduce the likelihood of churn.

3. Product and Service Enhancement

■ **Continuous Improvement:** Regularly update and enhance your product and service offerings based on client feedback and market trends. By continuously improving, you make it harder for competitors to offer a superior alternative.

■ **Customization:** Offer customized solutions that are specifically tailored to meet the unique needs of your key clients. This level of personalization can create a strong barrier to entry for competitors, as clients will be less likely to switch to a generic offering.

4. Competitive Intelligence

■ **Monitor Competitors:** Maintain a strong focus on competitive intelligence to keep track of competitors' moves, new product launches, and marketing strategies. By staying informed, you can anticipate and counteract their efforts to encroach on your territory.

■ **Preemptive Actions:** Use the insights gained from competitive intelligence to take preemptive actions, such as launching new features, adjusting pricing, or increasing client outreach, to neutralize potential threats before they materialize.

5. Client Satisfaction Focus

■ **Enhance Client Support:** Invest in high-quality client support that goes above and beyond, ensuring that any issues are resolved quickly and effectively. Exceptional service can be a powerful differentiator and a key factor in retaining clients.

■ **Feedback Loops:** Establish regular feedback loops with clients to understand their needs and concerns. Use this feedback to make necessary adjustments and demonstrate that you are responsive and committed to their success.

6. Barrier Creation

■ **Increase Switching Costs:** Implement strategies that increase the cost or complexity for clients to switch to a competitor. This could involve integrating your products more deeply into their operations or offering bundled solutions that would be difficult to replace.

■ **Exclusive Features:** Develop and promote features or services that are exclusive to your offerings, making it harder for competitors to match your value proposition and enticing clients to stay with you. Never let a comparison be "apples to apples." Force it to be "apples to oranges."

7. Brand Strengthening

- **Build Brand Loyalty:** Invest in building a strong, trusted brand that resonates with your target market. A strong brand can function as a defensive moat, making clients less likely to consider alternatives.

- **Thought Leadership:** Position your company as a thought leader in the industry through content marketing, speaking engagements, and participation in industry events. This can help solidify your reputation and make it harder for competitors to challenge your position.

8. Pricing Defense

- **Price Matching:** Implement a price-matching policy to counteract competitors attempting to undercut your prices. By matching or slightly beating competitors' prices, you can retain price-sensitive clients without significantly impacting your margins.

- **Value Emphasis:** Rather than engaging in a price war, focus on emphasizing the total value your products or services provide, including superior quality, better support, and additional features that justify your pricing.

9. Client Community Building

- **Foster a User Community:** Create and nurture a community around your product or service where clients can share experiences, solutions, and best practices. A strong community can build loyalty and make clients more resistant to switching to a competitor.

- **Client Advocacy:** Develop a client advocacy program where satisfied clients can share their success stories and refer new business. Advocates can become a powerful defense against competitors trying to win over your clients.

10. Internal Capability Enhancement

- **Strengthen Internal Processes:** Continuously improve your internal processes to ensure high efficiency and responsiveness. Streamlined operations can lead to better client service, quicker turnaround times, and a more resilient sales organization.

- **Sales Team Training:** Invest in ongoing training for your sales team to keep them sharp, knowledgeable, and well-equipped to manage competitive pressures. A well-prepared sales force is better positioned to defend existing accounts and secure new business.

By implementing these *Defense Strategies*, you can protect your market position, ensure client loyalty, and create barriers that make it difficult for competitors to erode your market share.

These strategies help safeguard your business against external threats while solidifying relationships with your clients.

Influence Strategies

> "Persuasion skills exert a far greater influence over others' behaviors than formal power structures do."
>
> **– Robert B. Cialdini**[53]

Utilizing *Influence Strategies* involves shaping the behaviors and decisions of clients, competitors, and other stakeholders to your advantage. This approach focuses on indirect methods of steering market dynamics, building alliances, and establishing your company as a leader in the industry. Here's how you could apply these strategies effectively:

1. Thought Leadership

- **Industry Authority:** Position your company as a thought leader by regularly sharing insights, research, and expertise through white papers, webinars, and industry events. This establishes your brand as an authority, influencing clients and competitors to follow your lead.

- **Content Marketing:** Develop a hefty content marketing strategy that educates and informs your target audience. By providing valuable content, you can shape

---

53   Robert B. Cialdini, Influence, New and Expanded: The Psychology of Persuasion (New York: Harper Business, 2021)

client perceptions and guide their buying decisions in your favor.

2. Strategic Partnerships

- **Form Alliances:** Build strategic partnerships with other companies that complement your offerings. These alliances can extend your influence in the market, opening new opportunities and creating a network effect that amplifies your reach.

- **Joint Initiatives:** Engage in joint initiatives, such as co-branded events or products, with partners to increase visibility and influence within your industry. This collaboration can help both parties gain credibility and attract new clients.

3. Client Advocacy

- **Leverage Satisfied Clients:** Encourage satisfied clients to become advocates for your brand by sharing their success stories, participating in case studies, or providing testimonials. Client advocacy can significantly influence the buying decisions of potential clients.

- **Referral Programs:** Implement referral programs that reward clients for bringing in new business. This not only incentivizes your existing clients but also leverages their influence within their networks to generate new leads.

4. Competitive Benchmarking

- **Highlight Strengths:** Use competitive benchmarking to demonstrate how your products or services outperform those of competitors. Sharing this data in marketing materials or sales pitches can influence prospects by providing clear, evidence-based reasons to choose your offerings.

- **Public Comparisons:** Publish comparisons that highlight your strengths relative to competitors, such as performance metrics, client satisfaction scores, or pricing advantages. These comparisons can subtly guide prospects towards viewing your company as the superior choice.

5. Industry Standards and Best Practices

- **Set Industry Standards:** Take an active role in defining industry standards and best practices. By leading or contributing to industry bodies, you can shape the rules and guidelines that others in the market will follow, positioning your company as an industry leader.

- **Best Practice Sharing:** Share best practices with your clients and partners, positioning your company as a source of valuable expertise. This can influence how others in the industry operate, often leading them to adopt practices that align with your offerings.

6. Social Proof

- **Showcase Case Studies:** Use case studies that demonstrate the success of your products or services across various industries. Social proof can be a powerful influencer, reassuring prospects that others have successfully chosen your solutions.

- **Awards and Recognitions:** Publicize any awards, certifications, or recognitions your company has received. These accolades serve as endorsements that can sway potential clients and partners in your favor.

7. Market Education

- **Educational Initiatives:** Launch educational initiatives, such as workshops, webinars, or training programs, which help your target market better understand their needs and how your products can meet them. Educating the market can influence buying decisions by positioning your company as a knowledgeable and helpful resource.

- **Consultative Selling:** Adopt a consultative selling approach where your sales team acts as advisors, helping prospects identify their challenges and solutions. This builds trust and positions your company as a valuable partner in their success. No one likes to be sold, but they do like to be helped.

8. Networking and Relationship Building

- **Industry Networking:** Actively participate in industry networking events, trade shows, and conferences to build relationships with key influencers and decision-makers. These connections can be leveraged to shape market perceptions and open doors to new opportunities.

- **Relationship Management:** Focus on maintaining strong relationships with key accounts, partners, and industry leaders. By being a trusted and dependable partner, you can influence their decisions and maintain a favorable position in the market.

9. Public Relations and Media Influence

- **Media Engagement:** Engage with industry media by contributing articles, giving interviews, or participating in panel discussions. By being visible in respected media outlets, you can influence public perception and establish your company as a thought leader.

- **Crisis Management:** Manage any public relations issues swiftly and transparently to maintain trust and influence over your stakeholders. Effective crisis management can prevent negative situations from escalating and protect your company's reputation.

10. Influencer Partnerships

- **Leverage Industry Influencers:** Partner with industry influencers or thought leaders who can advocate for your products and services. Their endorsement can carry significant weight with potential clients and help steer the market in your favor.

- **Co-Creation with Influencers:** Collaborate with influencers to create content, host events, or develop new products. This not only extends your reach but also leverages their influence to shape market trends and client preferences.

By applying these *Influence Strategies*, you can shape the market environment, guide client and competitor behaviors, and strengthen your position as a leader in your industry. These strategies are about subtly steering market dynamics and building a network of influence that supports your sales goals and long-term business success.

Movement Strategies

> "Water shapes its course according to the nature of the ground over which it flows; the soldier works out his victory in relation to the foe whom he is facing."
>
> - Sun Tzu

Utilizing *Movement Strategies* involves strategically repositioning your company within the market, expanding into new territories, or shifting your focus to adapt to changing conditions. These strategies help you stay ahead of the competition, capture new opportunities, and ensure sustained growth. Here's how you could apply these strategies effectively:

1. Market Expansion

- **Geographic Expansion:** Identify and target new geographic markets where there is demand for your products or services. This could involve entering new regions or countries that have been underserved or where competition is weak.

- **New Industry Verticals:** Explore opportunities in new industry verticals that align with your core capabilities. Tailor your offerings to meet the specific needs of these industries, allowing you to capture additional market share.

2. Customer Segment Shifts

- **Target New Client Segments:** Identify new client segments that could benefit from your offerings, such as small businesses, mid-market companies, or specific niches within your existing market. Adjust your sales approach and messaging to appeal to these new segments.

- **Reposition Existing Products:** Reposition your existing products to meet the needs of different client segments. This might involve rebranding, adjusting pricing, or highlighting different product features that resonate more with the new target audience.

3. Product Line Diversification

- **Expand Product Portfolio:** Introduce new products or services that complement your existing offerings, allowing you to enter new markets or appeal to a broader client base. This diversification can help mitigate risk and drive growth.

- **Vertical Integration:** Consider vertical integration by adding products or services that are either upstream (suppliers) or downstream (distribution) of your current offerings. This can help you capture more of the value chain and provide a more comprehensive solution to clients.

4. Channel Development

- **Develop New Sales Channels:** Explore and develop new sales channels, such as online platforms, third-party distributors, or strategic partnerships, to reach additional clients. Expanding your distribution network can help you penetrate new markets more effectively.

- **Enhance Existing Channels:** Optimize and expand your existing sales channels to improve reach and efficiency. This could involve improving e-commerce capabilities, enhancing your partner network, or increasing direct sales efforts.

5. Strategic Repositioning

- **Reposition Your Brand:** Shift your brand positioning to better align with market trends or changes in client preferences. This could involve rebranding efforts, changing your value proposition, or updating your messaging to better reflect your company's strengths.

- **Focus on Emerging Trends:** Identify and capitalize on emerging market trends, such as technological advancements or shifts in client behavior. Position your company as a leader in these areas to attract clients looking for innovative solutions.

6. Service Offering Expansion

- **Add Complementary Services:** Expand your service offerings to include complementary services that enhance the value of your core products. This could involve adding consulting, training, or support services that make your offerings more attractive to clients.

- **Bundling Products and Services:** Create bundled solutions that combine products and services into a single offering. Bundling can increase client value, simplify the purchasing process, and create a more compelling proposition.

7. Strategic Alliances for Market Entry

- **Form Alliances to Enter New Markets:** Partner with

companies that already have a presence in new markets you wish to enter. These strategic alliances can provide you with the local expertise, client base, and distribution networks needed to quickly establish a foothold.

■ **Joint Ventures:** Consider joint ventures with local or complementary companies to share resources and risks when entering new markets. Joint ventures can accelerate market entry and enhance your competitive position.

8. Technology Adoption

■ **Adopt Emerging Technologies:** Leverage emerging technologies to enhance your product offerings, improve operational efficiency, or create new revenue streams. Staying at the forefront of technology can help you maintain a competitive edge and appeal to tech-savvy clients.

■ **Digital Transformation:** Invest in digital transformation initiatives to streamline your sales processes, improve client engagement, and enhance data-driven decision-making. A strong digital presence can help you move into new markets more effectively.

9. Adapting to Market Changes

■ **Pivot Strategy:** Be prepared to pivot your sales strategy in response to significant market changes, such as economic shifts, new regulations, or changing client preferences. Quick adaptation can help you maintain momentum and avoid being left behind.

- **Agility in Sales Approach:** Foster agility within your sales team, encouraging them to adapt quickly to new market conditions, client needs, or competitive pressures. This can involve cross-training, flexible roles, and a culture of continuous improvement.

10. Competitive Positioning

- **Move to a Market Leadership Position:** Aim to shift your company's position within the competitive landscape by targeting leadership in key areas, such as product quality, client service, or innovation. Establishing a clear leadership position can attract more clients and create a strong market presence.

- **Focus on Niche Markets:** Identify and dominate niche markets where you can offer specialized solutions that meet specific client needs. Niche markets often have less competition and can provide higher margins. Think Blue Ocean Strategy.[54]

By implementing these *Movement Strategies*, you can strategically reposition your company within the market, expand into new areas, and adapt to changing conditions. These strategies

---

54 W. Chan Kim and Renée Mauborgne, Blue Ocean Strategy: How to Create Uncontested Market Space and Make the Competition Irrelevant (Boston: Harvard Business School Press, 2005)

allow you to stay ahead of competitors, capture new opportunities, and ensure long-term growth and success.

Repositioning Strategies

> "Positioning is not what you do to a product. Positioning is what you do to the mind of the prospect."
>
> **- Jack Trout**[55]

Utilizing *Repositioning Strategies* involves strategically changing the way your company, products, or services are perceived in the market. This could involve shifting your focus, adjusting your value proposition, or rebranding to better align with client needs or market trends. These strategies help you stay relevant, attract new clients, and differentiate yourself from competitors. Here's how you could apply these Strategies effectively:

1. Value Proposition Shift

- **Refine Value Proposition:** Reassess and refine your value proposition to better resonate with your target market. This could involve emphasizing different product features, highlighting cost savings, or focusing on how your solution addresses emerging client challenges.

- **Target Different Customer Needs:** Adjust your messaging to focus on different pain points or benefits that

---

55   Al Ries and Jack Trout, Positioning: The Battle for Your Mind, 20th Anniversary ed. (New York: McGraw Hill, 2003)

are more relevant to current market conditions. This shift can attract new clients who are looking for specific solutions.

2. Brand Repositioning

- **Rebrand or Refresh Your Image:** Consider a rebranding effort if your current brand no longer aligns with your company's direction or market trends. This could involve updating your logo, messaging, and overall brand identity to better reflect your company's strengths and vision.

- **Change Market Perception:** Actively work to change how the market perceives your brand. This might involve focusing on sustainability, innovation, or client service excellence to differentiate from competitors.

3. Product Repositioning

- **Reposition Existing Products:** Shift the positioning of existing products to appeal to different client segments or uses. For example, a product initially marketed for large enterprises could be repositioned for mid-market companies by highlighting ease of use and cost-effectiveness.

- **Introduce Product Variants:** Launch new variants of existing products that cater to different market needs, such as a premium version for high-end clients or a simplified version for cost-sensitive buyers.

4. Pricing Strategy Adjustment

- **Adopt a New Pricing Model:** Change your pricing strategy to better align with client expectations or competitive pressures. This could involve shifting to a subscription model, introducing tiered pricing, or offering value-based pricing to highlight the ROI of your products.

- **Price Repositioning:** Reposition your products in the market by adjusting their price points. This could mean positioning a product as a premium offering or making it more accessible by lowering the price to appeal to a broader audience.

5. Target Market Repositioning

- **Shift Focus to New Markets:** Reposition your company by shifting focus to a new target market that offers better growth opportunities. This could involve entering a different industry vertical or targeting smaller businesses if your current focus is on large enterprises.

- **Expand Market Reach:** Broaden your market reach by repositioning your offerings to appeal to a global audience or entering emerging markets where there is less competition.

6. Service Repositioning

- **Enhance Service Offerings:** Reposition your services by adding value-added components, such as personalized support, consulting, or training. This can differentiate your company from competitors who may only offer basic services.

■ **Focus on Client Experience:** Shift the focus of your services to prioritize client experience, making it a key selling point. This can involve improving response times, offering dedicated account management, or providing a seamless client journey.

7. Sales Strategy Repositioning

■ **Consultative Selling Approach:** Reposition your sales approach to be more consultative, focusing on understanding and solving client problems rather than just selling products. This can help build stronger relationships and position your company as a trusted partner.

■ **Account-Based Selling:** Shift to an account-based sales strategy where you focus on key accounts with high growth potential. This approach can help you reposition your sales efforts to drive more significant, long-term wins.

8. Channel Strategy Repositioning

■ **Develop New Sales Channels:** Reposition your channel strategy by exploring new sales channels, such as e-commerce platforms, to reach different client segments. This can help you access markets that were previously difficult to penetrate.

- **Strengthen Partner Relationships:** Reposition your company as a preferred partner by offering better incentives, co-marketing opportunities, or exclusive products to your channel partners. This can enhance your distribution network and improve market penetration.

9. Marketing Strategy Repositioning

- **Shift Marketing Focus:** Reposition your marketing strategy to highlight various aspects of your business, such as innovation, sustainability, or client success stories. This can help you connect with new audiences and refresh your brand image.

- **Leverage Digital Marketing:** Reposition your marketing efforts to focus more on digital channels, such as social media, content marketing, and SEO. This can help you reach a broader audience and improve lead generation.

10. Competitive Repositioning

- **Differentiate from Competitors:** Reposition your company by differentiating your offerings from competitors. This could involve focusing on unique product features, superior client service, or a more compelling value proposition.

- **Attack Competitor Weaknesses:** Reposition your messaging to highlight areas where your competitors are weak, such as limited product capabilities or poor client support. This can help you capture market share from competitors.

By applying these *Repositioning Strategies*, you can strategically shift your company's market position, making your products, services, and brand more appealing to clients. These strategies help you stay competitive, attract new clients, and adapt to changing market dynamics, ensuring long-term success and growth.

Escalation Strategies

> "The principle of war is the concentration of force against weakness."
>
> **—Napoleon Bonaparte**[56]

Utilizing *Escalation Strategies* involves intensifying your sales efforts, increasing competitive pressure, and leveraging your resources to dominate the market. These strategies are about taking aggressive actions to accelerate growth, overwhelm competitors, and secure a leading position in the market. Here's how you could apply these strategies effectively:

1. Sales Force Expansion

- **Increase Sales Team Size:** Rapidly expand your sales force to cover more ground, reach more clients, and close more deals. A larger team allows you to increase your market presence and increase sales velocity.

---

56   Andrew Roberts, Napoleon: A Life, Illustrated ed. (New York: Penguin Books, 2015)

- **Specialized Roles:** Create specialized roles within your sales team focused on key products, industries, or client segments. This ensures that each area receives focused attention and expertise, driving more targeted sales efforts.

2. Aggressive Market Penetration

- **High-Intensity Campaigns:** Launch high-intensity marketing and sales campaigns aimed at quickly capturing market share. This could include aggressive promotional offers, limited-time discounts, or bundling deals designed to attract new clients rapidly.

- **Target Competitors' Weak Points:** Identify and exploit weaknesses in your competitors' market coverage, such as underserved regions or client segments. Focus your sales efforts on these areas to quickly gain an advantage.

3. Product Launch Acceleration

- **Rapid Product Development:** Accelerate the development and launch of new products or features to stay ahead of competitors and meet emerging client needs. A fast-paced product launch strategy can help you capitalize on market opportunities before others do.

- **Frequent Updates:** Regularly release product updates or enhancements to maintain momentum and keep your offerings fresh in the eyes of clients. This can also help prevent competitors from catching up.

4. Pricing Pressure

- **Aggressive Discounting:** Implement aggressive discounting strategies to undercut competitors and quickly gain market share. This approach can be particularly effective in price-sensitive markets where cost is a major decision factor. For obvious reasons, use this sparingly.

- **Dynamic Pricing:** Use dynamic pricing strategies to respond quickly to competitive pricing moves or market demand changes. By adjusting prices in real time, you can stay competitive and maximize revenue.

5. Increased Customer Engagement

- **Intensify Customer Touchpoints:** Increase the frequency and quality of interactions with your clients through more frequent meetings, follow-ups, and personalized communication. Enhanced engagement can lead to stronger relationships and higher client retention.

- **Proactive Account Management:** Implement proactive account management practices where your team regularly reviews client needs and offers solutions before they even ask. This can help you stay ahead of competitors and maintain client loyalty.

6. Market Dominance Initiatives

- **Exclusive Contracts:** Pursue exclusive contracts or long-term agreements with key clients to lock in business and prevent competitors from gaining a foothold. This can solidify your market position and provide a stable revenue stream.

- **Strategic Alliances:** Form strategic alliances with other companies to create a more comprehensive offering, making it difficult for competitors to compete. These partnerships can also help you expand your market reach more quickly.

7. Sales Process Optimization

- **Accelerate Sales Cycles:** Optimize your sales processes to shorten the sales cycle, allowing you to close deals faster. This could involve streamlining approval processes, improving lead qualification, or enhancing proposal generation.

- **Automate Routine Tasks:** Implement automation tools to manage routine tasks, freeing up your sales team to focus on high-value activities like client interactions and closing deals. This can increase overall efficiency and productivity. Salespeople already spend too much time on administrative tasks.[57] Anything to relieve that burden will help improve sales efforts.

---

57   Salesforce. (2022). New Research Reveals Sales Reps Need a Productivity Overhaul – Spend Less than 30% Of Their Time Actually Selling. https://www.salesforce.com/news/stories/sales-research-2023/

8. Competitive Benchmarking

- **Aggressive Positioning:** Use competitive benchmarking to position your offerings aggressively against competitors. Highlight areas where your products outperform others and use this data to win over potential clients who are considering alternatives.

- **Public Comparisons:** Make public comparisons between your products and those of competitors in your marketing materials. This direct approach can sway undecided clients by clearly illustrating your superiority.

9. Marketing and Sales Alignment

- **Coordinated Campaigns:** Ensure close alignment between your marketing and sales teams to execute coordinated campaigns that maximize impact. This could involve joint planning sessions, shared goals, and integrated messaging that amplifies your market presence.

- **Resource Intensification:** Allocate more resources to high-impact marketing and sales activities, such as digital advertising, events, or direct outreach. By concentrating resources where they can make the most difference, you can drive faster and have more significant results.

10. Customer Acquisition Drives

- **Lead Generation Blitz:** Launch an intensive lead generation campaign to rapidly fill your sales pipeline. This could involve doubling down on content marketing, increasing your budget for paid ads, or running a series of targeted webinars or events.

- **Referral Program Expansion:** Expand or intensify your referral programs, incentivizing current clients to bring in new business. A well-structured referral program can significantly accelerate client acquisition and expand your network.

By applying these *Escalation Strategies*, you can aggressively push for market dominance, rapidly increase sales, and outpace your competitors. These strategies are about maximizing your impact in the market, leveraging all available resources, and taking decisive actions to secure a leadership position.

Deterrence Strategies

> "The supreme art of war is to subdue
> the enemy without fighting."
> —Sun Tzu

Utilizing *Deterrence Strategies* involves implementing strategies to discourage competitors from entering your market, challenging your position, or taking actions that could undermine your business. These strategies are about creating barriers, demonstrating strength, and signaling to competitors that challenging your position will be costly or unsuccessful. Here's how you could apply these strategies effectively:

1. Barrier Creation

- **Increase Switching Costs:** Design your products and services in a way that makes it difficult or costly for clients to switch to competitors. This could involve integrating deeply with clients' existing systems, offering bundled solutions, or providing long-term contracts with incentives for renewal.

- **Exclusive Features:** Develop and promote unique features that are only available through your products. These exclusive offerings can create a competitive moat, making it harder for competitors to match your value proposition.

2. Contractual Lock-In

- **Long-Term Contracts:** Secure long-term contracts with key clients that include terms favorable to your company, such as automatic renewals or penalties for early termination. This strategy makes it difficult for competitors to poach your clients.

- **Preferred Vendor Status:** Work towards becoming a preferred or sole supplier for your clients. Achieving this status can effectively lock out competitors from key accounts and solidify your market position.

3. Aggressive Pricing Defense

- **Price Matching:** Implement a price-matching policy to deter competitors from trying to undercut your pricing.

By signaling that you will match any competitive offer, you can discourage price wars and maintain market stability.

- **Sustained Discounting:** Offer sustained or strategic discounts to key clients, making it less attractive for them to consider competitors. This approach can dissuade competitors from attempting to win over your clients on price alone.

4. Capacity Signaling

- **Demonstrate Excess Capacity:** Publicly demonstrate or communicate your company's ability to scale production or service delivery quickly. This signals to competitors that you can easily meet increased demand, making it risky for them to enter the market or ramp up their efforts.

- **Showcase Operational Strength:** Highlight your operational efficiencies, such as superior logistics, faster delivery times, or unmatched client service. This can deter competitors who may struggle to compete on these operational fronts.

5. Client Loyalty Programs

- **Reward Loyalty:** Implement or enhance client loyalty programs that reward long-term relationships and repeat business. By offering exclusive benefits, discounts, or early access to new products, you can foster strong client loyalty that competitors will find difficult to break.

- **VIP Treatment:** Provide VIP treatment to your top clients, such as dedicated account managers, priority support, or customized solutions. This level of service can create a strong deterrent to competitors attempting to lure away your most valuable clients.

6. Public Commitment

- **Make Public Commitments:** Announce public commitments to your clients, such as guaranteed pricing, service levels, or innovation timelines. By setting these expectations, you can deter competitors by making it clear that your clients are well-protected and valued.

- **Visible Investments:** Publicize your investments in new technologies, infrastructure, or client support initiatives. This signals to competitors that you are committed to maintaining and strengthening your market position.

7. Strategic Litigation

- **Protect Intellectual Property:** Actively defend your intellectual property through patents, trademarks, or legal action if necessary. This can discourage competitors from copying your innovations or infringing on your market space.

- **Preemptive Legal Actions:** If a competitor appears to

be infringing on your market space or rights, consider preemptive legal actions to set a strong deterrent. Even the threat of litigation can often be enough to make competitors think twice.

8. Market Signaling

- **Announce Strategic Moves:** Use market signaling to announce strategic moves, such as new product launches, expansions, or partnerships, before they occur. This can deter competitors by making them wary of entering a market where you're already planning significant investments.

- **Competitive Intelligence:** Use competitive intelligence to send signals that you are aware of and ready to counteract competitors' moves. This can make competitors more cautious in their actions, knowing they are being closely monitored.

9. Sales Force Strength

- **Deploy Sales Power:** Allocate your best sales talent to key accounts or competitive hotspots to defend against potential encroachments. A strong, visible sales presence can deter competitors from attempting to make inroads into your client base.

- **Intensify Client Engagement:** Increase the frequency and depth of engagement with your key clients, ensuring that they feel valued and well-supported. This can prevent competitors from finding opportunities to offer better service or solutions.

10. Strategic Alliances

- **Strengthen Partnerships:** Forge or strengthen strategic alliances with complementary companies to create a united front against competitors. These alliances can increase your market power and make it more challenging for competitors to disrupt your position.

- **Exclusive Collaborations:** Enter into exclusive collaborations with key partners, ensuring that they do not collaborate with your competitors. This can effectively block competitors from accessing critical resources or capabilities.

By applying these *Deterrence Strategies*, you can create significant barriers that discourage competitors from challenging your market position. These strategies help protect your client base, defend against competitive threats, and maintain your company's leadership in the industry. The focus is on making it costly, difficult, or unappealing for competitors to engage in direct competition with your business. By letting your competitors know it will be painful for them to go against you, they will turn their sights on a less formidable target.

Integration Strategies

> "The whole is greater than the sum of its parts."
>
> – Euclid

Utilizing *Integration Strategies* involves strategies that combine or integrate resources, capabilities, or operations to create collaboration, increase efficiency, and deliver more comprehensive solutions to clients. These strategies can help you strengthen your market position, enhance value propositions, and streamline operations. Here's how you could apply these strategies effectively:

1. Product and Service Bundling

- **Bundle Offerings:** Create bundled packages that combine multiple products or services into a single offering. This not only increases the perceived value but also simplifies the purchasing decision for clients, making it harder for competitors to match your comprehensive solutions.

- **Customized Bundles:** Offer customized bundles tailored to specific client needs, allowing for greater flexibility and personalization. This approach can increase client satisfaction and loyalty by providing more targeted solutions.

2. Cross-Selling and Up-Selling

- **Integrate Cross-Selling Strategies:** Train your sales team to effectively cross-sell complementary products or services during the sales process. This strategy maximizes the value of each client interaction and increases overall revenue per client.

- **Up-Sell Opportunities:** Identify and promote up-sell opportunities by offering enhanced or premium versions of products and services. Integrating up-sell strategies into your sales process can lead to higher client lifetime value and stronger relationships.

3. Unified Client Experience

- **Integrated Client Support:** Streamline client support by integrating various support channels (e.g., phone, email, chat) into a unified system. This ensures a seamless experience for clients, improving satisfaction and retention.

- **Consistent Branding Across Touchpoints:** Ensure that your brand messaging, tone, and quality are consistent across all client touchpoints, including sales, marketing, and client service. This creates a cohesive brand experience that reinforces client trust and loyalty.

4. Sales and Marketing Alignment

- **Unified Sales and Marketing Strategy:** Align your sales and marketing teams around shared goals and strategies to create a more cohesive and effective approach to client acquisition and retention. This integration can lead to more consistent messaging, better-qualified leads, and increased sales efficiency. This seems obvious, but it's shocking how many organizations fail to do this.

- **Shared Metrics and KPIs:** Develop shared metrics and KPIs for both sales and marketing teams to ensure alignment and accountability. By measuring success against the same goals, both teams can work more effectively together to drive growth.

5. Supply Chain Integration

- **Integrate Supply Chain Operations:** Work closely with your supply chain partners to integrate processes, reduce lead times, and improve inventory management. This can lead to cost savings, faster delivery times, and improved client satisfaction.

- **Collaborative Forecasting:** Engage in collaborative forecasting with key suppliers and partners to better predict demand and align production schedules. This integration can reduce the risk of stockouts or overproduction, ensuring a more reliable supply chain.

6. Technology Integration

- **Integrated CRM Systems:** Implement a unified CRM system that integrates with other business tools, such as marketing automation and client support platforms. This ensures that your sales team has access to comprehensive client data, enabling more personalized and effective sales interactions.

- **Data Integration:** Integrate data from various sources (e.g., sales, marketing, client support) into a centralized database or analytics platform. This enables better decision-making and more strategic sales efforts by providing a holistic view of client behavior and trends.

7. Partner Ecosystem Development

- **Build a Partner Ecosystem:** Develop a strong partner ecosystem by integrating your offerings with those of complementary businesses. This can enhance your value proposition and provide clients with more comprehensive solutions that address a wider range of needs.

- **Co-Development and Co-Marketing:** Engage in co-development and co-marketing initiatives with partners to create integrated solutions that offer greater value to clients. These collaborations can also help you reach new markets and client segments.

8. Client Feedback Integration

- **Incorporate Client Feedback:** Integrate client feedback into your product development and sales strategies to ensure that your offerings meet client needs. This can lead to higher client satisfaction and more successful product launches.

■ **Feedback Loops:** Establish feedback loops between sales, client support, and product teams to continuously improve your offerings based on real-world client experiences. This integration fosters innovation and responsiveness to market demands.

9. Vertical and Horizontal Integration

■ **Vertical Integration:** Consider vertical integration by acquiring or partnering with suppliers or distributors, allowing you to control more of the supply chain. This can lead to cost efficiencies, better quality control, and a stronger market position.

■ **Horizontal Integration:** Explore horizontal integration by acquiring or merging with companies in the same industry that offer complementary products or services. This can expand your product portfolio, increase market share, and reduce competition.

10. Process Integration

■ **Streamline Internal Processes:** Integrate and streamline internal processes across departments, such as sales, marketing, finance, and operations, to improve efficiency and reduce costs. This can lead to faster decision-making and a more agile organization.

■ **Automation and Workflow Integration:** Implement automation tools and integrated workflows to reduce manual tasks and improve productivity. This integration ensures that your sales team can focus on high-value activities, such as building relationships and closing deals.

By applying these *Integration Strategies*, you can create synergies across your organization, improve client experiences, and enhance your competitive position. These strategies help you deliver more comprehensive and cohesive solutions to your clients, streamline operations, and drive long-term growth and success.

Leverage Strategies

> "Give me a lever long enough and a fulcrum on which to place it, and I shall move the world."
> - Archimedes

Utilizing *Leverage Strategies* involves strategies that maximize the impact of your resources, relationships, and market position to create disproportionate advantages. These strategies focus on amplifying your strengths, using your assets more effectively, and influencing market dynamics to your benefit. Here's how you could apply these strategies effectively:

1. Strategic Partnerships

- **Leverage Key Partnerships:** Form and nurture strategic partnerships with companies that complement your offerings. By leveraging the strengths and networks of your partners, you can expand your market reach, access new client segments, and offer more comprehensive solutions.

- **Co-Marketing Initiatives:** Collaborate with partners on co-marketing campaigns to share costs, broaden your audience, and enhance the perceived value of your combined offerings. This approach allows you to maximize the impact of your marketing budget.

2. Client Relationships

- **Maximize Key Account Potential:** Focus on deepening relationships with your key accounts, leveraging these relationships to expand your business within these organizations. This could include cross-selling additional products, securing long-term contracts, or developing customized solutions that further integrate your offerings into their operations.

- **Referral Programs:** Leverage satisfied clients to generate new business through a structured referral program. By incentivizing referrals, you can extend your reach and credibility through trusted client networks.

3. Brand Equity

- **Leverage Strong Branding:** Use your established brand reputation to enter new markets or introduce new products more effectively. A strong brand can reduce client acquisition costs and accelerate market penetration.

- **Brand as a Differentiator:** Position your brand as a key differentiator in competitive markets, leveraging your reputation for quality, innovation, or client service to win deals and retain clients.

4. Technology and Data

- **Leverage Data Analytics:** Utilize data analytics to identify high-potential leads, optimize pricing strategies, and improve sales forecasting. By leveraging data-driven insights, you can make more informed decisions and increase your sales efficiency.

- **Automate for Scale:** Leverage automation tools to streamline routine tasks, freeing up your sales team to focus on higher-value activities. Automation can help you scale your efforts without a corresponding increase in resources.

5. Market Position

- **Leverage Market Leadership:** If your company is a market leader, leverage this position to influence market standards, set pricing trends, and shape client expectations. Use your dominance to create barriers for competitors and maintain your leadership.

- **First-Mover Advantage:** If you're first to market with a new product or service, leverage this position to establish strong client relationships and brand loyalty before competitors enter the space.

6. Economies of Scale

- **Maximize Cost Efficiency:** Leverage economies of scale by increasing production or sales volume to reduce costs per unit. This can allow you to offer more competitive pricing or improve margins, giving you an advantage in price-sensitive markets.

- **Bulk Purchasing Power:** Use your purchasing power to negotiate better terms with suppliers, which can be passed on to clients as added value or used to improve your profitability.

7. Intellectual Property

- **Leverage Patents and Trademarks:** Use your intellectual property, such as patents and trademarks, to protect your market position and create licensing opportunities. This can generate additional revenue streams and deter competitors from entering your space.

- **Monetize IP:** Consider licensing your intellectual property to other companies, creating a new revenue stream while also extending your influence across the industry.

8. Human Capital

- **Leverage Expertise:** Highlight the expertise of your team as a key selling point. Leverage your sales team's deep industry knowledge or technical skills to build trust with potential clients and differentiate your company from competitors.

- **Employee Advocacy:** Encourage and empower your employees to become advocates for your brand on social media and at industry events. Employee advocacy can amplify your brand's reach and credibility in the market.

9. Customer Insights

- **Leverage Customer Data:** Use insights from client data to tailor your sales approach, develop targeted marketing campaigns, and identify upsell or cross-sell opportunities. Understanding client behavior and preferences allows you to provide more personalized and effective solutions.

- **Voice of the Client:** Leverage client feedback to continuously improve your products and services. By acting on feedback, you can enhance client satisfaction and loyalty, leading to repeat business and positive word-of-mouth.

10. Financial Leverage

- **Leverage Financing Options:** Offer flexible financing or payment options to clients to make your products more accessible and attractive. Financial leverage can help close deals that might otherwise be lost due to budget constraints.

■ **Invest in Growth:** Leverage available capital to invest in growth opportunities, such as expanding your sales team, entering new markets, or acquiring complementary businesses. Strategic investments can amplify your market presence and accelerate revenue growth.

By applying these *Leverage Strategies*, you can amplify the effectiveness of your resources, enhance your market position, and create significant advantages over competitors. These strategies help you maximize the impact of your existing assets, drive growth, and achieve your sales goals more efficiently and effectively.

Deception Strategies

"Never attempt to win by force what can be won by deception."

– Niccolò Machiavell

Utilizing *Deception Strategies* involves using strategies that deliberately mislead competitors or create ambiguity to gain a strategic advantage. These tactics are designed to protect your market position, create opportunities, and outmaneuver competitors by keeping them off-balance or misinformed. If you work for a publicly traded company, you won't be able to use some of these strategies. Do not break any laws, whether they be local, state, or federal. Misdirection is one thing; breaking laws is another. Make sure your legal team approves any of these strategies.

Here's how you could apply these strategies effectively:

1. Selective Information Sharing

- **Control Information Flow:** Carefully manage the information you share with the market and competitors. By selectively releasing details about your products, pricing, or strategies, you can create uncertainty and prevent competitors from fully understanding your plans.

- **Misinformation Tactics:** Occasionally release misleading or incomplete information about your future product launches or strategic moves. This can cause competitors to misallocate resources or make erroneous strategic decisions. Don't break any laws but do think of creative ways to mislead your competition.

2. False Signals

- **Market Distraction:** Send out false signals about entering a new market or launching a new product. This can distract competitors, leading them to invest resources in areas where you have no intention of competing, thereby weakening their position in their core markets.

- **Feign Weakness:** Deliberately understate your strengths or overstate challenges your company is facing. This can lead competitors to underestimate your capabilities, giving you the upper hand when you make your actual move.

3. Ambiguous Communication

- **Vague Announcements:** Make vague public announcements about upcoming changes or strategic shifts without providing specific details. This creates uncertainty and speculation among competitors, making it harder for them to anticipate your next move.

- **Ambiguous Positioning:** Use ambiguous product positioning that makes it difficult for competitors to clearly understand your market focus or target audience. This can prevent them from effectively countering your strategies.

4. Controlled Leaks

- **Strategic Leaks:** Intentionally leak selective information to the market through unofficial channels. These controlled leaks can be used to mislead competitors about your true intentions, causing them to react to false or incomplete information.

- **Leak Decoys:** Use decoy projects or initiatives as part of your controlled leaks. Competitors might waste time and resources trying to counter these non-existent or insignificant threats.

5. Decoy Products or Services

- **Launch Decoy Products:** Introduce a product or service that appears to be a major new offering but is designed to distract competitors from your core innovations. This can lead competitors to focus on the wrong areas, allowing you to advance your true strategic objectives.

- **Announce Non-Existent Features:** Officially announce new product features or capabilities that are still in development or not yet available. This can cause competitors to scramble to match these features, diverting their attention and resources.

6. Overt Collaboration

- **Appear to Collaborate:** Publicly engage in discussions or partnerships with potential collaborators that lead competitors to believe you're pursuing a specific strategy. This can mask your true intentions and lead competitors to misjudge your moves.

- **Fake Alliances:** Create the impression of alliances or partnerships that don't exist. This can confuse competitors about your market strategy and prevent them from accurately assessing your strengths and weaknesses.

7. Timing Misdirection

- **Announce Prematurely:** Announce product launches, expansions, or strategic moves earlier than planned to mislead competitors about your timeline. This can cause them to rush their own plans or make strategic errors based on incorrect timing assumptions.

- **Delayed Execution:** Delay the execution of officially announced plans to mislead competitors into thinking you've encountered obstacles. This can lull them into a false sense of security, giving you time to refine your strategy or execute it more effectively.

8. Underplaying Success

- **Downplay Achievements:** Publicly underplay your successes or growth to create the impression that you're not a significant threat. This can lead competitors to underestimate your potential, allowing you to build strength without drawing attention.

- **Feigning Challenges:** Communicate exaggerated difficulties or setbacks, making competitors believe you're struggling. This can lead them to ease off their competitive efforts, giving you breathing room to regroup and strengthen your position.

9. False Vulnerabilities

- **Showcase Weaknesses:** Deliberately highlight minor or controlled weaknesses in your business to mislead competitors into attacking areas where you're actually strong. This can set traps for competitors, causing them to overextend or make strategic errors.

- **Create Artificial Gaps:** Intentionally leave small gaps in your market coverage or product features to lure competitors into areas where you're prepared to defend or counterattack effectively.

10. Competitive Misdirection

- **False Competitive Focus:** Publicly focus on competing with a specific company or product to divert attention from your true competitive target. This can lead your real competitors to underestimate your threat and leave them vulnerable to your actual strategy.

- **Fake Strategic Priorities:** Communicate false strategic priorities that lead competitors to focus on the wrong areas. This can create openings in your real areas of focus, allowing you to advance your true objectives with less resistance.

By applying these *Deception Strategies*, you can strategically mislead competitors, protect your market position, and create opportunities to outmaneuver your rivals. These tactics help you control the narrative, keep competitors off-balance, and execute your strategies with a higher degree of success by exploiting their misunderstandings or miscalculations.

Mastering the Art of Conquest: Putting the Ten Strategies into Historical Perspective with Alexander the Great

Alexander the Great's military campaigns against Persia from 334 BC to 323 BC not only shaped the ancient world but also offer profound lessons for modern sales leadership.[8] His strategies can be directly mapped to advanced sales tactics, demonstrating how historical principles of warfare can be adapted to conquer contemporary market challenges.

Attack Strategies: Aggressive Market Entry

Alexander initiated his Persian campaign with bold, decisive strikes, exemplified by his victory at the Battle of Granicus. This aggressive approach disrupted the status quo and quickly established his presence in new territories. Similarly, a sales leader can adopt aggressive market penetration tactics, like introducing groundbreaking products or entering under-served markets to disrupt competitors and capture market share.

Defense Strategies: Securing Market Gains

After his conquests, Alexander didn't merely move on; he consolidated his gains by founding cities and establishing garrisons, like Alexandria. These strongholds ensured the sustainability of his conquests. In sales, this strategy translates to solidifying gains in new markets with solid support structures, such as customer service centers or local partnerships, ensuring long-term client relationships and market stability.

Influence Strategies: Shaping Stakeholder Behavior

Alexander adeptly used cultural integration to stabilize and legitimize his rule, adopting local customs and placing Persians in governmental roles. In a sales context, this strategy involves understanding and aligning with customer and partner cultures, tailoring marketing messages to fit local sensibilities, and positioning products to resonate deeply with target demographics.

Movement Strategies: Dynamic Positioning in the Market

Known for the incredible speed and mobility of his forces, Alexander's ability to maneuver swiftly allowed him to outpace and overwhelm his enemies. For sales leaders, this highlights the importance of agility in business practices—rapidly adapting to market changes, reallocating resources swiftly, and exploiting market opportunities before competitors can react.

Repositioning Strategies: Altering Market Perceptions

By proclaiming himself "King of Asia," Alexander changed his image from that of a conqueror to a ruler, gaining legitimacy. Similarly, a sales strategy might involve rebranding efforts or pivoting product features to better meet the market's needs, thus changing the company's perception to better align with customer expectations and market trends.

Escalation Strategies: Intensifying Sales Efforts

Alexander escalated his military efforts when faced with resistance, committing more resources to ensure victory. This is mirrored in sales by increasing investments in key markets or ramping up promotional activities to overcome competitive challenges or capitalize on peak market interest.

Deterrence Strategies: Establishing a Competitive Edge

Alexander's fearsome reputation often led enemies to surrender without a fight. In sales, building a strong brand reputation through quality products and superior customer service can deter competitors from entering your key markets or dissuade customers from switching to rival products.

Integration Strategies: Combining Resources Effectively

Alexander's integration of diverse cultures under his rule not only secured his empire but also enriched it. A sales leader can emulate this by integrating diverse teams, technologies, and business units to innovate and deliver solutions that are more effective and appealing to a broad customer base.

Leverage Strategies: Maximizing Resource Impact

In his conquests, Alexander made strategic use of the resources of newly acquired territories to sustain his campaign. Similarly, in sales, effective utilization of available data, technology, and human resources can enhance productivity and impact, driving better outcomes with less expenditure.

Deception Strategies: Strategic Ambiguity

At the Battle of Issus, Alexander's use of deception and terrain mastery played crucial roles in his victory. In sales, strategic ambiguity about upcoming product launches or market moves can keep competitors uncertain, providing the element of surprise that can lead to significant market advantages.

Through the lens of Alexander's ancient conquests, modern sales leaders can see the value of strategic diversity and execution excellence. His multifaceted approach underscores the effectiveness of combining various tactics to achieve your overarching business goals and secure lasting success in your marketplace. Now it's your turn to do the same.

CHAPTER 6

Strategic Tools and Frameworks

"Structure follows strategy."

- Alfred Chandler[58]

"Strategy is a pattern in a stream of decisions."

- Henry Mintzberg[59]

"The good-to-great companies did not focus princi-
pally on what to do to become great; they focused
equally on what not to do and what to stop doing.

- Jim Collins[60]

Before we dive into this very heavy topic, I want to give you a warning. Some or all of your executive leadership team may reject these strategic tools and frameworks. And as we'll discuss in depth later, getting buy-in from as many leaders

58   Chandler, A. D., Jr. (2023). Strategy and structure: Chapters in the history of the industrial enterprise. Sothis Press

59   Mintzberg, H. (1978). Patterns in Strategy Formation. Management Science, 24(9), 934-948

60   Jim Collins, Good to Great: Why Some Companies Make the Leap...And Others Don't (New York: Harper Business, 2001)

and stakeholders is critical to maximizing the results of your strategic sales efforts. Note that I said maximize. We don't live in a perfect world, so read through this chapter, think about the mindset of your executive leadership team and how they might accept or reject these. Then decide which ones you can get buy-in and the ones you'll have to implement on your own. My goal is to give you as many tools as possible to ensure your success. Your job is to decide which ones you can realistically implement.

Introduction to OKRs, SWOT, and More

In the world of strategic sales leadership, utilizing structured tools and frameworks can enhance the effectiveness of planning and execution. This chapter introduces some of the most powerful strategic tools, including Objectives and Key Results (OKRs), SWOT Analysis, and other essential methodologies that you can employ to drive clarity, alignment, and superior performance in their teams. While you may have heard of these strategic tools, you may not be using them in a way to maximize your sales.

Let's begin by explaining what they are and how they can help you on your path to success.

Objectives and Key Results (OKRs)

Definition and Purpose: OKRs are a goal-setting framework used to define measurable goals and track their outcomes. The primary purpose of OKRs is to connect company, team, and personal objectives to measurable results, ensuring all members of the organization are moving in the same direction with clear priorities.[61] Sounds simple enough, but there's more.

Components:

- **Objectives**: These are significant, concrete, action-oriented, and (ideally) inspirational statements. Objectives should be short, memorable, and engaging. Keep the emphasis on short.

- **Key Results**: These are a set of metrics that measure your progress towards the Objective. Key Results should be quantifiable, achievable, and difficult, but not impossible. They should also be time-bound. Make sure they're challenging to achieve, but not so hard that they de-motivate your team.

Implementation:

- Set objectives that are aligned with your organization's strategic goals.

- Define key results that are actionable and quantifiable.

- Review OKRs regularly (typically quarterly) to ensure alignment and adjust as necessary based on performance and changing conditions. You need time to give your "seeds" a chance to sprout. Figure out your sales cycle and

---

61   Ben Lamorte, The OKRs Field Book: A Step-by-Step Guide for Objectives and Key Results Coaches (Wiley, 2022)

how often it makes sense to check. For most organizations, quarterly works. For shorter sales cycles you may need to set monthly reviews.

Benefits:

- Focus efforts on measurable outcomes.

- Foster coordination and alignment across different levels of the organization.

- Encourage accountability through clear, measurable benchmarks.

Now let's create some sample OKRs with a focus on growth, team development, and operational excellence. These are just examples. Make ones that fit your organization's needs.

Objective 1: Expand Business and Increase Revenue Growth

Key Results:

1. **Achieve a 15% year-over-year increase in revenue** by developing and executing targeted sales strategies for high-value accounts.

2. **Secure five new major client accounts** within key target industries by the end of the fiscal year.

3. **Increase average deal size by 10%** through upselling and cross-selling initiatives within the existing client base.

Objective 2: Elevate Sales Team Performance and Engagement

Key Results:

1. **Implement a comprehensive sales training program** focusing on advanced selling techniques and product knowledge, with at least 90% team participation by Q3.

2. **Improve sales team job satisfaction rate by 20%** as measured by bi-annual employee surveys.[62]

3. **Increase the conversion rate of proposals to closed deals by 25%** through enhanced sales enablement tools and support.

Objective 3: Strengthen Strategic Partnerships and Channel Development

Key Results:

1. **Form at least three new strategic partnerships** that open access to new markets or enhance product offerings.

2. **Increase revenue generated from channel partners by 20%** through joint marketing efforts and partner training programs.

3. **Host quarterly partnership review meetings** to ensure alignment and explore new opportunities for joint ventures.

---

62   Freshworks. (n.d.). Key Ingredient of Successful Companies: Sales Team Happiness. Retrieved from https://www.freshworks.com/crm/sales/sales-team-happiness/

Objective 4: Optimize Sales Processes and Utilize Advanced Analytics

Key Results:

1. **Reduce the sales cycle time by 15%** by optimizing and automating key sales processes.

2. **Achieve 90% adoption rate of the new CRM system** across the sales department to improve data accuracy and lead management.

3. **Launch a sales dashboard** that provides real-time data on sales performance, pipeline status, and market conditions, aiming for daily use among the sales leadership team.

These OKRs emphasize not just financial targets but also the strategic development of your sales force and partnerships, as well as the effective use of technology to enhance sales operations. They are designed to promote a balanced approach to achieving consistent sales growth, enhancing team capabilities, and improving your operational efficiencies.

Now let's explore SWOT.

SWOT Analysis

Definition and Purpose: SWOT stands for Strengths, Weaknesses, Opportunities, and Threats. It is a strategic planning tool used to identify and understand the internal and external factors that can impact the viability of a project, product, place, or person.[63] You've probably done your share of PowerPoint presentations with a SWOT analysis.

Components:

- **Strengths**: Characteristics of your business or project that give it an advantage over others.

- **Weaknesses**: Characteristics that place your team at a disadvantage relative to others.

- **Opportunities**: Elements that the project could exploit to its advantage.

- **Threats**: Elements in the environment that could cause trouble for the business or project.

Implementation:

- Conduct regular SWOT analyses for different segments of your business to identify strategic positions and potential growth areas.

- Use the insights gained to guide strategic decision-making and resource allocation.

Benefits:

- Provides a clear snapshot of internal and external factors affecting your business.

---

63   Marcel Planellas and Anna Muni, Strategic Decisions: The 30 Most Useful Models (New York: Cambridge University Press, 2019)

- Helps anticipate or respond to changes in the business environment.

- Enhances strategic planning by identifying where to compete and where to defend.

Additional Strategic Tools[47]

There are some additional strategic tools that you can add to your arsenal.

1. PESTLE Analysis:

- Analyzes Political, Economic, Social, Technological, Legal, and Environmental factors to assess external factors impacting your business.

- Helps in understanding market growth or decline, business position, potential and direction for operations. Ignore this one at your own peril.

2. Porter's Five Forces:

- Analyzes competitive forces within the market to determine the intensity of competition and its attractiveness in terms of profitability.

- Includes the bargaining power of buyers and suppliers, the threat of new entrants, the threat of substitute products, and competitive rivalry. This is more geared to CEO's, CFO's and such, but it can help you by giving you a very deep understanding of your competitors.

3. Value Chain Analysis:

- Involves examining the business activities and how they affect the company's competitive strength.

- Provides a clear understanding of how value is added throughout the organization and helps identify where value can be increased or costs reduced.

4. Balanced Scorecard:

- Combines financial measures with other key performance indicators around client perspectives, business processes, and organizational growth.

- Encourages balanced company performance against a range of objectives. There's a good probability that your organization uses this one already.

These additional tools can be intimidating, but the effort to understand, and implement them into your sales efforts will be massively rewarded. By mastering these tools, you and your sales leaders can craft detailed and nuanced strategies that not only drive sales performance but also align closely with your broader business objectives. These frameworks support a systematic approach to strategic decision-making, allowing you to leverage insights and foster a culture of accountability and strategic awareness across their teams.

If you remember that few of your competitors will be doing this, you can imagine the advantage you will gain.

For sales leaders eager to harness the value of strategic tools and frameworks, it's crucial to navigate around several common pitfalls that can obstruct their effective use. Here are some typical mistakes that sales leaders often encounter:[64]

Overcomplication: A frequent error is the overuse of complex strategic tools, which can muddy the clarity and focus essential for team success. The aim should be simplicity and precision, selecting and adapting tools that specifically meet the team's needs.

Misalignment with Business Goals: Occasionally, sales leaders might deploy these tools without aligning them closely with the company's main objectives. This misalignment can lead to initiatives that might succeed on their own but don't advance the organization's overall goals, squandering resources and opportunities.

Poor Communication and Integration: Even the most well-conceived strategies can stumble if they're not effectively communicated and integrated within the team. It's vital for sales leaders to ensure that everyone on the team understands how to utilize the tools and how they fit into the broader strategy to foster widespread buy-in and effective execution.

Static Usage: The business landscape is always evolving, yet some leaders treat strategic tools like SWOT analysis or OKRs as static, one-time actions. To truly benefit, these tools should be used dynamically, updated regularly to reflect new challenges, market conditions, and opportunities. They're not just for planning but for continuous strategic adjustment.

---

64   Martin Reeves, Knut Haanaes, and Janmejaya Sinha, Your Strategy Needs a Strategy: How to Choose and Execute the Right Approach (Boston: Harvard Business Review Press, 2015)

Lack of Proper Training: Effective implementation of strategic tools often requires specific skills that your sales team may not have. Without adequate training, the use of these tools can lead to misguided strategies and suboptimal decisions.

Undervaluing Qualitative Insights: While many strategic tools focus on quantifiable data, it's also important not to overlook qualitative insights such as client feedback, employee input, and subtle market shifts. These insights are invaluable for developing a well-rounded strategy.

Inadequate Follow-Up and Evaluation: After setting strategies in motion, some sales leaders fail to track progress or assess the effectiveness of their initiatives. This oversight can hamstring the organization from learning and evolving its strategies based on actual outcomes.

Over Reliance on Familiar Tools: There's a tendency among some leaders to depend too heavily on specific tools or methodologies simply because they are familiar or comfortable with them. This can prevent them from exploring other, potentially more suitable tools that could better address strategic challenges. To succeed you're going to need to get comfortable being uncomfortable.

By staying aware of these pitfalls, you and your sales leaders can more effectively employ strategic tools and frameworks to enhance decision-making, drive impactful actions, and secure a competitive edge and sales success.

Okay, now we turn our attention to applying all this stuff.

Your Guide to Applying Strategic Frameworks

Strategic frameworks are essential for providing structure and clarity to the complex decisions and activities that define your sales process. Effective application of these frameworks can enhance decision-making, align efforts with organizational objectives, and improve the overall strategic agility of your sales team. This guide provides a detailed and insightful approach to applying strategic frameworks effectively within your sales organization.

Step 1: Selecting the Right Frameworks

The first step in effectively applying strategic frameworks is to choose the right tools based on your specific strategic needs. Consider the following factors:

- **Organizational Goals**: Align frameworks with your long-term objectives. For instance, use SWOT for strategic positioning or OKRs for goal setting and execution.

- **Market Environment**: Choose frameworks that reflect the dynamics of your market. PESTLE is excellent for understanding macro-environmental factors, while Porter's Five Forces provides insight into industry competitiveness.

- **Team Capabilities**: Select frameworks that your team can understand and use effectively, while also considering the need for potential training.

- **Integration Possibilities**: Opt for tools that integrate well with each other, ensuring that insights from one can inform and enhance the application of another.

Step 2: Training and Dissemination

Before implementation, ensure that your team understands how to use the chosen frameworks effectively:

- **Training Sessions**: Conduct workshops or training sessions to introduce the frameworks. Focus on practical applications and real-world examples.

- **Documentation**: Provide comprehensive documentation and resources that team members can refer to when needed.

- **Expert Sessions**: Consider bringing in external experts for specialized frameworks to provide deeper insights and training.

Step 3: Customization and Contextualization

No strategic framework is one-size-fits-all. Customize and contextualize frameworks to fit your organizational context:

- **Adaptation**: Modify frameworks to address specific challenges or opportunities your sales team faces.

- **Simplification**: Simplify complex frameworks to ensure they are usable and practical for daily decision-making processes. Complexity is the enemy of implementation.

- **Continuous Update**: Revise and update frameworks as

your market and organizational context evolves. This is an ongoing process.

Step 4: Integration into Decision-Making Processes

Effectively integrate strategic frameworks into the regular decision-making processes:

- **Strategic Meetings**: Utilize frameworks during strategic meetings to guide discussion and analysis.

- **Decision Criteria**: Incorporate insights from frameworks as criteria for making strategic decisions, ensuring that all decisions are data informed.

- **Collaborative Tools**: Use collaborative digital tools to make the frameworks accessible and editable to all team members involved in strategic planning.

Step 5: Monitoring and Evaluation

Regularly monitor and evaluate the effectiveness of the strategic frameworks:

- **Performance Metrics**: Establish metrics to assess how well the frameworks are contributing to achieving strategic goals.

- **Feedback Loops**: Create mechanisms for team members to provide feedback on the frameworks' usability and effectiveness.

- **Iterative Improvement**: Use feedback and performance

data to make iterative improvements to how frameworks are applied.

Step 6: Reporting and Refinement

Ensure that the application of strategic frameworks leads to actionable insights and visible improvements:

- **Regular Reporting**: Develop regular reporting procedures to communicate the outcomes and insights from strategic frameworks to all relevant stakeholders.

- **Actionable Insights**: Focus on translating the abstract outcomes of framework analyses into concrete, actionable steps.

- **Refinement Sessions**: Schedule periodic sessions to refine the use of frameworks based on past applications and evolving business needs.

Step 7: Fostering a Strategic Culture

Promote a culture that values strategic thinking and continuous learning:

- **Encourage Experimentation**: Encourage team members to experiment with different applications of strategic frameworks. Don't punish them if things don't go as planned.

- **Recognize Contributions**: Acknowledge and reward contributions that enhance the effectiveness of strategic frameworks. A public acknowledgement goes a long way towards motivating others to do the same.

■ **Promote Continuous Learning**: Foster an environment where continuous improvement and learning are valued and supported. Offer things like cash and gift cards to reward those that take the extra time out of their day to learn.

By following this guide, you can effectively implement and leverage strategic frameworks to enhance the coherence, efficiency, and effectiveness of your sales strategies. This practical approach not only aligns daily sales activities with broader business objectives but also empowers your teams to navigate complex market environments with greater agility and confidence.

Putting It All Together: Drafting Your Strategy Using Frameworks

Implementing strategic frameworks effectively requires a systematic approach to ensure that they genuinely influence the sales strategy and lead to measurable results. Below are detailed action items for drafting your strategy using these frameworks, which can guide sales leaders through a practical and actionable strategy development process.[65]

---

65   Robert M. Grant, Contemporary Strategy Analysis, 11th ed. (Hoboken, NJ: Wiley, 2022)

Step 1: Define Strategic Objectives

Before diving into specific frameworks, clearly define what you aim to achieve with your sales strategy. These objectives should be aligned with the broader goals of the organization and should be specific, measurable, achievable, relevant, and time-bound (SMART).

- **Action**: Conduct a goal-setting workshop with key stakeholders to identify and agree on strategic sales objectives for the upcoming period. You may be tired of me saying this, but the more people you can get to buy-in on this, the easier your job will be.

Step 2: Select Appropriate Frameworks

Choose frameworks that best suit your strategic needs and the objectives previously defined. For example, use SWOT to understand your current strategic position, PESTLE to explore external factors, and OKRs to set specific goals.

- **Action**: List potential frameworks and evaluate their relevance and impact on your strategic objectives. Decide on a combination of frameworks that cover both internal capabilities and external market conditions.

Step 3: Gather Necessary Data and Insights

Collect the data needed to fill out the selected frameworks. This involves both internal data, such as sales performance and client feedback, and external data, such as market trends and competitor analysis.

- **Action**: Assign team members to gather specific types of data. Use both qualitative insights from stakeholder interviews and quantitative data from market research. If you have a sales operations team, they can do a lot of the heavy lifting on this.

Step 4: Workshop to Fill Frameworks

Organize a strategic workshop with key team members to fill out the selected frameworks. This collaborative approach ensures that multiple perspectives are considered and enhances the buy-in from different departments.

- **Action**: Schedule and conduct a workshop where each framework is discussed and completed. Ensure that all participants are prepared with pre-workshop assignments to bring necessary data and insights. Do not let anyone show up without having completed the pre-work!

Step 5: Synthesize Insights and Formulate Strategy

Once the frameworks are completed, synthesize the insights gained to formulate a cohesive sales strategy. Look for common themes, opportunities, and challenges that have emerged across the different frameworks.

- **Action**: Create a synthesis report that combines insights from all frameworks. Use this report to draft a strategic document outlining key strategic initiatives.

Step 6: Define Tactics and Actions

Break down the strategic initiatives into specific tactics and actionable steps. Assign responsibilities and timelines for each action to ensure accountability. Do not skip over this part.

- **Action**: Develop an action plan that includes specific tasks, responsible persons, deadlines, and required resources. Ensure each action is directly linked to the strategic objectives.

Step 7: Establish KPIs and Monitoring Plans

To measure the effectiveness of your strategic plan, establish clear key performance indicators (KPIs) and set up regular monitoring and reporting mechanisms.

- **Action**: Define KPIs that will measure the success of each strategic initiative. Set up a schedule for regular strategy review meetings.

Step 8: Communicate the Strategy

Communicate the finalized strategy across the organization to ensure everyone understands their role in its execution. Effective communication is crucial for alignment and motivation. The simpler the message the easier it will stick and spread.

- **Action**: Organize a launch meeting to communicate the new sales strategy. Use diverse communication tools such as emails, newsletters, and intranet posts to reach everyone in the organization.

Step 9: Implement, Monitor, and Adapt

With the strategy in place, focus on implementation, continuous monitoring, and readiness to adapt the strategy based on performance and external changes.

- **Action**: Implement the strategy according to the action plan. Monitor ongoing performance and adjust the strategy as needed based on KPIs and external market conditions.

Yes, I know, this is a lot to do and implement. But the increase in market share and sales revenue will make all your efforts pay off many times over. By following these detailed steps and systematically applying strategic frameworks, you and your sales leaders can ensure that your strategy is not only well-crafted and comprehensive but also dynamically aligned with the changing business environment and capable of driving significant sales growth.

You might be thinking, "Meh, I have never done this before and managed to be successful." That old world is gone. This is a new world that will show no mercy to you or any of us. Whether you fail or succeed is up to you. My goal is to improve the probability of your success.

Research shows that between 60% to 90% of all strategic initiatives fail.[66] Part III (Execution) of this book goes into detail about this and how to be among the few that succeed.

When sales leaders draft their strategies using frameworks, several common pitfalls can undermine the effectiveness of

---

66   Carucci, R. (2017, November 13). Executives Fail to Execute Strategy Because They're Too Internally Focused. Harvard Business Review. https://hbr.org/2017/11/executives-fail-to-execute-strategy-because-theyre-too-internally-focused

their strategic plans. Here are some key issues that sales leaders often encounter:

1. Lack of Alignment with Corporate Strategy:

- **Problem**: Sales leaders sometimes develop sales strategies in isolation, which can result in a misalignment with the broader corporate strategy. This disconnection can lead to conflicting goals within the organization.

- **Impact**: Resources might be misallocated, and departments could end up working at cross-purposes, reducing the overall effectiveness of the organization.

2. Over-Reliance on Specific Frameworks:

- **Problem**: Sales leaders might become overly reliant on frameworks that they are comfortable with, potentially ignoring other tools that might be more appropriate given the context or specific challenges faced.

- **Impact**: This can lead to a skewed understanding of the market or the organization's strategic position, resulting in flawed strategies.

3. Failure to Customize Frameworks:

- **Problem**: Not all strategic frameworks fit all situations directly out of the box. Failing to adapt these tools to the specific needs and realities of your organization is a common oversight.

- **Impact**: The resulting strategy might not fully capture the unique challenges or opportunities your sales team faces, making the strategy less effective.

4. Inadequate Data and Insights:

- **Problem**: Effective strategy formulation requires accurate and comprehensive data. Sometimes, sales leaders rush the process or rely on incomplete or outdated data.

- **Impact**: Strategies based on inadequate data may lead to poor decisions, missed opportunities, and underperformance against competitors who better understand the market dynamics. As Mark Twain reportedly once said, "It ain't what you don't know that gets you into trouble. It's what you know for sure that just ain't so."

5. Insufficient Involvement of Key Stakeholders:

- **Problem**: If sales strategies are drafted without sufficient input from key stakeholders, including those from other departments such as marketing, finance, and operations, the strategies may not be comprehensive.

- **Impact**: Lack of stakeholder involvement can lead to resistance during implementation, as teams may not feel ownership or see the relevance of the strategy to their specific roles.

6. Poor Communication and Implementation:

- **Problem**: Even the best strategies will fail if they are not communicated effectively and implemented efficiently. Poor communication and vague implementation plans are significant pitfalls.

- **Impact**: The strategy may be misunderstood or poorly executed, leading to confusion and suboptimal results.

7. Neglecting Continuous Review and Adaptation:

- **Problem**: The business environment is dynamic, but sometimes sales strategies are treated as static documents.

- **Impact**: Strategies that are not regularly reviewed and adapted can quickly become obsolete as market conditions, technology, and client preferences evolve. Strategies ripen like bananas and avocados.

8. Underestimating the Importance of Execution:

- **Problem**: There can be a tendency to focus too much on the strategic planning process itself and not enough on how it will be executed.

- **Impact**: Without clear execution steps, accountability measures, and follow-ups, even the most well-thought-out strategies can flounder.

To avoid these pitfalls, you must ensure your strategies are aligned with overall corporate objectives, involve key stakeholders, base decisions on solid data, communicate plans clearly, and establish mechanisms for ongoing review and adaptation. This approach helps to create a sturdy, responsive, and effective sales strategy that can drive sustained success in any economic environment.

The Roman Legion System Used Strategic Frameworks and Tools

In the tapestry of ancient history, Roman General Scipio Africanus stands out as a master strategist whose life and military campaigns offer timeless lessons for modern business leaders, particularly those navigating the complex world of sales.[67]

Embracing Simplicity Amid Complexity

Scipio's early campaigns, particularly during the Second Punic War, exemplified his embrace of simplicity in strategy. When Scipio took command, he inherited a chaotic situation with Carthaginian forces, under Hannibal, spread across Italy. Scipio's response was not to match complexity with complexity but to simplify Rome's military focus, concentrating on a clear and attainable goal: the invasion of Carthage's homeland in North Africa. This move forced Hannibal to withdraw from Italy to defend his home base, simplifying the conflict for Rome.

---

67   Richard A. Gabriel, Scipio Africanus: Rome's Greatest General, Illustrated ed. (Washington, D.C.: Potomac Books, 2008)

In sales, this reflects the need to avoid overcomplicating strategies with too many frameworks and tools. Instead, like Scipio, sales leaders should aim for clear, straightforward objectives that can decisively impact the market and force competitors to respond on their terms.

Alignment with Broader Objectives

Scipio's strategic brilliance was not just in battlefield tactics but in aligning his military goals with the broader objectives of Rome—to weaken Carthage and end its threat permanently. By attacking Carthage in North Africa, Scipio aligned his tactical decisions with the strategic aim of securing peace and stability for Rome, ensuring that his victories contributed directly to Rome's long-term objectives.

Similarly, in the corporate realm, sales strategies must align with the company's overarching goals. Every tactical move in sales should support the broader business objectives, ensuring that each success in the field translates into progress for the entire organization.

Effective Communication and Strategy Integration

Throughout his military career, Scipio was known for his ability to communicate effectively with his troops, allies, and even enemies. He integrated diverse forces—Roman legions, Numidian cavalry, and local allies—into a cohesive fighting force. This integration was possible because of clear, consistent communication and a shared understanding of common goals.

In a sales context, the success of strategic tools hinges on their effective communication and integration across the team. Sales leaders must ensure that every member of their team understands the strategic tools at their disposal and how they fit into the larger strategy, creating a unified force moving towards common sales targets.

Dynamic Use of Tools

Scipio was adept at adapting his strategies to the evolving circumstances of war. He recognized the fluid nature of military conflict and adjusted his tactics based on enemy movements, local political situations, and the physical environment. This dynamic approach allowed him to stay several steps ahead of his adversaries.

For sales leaders, this teaches the importance of not treating strategic tools as static. Tools like SWOT analysis or OKRs need to be regularly updated to reflect new market conditions and competitive landscapes, encouraging ongoing strategic thinking and adaptation.

Training for Mastery

Scipio ensured that his troops were well-trained and capable of executing complex maneuvers in battle. This emphasis on training was crucial for the successful implementation of his innovative strategies.

In sales, the effectiveness of any strategic tool is contingent upon the team's ability to understand and utilize it proficiently. Sales leaders should invest in training programs that equip their teams with the necessary skills to implement strategic tools effectively, ensuring clarity and competence in execution.

Harnessing Qualitative Insights

Scipio valued the qualitative insights gathered from local informants, scouts, and even captured enemies, using this information to enhance his battlefield strategies. He understood that qualitative insights could provide a nuanced understanding of the situation beyond what standard intelligence methods could offer.

In modern sales strategies, while quantitative data is invaluable, qualitative insights from client feedback, market trends, and employee input are crucial. These insights provide a richer, more detailed picture that can guide strategic decision-making.

Continuous Assessment and Adaptation

After each campaign, Scipio reviewed his strategies, assessed his victories and setbacks, and adapted his approaches. This continuous loop of assessment and adaptation was key to his sustained success.

Effective sales strategies require similar mechanisms for tracking progress and evaluating the impact of initiatives. This helps in learning from experiences and adapting strategies effectively, ensuring continuous improvement and success.

Embracing New Methods

Scipio was open to adopting new methods and technologies, often integrating tactics from different cultures into his military strategy. This adaptability was a significant factor in his victories.

Sales leaders should similarly be open to exploring new and potentially more effective strategic frameworks that better meet specific challenges, ensuring they remain competitive and innovative.

Scipio Africanus' life gives sales leaders a blueprint for strategic mastery, demonstrating that the principles of clear strategy, effective communication, and continuous adaptation are as relevant today as they were on the ancient battlefields.

CHAPTER 7

Maximizing Customer Lifetime Value (CLV)

"At the heart of strategy is the question of competition. At the heart of competition is delivering superior value."

—Kenichi Ohmae

"The purpose of a business is to create a customer who creates customers."

—Peter Drucker

As sales leaders, we are so focused on closing the next deal or finishing the quarter strong that we often lose sight of the big picture. We don't stop and think about what is the potential lifetime value of a client. It's significantly easier to sell more to an existing client who likes, knows and trusts you than it is to find a brand new client. The sales cycle is also much shorter with an existing client. Yet many organizations fail to maximize client lifetime value.

Maximizing customer lifetime value (CLV) is crucial for sustained business success, especially in competitive markets where acquiring new clients can be costly. Too many decisions are made without stopping for a moment to think through what the client lifetime value is or how to maximize it. By focusing on maximizing CLV, sales teams not only improve profitability but also foster long-term loyalty and advocacy among their client base. The chapter will cover the importance of understanding client needs, building strong relationships, employing strategic account management, and leveraging data to personalize interactions and anticipate client needs.

Why You Should Care

Research consistently shows that acquiring a new client is significantly more expensive than retaining and selling to an existing one. While exact figures can vary depending on industry and specific studies, here are some key findings you need to be aware of:

1. **Cost difference:** Acquiring a new customer is generally estimated to be 5 to 25 times more expensive than retaining an existing one.[68]

2. **Probability of sales:** The probability of selling to an existing customer is 60%-70%, while the probability of selling to a new prospect is only 5%-20%.[69]

3. **Profitability:** Increasing customer retention rates by just 5% can increase profits by 25%-95%, according to research by Frederick Reichheld of Bain & Company.[70]

---

68   The Value of Keeping the Right Customers https://hbr.org/2014/10/the-value-of-keeping-the-right-customers

69   Customer Acquisition Vs.Retention Costs – Statistics And Trends https://www.invespcro.com/blog/customer-acquisition-retention/

70   Loyalty Rules https://www.bain.com/contentassets/29f74ec417fa4e36a1d7d7e7479badc5/loyalty_rules_chapter_one.pdf

4. **Spending patterns:** Repeat customers tend to spend more overtime. One study found that customers spend 67% more in their 31st to 36th months with a business than in their first six months.[71]

5. **Word-of-mouth marketing:** Satisfied existing customers are more likely to refer new customers, effectively reducing acquisition costs.[72]

6. **Lower marketing costs:** Targeted marketing to existing clients who already know and trust your brand is often more cost-effective than broad campaigns to attract new clients.[73]

7. **Easier upselling and cross-selling:** Existing clients are more receptive to additional products or services, as they're already familiar with your brand.

These findings underscore the importance of client retention strategies and the value of nurturing existing client relationships. A great sales leader will make sure their team balances their time between new client acquisition and maintaining and growing the existing client base.

---

71   Small Business Owners Shift Investment from Customer Acquisition to Customer Engagement https://www.bia.com/press-releases/small-business-owners-shift-investment-from-customer-acquisition-to-customer-engagement-new-report-by-manta-and-biakelsey/

72   Referral Rate https://www.madx.digital/glossary/referral-rate

73   Word of Mouth Marketing: Stats and Trends for 2023 https://www.lxahub.com/stories/word-of-mouth-marketing-stats-and-trends-for-2023

Client or Customer?

Before we move forward, we need to clarify an important point. A client and a customer are two different things. The words "client" and "customer" are often used interchangeably in everyday language, but they can have distinct meanings, especially in business contexts:

Client:

Relationship: The term "client" typically refers to a person or entity that engages the professional services of another. These relationships are often ongoing and involve a deeper level of interaction and customization. For example, clients of lawyers, consultants, and architects expect tailored advice or services. If we want our sales team to become the Trusted Advisor, we must view the people we serve as clients. In turn our clients must view us as subject matter experts whom they can trust and turn to help them grow their organizations.

Engagement: Clients might work with the service provider over an extended period, where the services are often complex, customized, or involve higher stakes.

Expectation: There is generally a higher expectation for a personal relationship or deeper understanding of needs and solutions. The client expects advice or expertise in a specific area.

Customer:

Relationship: The term "customer" is typically used for someone who purchases goods or services. The relationship is usually transactional and might not be as personal or ongoing as with a client. Think of when you go to your local grocery store, restaurant, or buy a car. These are transactional in nature.

Engagement: Customers often engage in one-off or short-term transactions. They might buy products or services that are already made or standardized.

Expectation: The interaction is usually simpler and more straightforward. Customers expect the product or service to meet the promised specification or need, but they might not expect as much personalized service or ongoing advice.

While both terms involve an exchange of goods or services for payment, "client" often refers to a more complex, ongoing professional relationship, whereas "customer" usually refers to a more transactional and potentially short-term interaction. The distinction can vary by industry and context, but, it's about the depth and nature of the relationship and the type of service or product being offered. If your goal is to get you and your team to the very highest levels of selling success, start seeing the people whose business you desire as clients.

Ask yourself, which do you want, a customer or a client? Make sure your sales team also understands the difference.

Techniques for Building Strong Client Relationships

Building strong, enduring client relationships is foundational to maximizing client lifetime value. Here are detailed strategies and insights into how sales leaders and their teams can foster these relationships:[74]

---

74   Bev Burgess and Dave Munn, A Practitioner's Guide to Account-Based Marketing: Accelerating Growth in Strategic Accounts (London: Kogan Page, 2021)

1. Understand and Segment Your Clients

- **Detailed Profiling**: Gather comprehensive data on your clients to understand their business needs, challenges, and goals. Use this information to segment your client base into groups with similar characteristics and needs. This is table stakes.

- **Action Steps**: Implement CRM systems to capture and analyze client data. Regularly update client profiles based on interactions, transactions, and feedback.

2. Consistent and Personalized Communication

- **Tailored Interactions**: Customize your communication based on the client's profile. Address their specific interests and pain points and provide solutions that resonate with their unique business context.

- **Action Steps**: Develop client-specific communication plans that include preferred channels, frequency, and personalized messaging that reflects the client's recent interactions with your company.

3. Proactive Problem Solving

- **Anticipate Challenges**: Stay one step ahead by anticipating potential challenges your clients might face and propose solutions proactively. This demonstrates commitment and adds value to the relationship. This will help cement your Trusted Advisor status.

- **Action Steps**: Conduct regular strategy sessions with your team to analyze client data and predict potential issues. Develop and propose preemptive solutions to clients before these issues impact their business.

4. Client Education and Training

- **Empower Clients**: Educate your clients about industry trends, product optimizations, and best practices. Workshops, webinars, and training sessions can empower clients to make better use of your products or services. Clients are overwhelmed with data. Add value by being the curator of all that data.

- **Action Steps**: Organize regular educational events for clients. Create and distribute helpful content, such as guides, how-to videos, and case studies that enhance their understanding and skills.

5. Regular Feedback and Adaptation

- **Feedback Mechanisms**: Implement structured feedback mechanisms to gather insights into client satisfaction and areas for improvement. This feedback should be actively used to adapt and improve services.

- **Action Steps**: Establish regular check-ins and satisfaction surveys. Create a closed-loop feedback process where every piece of feedback is evaluated, and appropriate changes are implemented.

6. Reward Loyalty

- **Loyalty Programs**: Develop programs that reward long-term clients. This could include tiered benefits, exclusive offers, or loyalty discounts that enhance client engagement and retention.

- **Action Steps**: Design a loyalty program that aligns with your clients' value to your business. Regularly review and adjust the rewards to keep the program engaging and relevant.

7. Foster Trust Through Transparency

- **Open Communication**: Build trust by being transparent about your processes, pricing, and policies. Clear, honest communication can prevent misunderstandings and build a stronger relational foundation. Many clients are used to being lied to or misled, this alone will separate you from your competitors.

- **Action Steps**: Ensure all client-facing employees are trained to communicate openly and uphold the highest integrity standards. Include clients in decision-making processes where appropriate.

8. Invest in Relationship Management Tools

- **Technology Support**: Use technology to enhance your relationship management capabilities. CRM systems, analytics tools, and communication platforms can help maintain the continuity and consistency of client interactions. We'll dive into technology tools and best practices in a later chapter.

- **Action Steps**: Invest in CRM software that suits your business size and needs. Train your team to effectively use these tools to manage and enhance client relationships.

By implementing these techniques, your sales team can build stronger relationships that not only increase the satisfaction and loyalty of existing clients but also maximize the revenue potential from each client over the lifetime of their engagement with the business.

Advanced Account Management Strategies

Advanced account management strategies are essential for deepening your client relationships, enhancing client satisfaction, and maximizing customer lifetime value (CLV).[59] These strategies involve sophisticated techniques that go beyond basic client service, focusing on developing comprehensive insights into client needs, customizing service approaches, and leveraging technology to deliver superior value. To achieve sales revenue you've never achieved, you're going to have to do things you've never done before. Most of your competitors won't take these extra steps.

Here are a few strategies you may want to add to your arsenal:

1. Strategic Account Planning

- **Purpose**: Develop a detailed plan for managing and growing key accounts. Strategic account planning involves understanding the client's business at a granular level to tailor services and solutions that align with their strategic objectives.

- **Action Steps**:

  - Conduct thorough research to understand the client's industry, competitors, and market trends.

  - Identify key stakeholders within the client organization and build relationships with them. Knowing who each is, their respective roles and power within their organization is critical.

  - Set specific, measurable goals for the account based on client expectations and potential growth opportunities.

2. Cross-Functional Account Teams

- **Purpose**: Create dedicated teams for major accounts to provide comprehensive support that meets all aspects of the client's needs, from technical support to business development. Wow your clients with the level of service and attention you bring them.

- **Action Steps**:

  - Assemble a team from sales, customer service, technical support, and other relevant departments.

  - Conduct regular team meetings to discuss the account status, synchronize efforts, and strategize improvements.

- Establish clear roles and responsibilities that align with the account's needs and goals.

3. Value Co-Creation

- **Purpose**: Engage clients in a collaborative process to co-create value, enhancing the product or service's relevance and effectiveness.

- **Action Steps**:

  - Invite clients to participate in product development meetings or brainstorming sessions.

  - Implement tools for ongoing collaboration, such as shared digital workspaces.

  - Regularly review the co-creation initiatives to ensure they meet the client's evolving needs and contribute to their strategic goals.

4. Customized Reporting and Analytics

- **Purpose**: Provide clients with customized reports and analytics that help them understand the value they are receiving and make informed decisions about their business. People give us money to solve their business problems. Make sure they understand the value you are providing them.

- **Action Steps**:

  - Develop tailored reporting templates that highlight key metrics relevant to the client's business.

- Schedule regular review sessions to go through the reports and discuss insights.

- Use analytics to identify trends, risks, and opportunities for the client.

5. Proactive Relationship Management

- **Purpose**: Anticipate client needs and issues before they become problems, demonstrating commitment and deep understanding of their business.

- **Action Steps**:

  - Implement a monitoring system to track client health indicators, such as product usage patterns and service ticket volumes.

  - Set up alerts for anomalies that might indicate potential issues or opportunities.

  - Engage with clients proactively when indicators suggest the need for attention.

6. Integration of Technology

- **Purpose**: Use technology to enhance account management capabilities, improving efficiency and the quality of interactions.

- **Action Steps**:

  - Deploy CRM systems with advanced features like AI-driven insights and automated interaction logs.

- Utilize communication platforms that facilitate seamless interactions across different channels.
- Invest in secure, scalable cloud technologies that support data sharing and collaboration.

7. Executive Sponsorship

- **Purpose**: Link some of your senior executives with client accounts to foster deeper engagement and demonstrate high-level commitment to the client's success.

- **Action Steps**:
  - Assign a member of your senior leadership team as an executive sponsor for key accounts.
  - Include executive sponsors in strategic meetings with the client.
  - Use executive sponsors to resolve high-level issues and to facilitate strategic discussions.
  - Ensure they have regular meetings with your key clients. This is not a one time a year event.

8. Continuous Learning and Adaptation

- **Purpose**: Ensure that account management strategies and tactics are continually refined and adapted based on feedback and evolving client needs.

- **Action Steps**:
  - Regularly solicit feedback from clients on the

effectiveness of your account management. Tell them to be brutally honest with you.

- Conduct periodic reviews of account management practices to identify areas for improvement. It could be quarterly or twice per year.

- Stay updated on best practices and emerging trends in account management to keep your strategies cutting-edge.

Implementing these advanced account management strategies can significantly enhance the ability of your team to not only meet but exceed client expectations, fostering loyalty and driving long-term revenue growth.

Reflection Points: Assessing Your Client Engagement Techniques

Regular assessment of client engagement techniques is critical to ensure that your strategies remain effective and continue to foster strong, value-driven relationships. This process involves scrutinizing the methods and practices used to interact with your clients, understanding their effectiveness, and identifying areas for improvement. Below are detailed reflection points to help you and your sales leaders evaluate their client engagement techniques systematically.

1. Clarity and Relevance of Communication

- **Reflection Point**: Assess whether the communications with clients are clear, relevant, and aligned with their needs and preferences. Are the messages tailored to address specific client concerns or objectives? Are complex ideas presented in an understandable way?

- **Action Steps**:
  - Review a sample of communications sent to clients, looking for clarity and relevance.
  - Gather feedback directly from clients on how well they understand the communications and if they find the information useful.

2. Responsiveness and Accessibility

- **Reflection Point**: Evaluate how quickly and effectively your team responds to client inquiries and requests. Consider whether clients can easily reach the right person within your organization when they need assistance. If you've ever experienced voicemail hell trying to get help on an issue, you'll understand the importance of getting this right.

- **Action Steps**:
  - Track response times and resolution rates.
  - Survey clients about their satisfaction with the accessibility and responsiveness of your team.

3. Proactivity in Client Management

- **Reflection Point**: Consider how proactive your engagement strategies are. Are you anticipating client needs and addressing potential issues before they arise? Are you offering solutions and improvements without client prompting? Always be proactive, not reactive. The first increases sales and margins, while the second just alienates your client base.

■ **Action Steps**:

- Review recent client interactions for examples of proactive versus reactive engagement.

- Develop a checklist of proactive behaviors and train your team on these practices.

4. Personalization of Interactions

■ **Reflection Point**: Assess the degree of personalization in your client interactions. Are you treating each client as an individual with unique challenges and needs, or are interactions more generic?

■ **Action Steps**:

- Implement or enhance the use of CRM systems to store detailed client preferences and history to tailor interactions.

- Encourage team members to make notes on personal details and preferences that can be referenced in future communications.

5. Consistency Across Touchpoints

■ **Reflection Point**: Evaluate the consistency of client

experiences across different touchpoints (e.g., sales, customer service, technical support). Inconsistencies can lead to client dissatisfaction and erosion of trust.

■ **Action Steps**:

- Map all client touchpoints and conduct an audit to ensure messaging and service quality are consistent.

- Train all client-facing employees on core messages and the importance of maintaining a uniform standard of service.

6. Feedback Utilization

■ **Reflection Point**: Reflect on how your organization collects and uses client feedback. Is feedback systematically collected and analyzed? Is it used to make meaningful changes?

■ **Action Steps**:

- Review the current feedback collection processes for efficiency and effectiveness.

- Ensure there are clear mechanisms for incorporating feedback into operational changes and strategy adjustments.

7. Relationship Depth

■ **Reflection Point**: Consider the depth of the relationships with clients. Are these relationships purely transactional, or do they reflect deeper partnerships? If members of your sales team are being invited to weddings, birthdays and such, you're doing it right.

- **Action Steps**:
  - Identify key clients and evaluate the current depth of the relationship using relationship matrices or scoring.
  - Develop specific strategies to deepen relationships, such as more frequent strategic review meetings or joint innovation initiatives.

8. Outcome and Impact Measurement

- **Reflection Point**: Assess how well you measure the outcomes and impacts of your client engagement efforts. Are you tracking the right metrics to ensure that your engagement strategies are effective?

- **Action Steps**:
  - Define key performance indicators (KPIs) for client engagement, such as client retention rates, Net Promoter Scores (NPS), and upsell/cross-sell rates.
  - Regularly review these metrics and adjust strategies accordingly to optimize outcomes.

By regularly reflecting on these points, you and your sales leaders can ensure that your client engagement techniques remain dynamic, effective, and aligned with both client needs and organizational goals. This ongoing assessment is key to building lasting relationships that maximize client lifetime value. The hard part is standing this up. Once you've got it started, ensure that it keeps going. The increase in sales, margins and client loyalty will more than make up for the effort.

Sands of Strategy: Maximizing Client Lifetime Value Through the Lens of T.E. Lawrence and the Arab Revolt

In the scorching deserts of the Middle East during the Arab Revolt of 1916-1918, the British officer T.E. Lawrence, better known as Lawrence of Arabia[75], employed revolutionary tactics to wage an unconventional war against the Ottoman Empire. His strategy wasn't merely about winning battles, it was about forging deep, enduring relationships with the Arab leaders, understanding their unique needs, and tailoring his support to maximize the effectiveness of their partnership. This historical narrative draws relevant parallels to the modern concept of maximizing Customer Lifetime Value (CLV) in business.

Understanding the Terrain

Just as Lawrence took the time to understand the physical and political landscape of the Arabian Peninsula, sales teams today must start by comprehensively understanding the market terrain in which their clients operate. Lawrence's deep knowledge of the region's geography allowed him to advise and lead guerrilla warfare tactics that leveraged the strengths of his Arab allies against the weaknesses of their enemies.

---

75   Hero: The Life and Legend of Lawrence of Arabia, Harper Perennial, November 1, 2011

Similarly, sales teams need to analyze their client's industry landscape, challenges, and opportunities. By developing a nuanced understanding of what drives the client's business, companies can tailor their solutions to add distinct value, enhancing the client's performance and, consequently, their own importance to the client.

Building Trust through Shared Victories

Lawrence's approach went beyond traditional alliances; he embedded himself with local tribes, sharing in their struggles and triumphs. This deep involvement built trust and loyalty, essential for the long-term motivation of his allies.

In business, shared victories come from collaborative projects that not only succeed but also align with the client's core goals. By celebrating these joint successes and recognizing the client's role in achieving them, a sales team can solidify trust and deepen the client relationship, increasing the likelihood of renewals and the willingness of the client to advocate for your organization within their industry.

Adapting to Changing Conditions

The Arabian desert is a land of extreme conditions, requiring constant adaptation. Lawrence thrived by being flexible in his strategies and tactics, often altering plans based on the evolving situation and the feedback from his allies.

For sales teams, this translates into adopting a flexible approach to client management, staying responsive to the client's evolving needs, and adjusting offerings accordingly.

Dynamic account management can help anticipate changes in the client's business environment and provide proactive solutions, thereby enhancing the perceived value of the service or product offered.

Long-Term Vision for Mutual Success

Lawrence was unique in that he looked beyond the immediate horizon of military victories. He envisioned a future where the Arabs would govern themselves, fostering a sense of ownership and commitment among his allies. This long-term vision was crucial for sustaining the morale and cooperation of the Arab forces.

In the world of sales, understanding and aligning with your client's long-term goals can transform a vendor from a mere supplier to a strategic partner. By investing in your client's future success, your company can align its innovations and services with the client's long-term success, maximizing the lifetime value through ongoing engagement and expanded service opportunities.

Legacy of the Desert Warrior

Just as the legacy of Lawrence of Arabia endures as a testament to strategic brilliance and deep respect for allied relationships, so too can your sales team create lasting legacies with their clients by maximizing CLV through strategic foresight, genuine partnership, and adaptive service. In the shifting sands of market and competition, the lessons from Lawrence's campaigns illuminate the path towards enduring client relationships and sustained business growth.

Through the lens of history, the strategies of Lawrence of Arabia provide a clear blueprint for understanding and maximizing Customer Lifetime Value. Just as he led through insight, alliance, and adaptation, so must sales professionals if they are to thrive in the ever-evolving commercial landscapes of today.

Part III

EXECUTION

"The future never just happened. It was created."

—Will Durant

"Make a simple plan, inform everyone involved with it, don't change it, and kick it in the ass."

—Delta Force Founder and Legendary Special Forces Operator Col. Charlie Beckwith

"It ought to be remembered that there is nothing more difficult to take in hand, more perilous to conduct, or more uncertain in its success, than to take the lead in the introduction of a new order of things. Because the innovator has for enemies all those who have done well under the old conditions, and lukewarm defenders in those who may do well under the new. This coolness arises partly from fear of the opponents, who have the laws on their side, and partly from the incredulity of men, who do not readily believe in new things until they have had a long experience of them."

—Niccolò Machiavelli, The Prince

We start part three of this book with a quote from Machiavelli as a reminder that most people do not like change. Yet the core aspect of strategic execution is change. Change is hard, even when it's a change that is good for you. Think about the typical New Year's resolutions. Most of those don't last more than 28 days tops, and these are changes that people want to make. These are changes that they're eager to make, yet most New Year's resolutions fail. One study conducted by the University of Scranton found that only about 8% of people successfully achieve their New Year's resolutions.[76] So it's incumbent on sales leaders to remember that when we are looking to execute on a strategy, change is going to be the foundation upon which the success of your strategy is built.

There was a study done a few years ago that took place at hospitals across the US, where people were told that if they didn't make significant lifestyle changes, they would die. Not get sicker. Not feel worse. Not have a reduced quality of life. Die! The shocking thing about the study is that only 10 percent of the people who were encouraged to change for the sake of saving their own lives could make the change.[77] It reminds us that one of the foundational aspects of human nature is that most people don't like change for any reason.

As Machiavelli warned us hundreds of years ago, a new order of things or change in an organization means that someone stands to gain, and someone stands to lose. For some people,

---

76   It's January 7: Are You Sticking to Your New Year's Resolution? https://knowledge. wharton.upenn.edu/article/its-january-7-are-you-sticking-to-your-new-years-resolution/

77   Change or Die https://www.fastcompany.com/52717/change-or-die

nothing will be gained or lost despite changes being made. For you to succeed with the execution of your strategy, you're going to have to get buy-in from every key person in the organization, from as many departments as possible. Begin with your sales team. They have to believe in your vision, and your plan on how to execute that vision. Then focus your efforts on winning over the right people in operations, marketing, engineering, R&D, or whatever departments you need on your side to succeed.

Make a list of all the people you need to win over, and the different organizations they have influence over. Write down what each of them will stand to gain or lose by helping to execute your strategy. Write down every organization that you'll be working with and what they stand to gain or lose by helping you execute your strategy.

If you realize that some key people will be losing or not benefiting from helping you execute on your strategy, you're going to be faced with one of two questions:

1) How do you modify your strategy and execution to sweeten the deal for them so that there is something to benefit them?

2) If you can't find a "Win" for them, do you just go around them or try to move forward without them?

Every decision we make has a political price to it. It's up to you to determine if "the juice is worth the squeeze." Decide who you're willing to go to battle against, and what's at stake if you do and lose. There will be consequences even if you win. Be clear on both. There's an old saying that goes, "Before you go in, know the way out."

This is one of the most important parts of this entire book. Once you launch your strategy and start asking people to execute it with you, if you didn't get this part right, the probability of you succeeding plummets. As we discussed in the first part of the book, the life expectancy of a sales leader in an organization isn't long. A Vice President of sales usually lasts on average about 19 months before being fired.[78] From the day you start at a new company and begin executing on your strategy, you're going to have about two quarters (180 days) to get things in place, and another two quarters to see if your strategy works. That gives you about one year to execute. If things go well and you're starting to get traction, and the execution is going reasonably smoothly, congratulations, you've bought yourself more time.

If you don't think you have enough people with power in the organization to support the execution of your strategy, think long and hard about staying on the same path. Course correction is often a wise choice.

Either change the parts of your strategy to ensure they benefit the key people whose support you need, or try to form enough alliances with those who are not on board yet by offering them assistance in other ways in exchange for their support,

How hard is it to bring change? The success rate of strategic plan implementation can vary widely across different companies and industries, however, in a vast majority of organizations, strategic execution ends in failure. Research indicates that about 60 to 90 percent of strategies never fully

---

78   The average VP of Sales tenure has shrunk — here's why https://www.gong.io/blog/vp-sales-average-tenure/

launch.[79] Furthermore, it is estimated that up to 67 percent of strategic planning efforts fail, partly due to outdated approaches to strategic thinking.[80] The failure rates for the execution of strategies can range as high as 60 to 90 percent, suggesting that successful strategy execution is a significant challenge for many organizations.[81]

These high failure rates have been noted by top consulting firms and in literature from the Harvard Business Review, with approximately 70 percent of strategies failing due to poor execution.[82] It's highlighted that while every organization engages in planning, only a few are successful in execution.[83]

These findings suggest that there is a pervasive gap in the ability to effectively translate strategic planning into action, pointing to the need for better alignment of management processes and a cultural shift towards ongoing strategic management within organizations.

Why do so many organizations fail in executing their strategy? At a high level it's because strategy is an abstraction. For example, you can eat an orange, an apple, or a banana, but you can't eat fruit. Fruit is an abstraction much in the way strategy is an abstraction. If eating an apple is the concrete version of

79   4 Common Reasons Strategies Fail https://hbr.org/2022/06/4-common-reasons-strategies-fail#

80   Why 67 Percent of Strategic Plans Fail https://www.inc.com/tanya-prive/why-67-percent-of-strategic-plans-fail.html#:

81   Creating the Office of Strategy Management https://hbswk.hbs.edu/item/creating-the-office-of-strategy-management#

82   70% of Strategies Fail https://www.linkedin.com/pulse/70-strategies-fail-set-up-strategic-management-office-david-tang/

83   90 Percent of Organizations Fail to Execute Their Strategies Successfully https://www.intellibridge.us/90-percent-of-organizations-fail-to-execute-their-strategies-successfully/

the abstraction eating fruit, then, what is the concrete aspect of strategy? Well, if we think of "strategy" as abstract because it refers to a plan or set of actions designed to achieve a long-term or overall aim and is not tangible, then the "implementation" or "execution" of that strategy would be the concrete aspect. This involves the actual steps, actions, and initiatives that bring the strategy to life and can be observed, measured, and evaluated. And that's where most organizations fall apart.... execution.

Let's drill down further. The reasons for the low success rate in strategic implementation can be multifaceted and may include factors like poor communication, lack of alignment between various levels of the organization, inadequate resource allocation, resistance to change, and shifting market conditions. As a sales leader one aspect of your job is to make your sales strategy work within the organization's overarching strategy. Assuming there is one in place.

To improve the success rate of strategic implementation, organizations need to foster a culture of alignment, collaboration, and adaptability. Strong leadership, effective communication, and continuous monitoring and evaluation of progress are also critical to achieving strategic objectives. Depending on the type of organization you're with, you may have a little, some, or a lot of influence on those things.

This impacts effective strategic execution in organizations and your ability to succeed in several ways:

1. **Ingrained Practices:** Organizations often have established practices and processes that have been passed down through the years. While some of these practices

might be relevant and effective, others might have lost their rationale over time. Leaders must critically assess and adapt these practices to ensure they align with the organization's current goals and objectives. Sales leaders must offer guidance so you're not stuck trying to implement your strategy which may be at odds with the organization's strategy.

2. **Resistance to Change:** Cultural transmission can lead to resistance to change, as employees may resist new strategies or ideas that deviate from the established norms. Leaders must be prepared to address this resistance and communicate the rationale behind changes to gain buy-in and cooperation. Frankly, this is the hardest part.

3. **Continuous Learning:** Effective strategic execution requires a culture of continuous learning and adaptation. Leaders must foster an environment where employees are encouraged to challenge existing norms, seek new information, and experiment with innovative approaches to achieve organizational goals and be rewarded when they do. A great sales team is constantly training and learning. The largest obstacle to this is normally upper leadership whose minds are calcified and remain convinced that the way they learned to do it decades ago is still relevant.

4. **Communication and Transparency:** Open and transparent communication is vital to combat misinformation and misinterpretation within an organization. Leaders must ensure that the reasons behind strategic decisions

are clearly communicated, allowing employees to make informed decisions and actively participate in strategic execution. After overcoming resistance to change, this is the second hardest part. Most divisions in an organization (sales, operations, marketing, etc.) are siloed from each other and don't have an open and ongoing habit of clear communication. We're not even going to discuss the constipated thinking that plagues many at the executive level. Constipated thinking stifles needed free thinking and speech.

Now that we've laid the groundwork on defining strategic execution, why it usually fails, let's explore how to ensure successful execution.

CHAPTER 8

Building High-Performing Sales Teams

"Great things in business are never done by one person. They're done by a team of people."

—Steve Jobs

"Generally, success or failure of the mission can be tracked down to the leadership void in the selection or training of personnel at the individual, team or organizational level of the tactical element."

—Special Forces/Delta Operator MSG Paul R. Howe of Black Hawk Down renown.

"Get the right people on the bus and the wrong people off the bus."

—Jim Collins

OVERVIEW

Sales teams are the backbone of any organization's revenue generation efforts. As a strategic sales leader, it is essential to understand how to recruit, develop, and motivate a team of top-notch sales professionals who are aligned with the organization's vision and equipped with the skills to excel in their roles.

We will begin by discussing the process of recruiting and selecting top sales talent. By defining the ideal characteristics, competencies, and cultural fit for your sales team, you can attract individuals who possess the right skills and mindset to thrive in a sales environment. We will explore effective recruitment strategies, including leveraging networks, utilizing assessments, and conducting comprehensive interviews to identify the best candidates for your team.

Once your sales team is in place, the next step is to focus on their development and continuous improvement. We will delve into the importance of training and coaching, equipping your sales professionals with the necessary skills, knowledge, and techniques to excel in their roles. We will also explore strategies for fostering a culture of learning and growth within the sales team, encouraging continuous development, and enabling individuals to reach their full potential.

Effective sales team management extends beyond individual development. We will discuss the significance of fostering collaboration and teamwork within the sales team, creating an environment where individuals can leverage each other's strengths, share best practices, and collaborate on complex deals. By cultivating a culture of trust, communication, and accountability, you can enhance team dynamics and drive collective success.

Throughout this chapter, we will draw inspiration from successful companies renowned for their high-performing sales teams. We will explore their approaches to talent acquisition and development, such as the rigorous selection process of Salesforce and the emphasis on continuous learning at companies like Google. By examining these examples, you can derive valuable insights and practical strategies for building your own high-performing sales teams.

By the end of this chapter, you will have the tools and knowledge to build and lead a high-performing sales team. Whether you are hiring new talent, developing existing team members, or fostering a culture of collaboration, you will be equipped to create a sales team that consistently achieves outstanding results and drives your organization's growth. So, let us embark on this journey of team building and unleash the full potential of your sales team.

The Pareto Principle (The 80/20 Rule) and Your Sales Team

The Pareto Principle, also known as the 80/20 rule, states that 80 percent of outcomes result from 20 percent of the causes or inputs.[84] In various contexts, it suggests that a small portion of efforts or factors tends to have a disproportionately significant impact on the overall results or outcomes. As we'll discuss below, the same 80/20 rule applies to us in sales.

Here are the key concepts behind Pareto Principle and a few ways you can use it with your sales team to increase revenue.

Revenue Distribution: Many studies and real-world observations have shown that a significant proportion of a sales

---

84   Richard Koch, The 80/20 Principle: The Secret to Achieving More with Less (New York: Currency, 1999)

team's revenue often comes from a small percentage of top-performing salespeople. This aligns with the Pareto Principle, where 20% of the salespeople generate about 80% of the sales revenue.

Client Segmentation: The Pareto Principle can also be applied to client segmentation. It suggests that around 20% of your clients may account for 80% of a company's sales. This insight can help you and your sales teams prioritize their efforts and resources on key accounts and high-value clients.

Time Management: Salespeople often find that a substantial portion of their time is spent on unproductive tasks or low-value prospects. Understanding the Pareto Principle can encourage your sales team to focus their efforts on the most promising leads and opportunities, leading to more efficient use of their time and increased sales. Leadership must set an example and encourage their team to focus on the precious few versus the trivial many.

Productivity Improvement: Use the Pareto Principle to identify your top-performing salespeople and analyze their strategies and techniques. This information can be used to train and develop other team members, potentially improving overall sales performance. Like the saying goes, "Success leaves footprints" Do not reinvent the wheel if you don't have to.

Sales Target Setting: Setting realistic and achievable sales targets for individual salespeople can be informed by the Pareto Principle. By recognizing the distribution of performance within your team, you can set targets that are challenging but attainable for each salesperson.

Client Retention: The principle can also be applied to your client retention efforts, where a small percentage of clients may account for a significant portion of repeat business. Identifying and nurturing these loyal clients can be a valuable strategy for long-term sales success. We already addressed this in an earlier chapter, but it's worth repeating.

Incentive Design: Compensation and incentive plans for sales teams can be structured to reward top performers more generously, aligning with the Pareto Principle. This can motivate your top salespeople to maintain their high performance and encourage others to improve.

The key takeaway is the recognition of the uneven distribution of results and the potential for optimizing your sales team performance by focusing on the most impactful areas. Do everything in your power to improve the sales capability of everyone on your sales team, while realizing that your best performers will always significantly outperform everyone else. Ignore this principle at your own peril.

What about the rest of your sales team?

How to Get More of Your 80% Into the Top 20%

Every sales leader dreams of having a sales team composed entirely of people like their number one salesperson. While statistically impossible to do, we can do something close.

A five percent performance improvement in the middle 60 percent of salespeople yields over 70 percent more revenue compared to the same five percent improvement in top performers.[85] [86] [87] This striking statistic highlights the immense potential that lies within an organization's average performers.

Composition of a Typical Sales Team

A typical sales team is generally composed of:

> Bottom 20%: Underperformers
> Middle 60%: Average performers
> Top 20%: High performers

Why Focus on the Middle?

There are several compelling reasons to invest in developing your middle performers:

1. **Sheer Numbers:** The middle 60 percent represents the largest segment of the sales force, providing a greater pool for improvement.[85]

2. **Untapped Potential:** Many middle performers have the capacity to become top performers with the right support and development.[86]

---

85   Buck, R. (n.d.). Improving your middle performers is the secret to improving your top & bottom line. Act!. Retrieved from https://www.act.com/blog/improving-your-middle-performers-is-the-secret-to-improving-your-top-bottom-line/

86   Cornerstone OnDemand. (n.d.). Employees Stuck in the Middle? How to Transform the Average Joe into an Everyday Superhero. Retrieved from https://www.dresserassociates.com/pdf/whitepapers/Employees-Stuck-in-the-Middle-How-to-Transform-the-Average-Joe-into-an-Everyday-Superhero.pdf

87   Sindell, T., & Sindell, M. (2013, September 1). Maximizing the Middle: Why Focusing Your Sales Talent Investment on Mid-Level Performers Will Exponentially Increase Sales Performance. Skyline Group. https://skylineg.com/resources/blog/maximizing-the-middle-why-focusing-your-sales-talent-investment-on-mid-level-performers-will-exponentially-increase-sales-performance

3. **Revenue Impact:** Even small improvements in this large group can lead to substantial revenue gains.[87]

4. **Succession Planning**: Developing middle performers creates a pipeline of future top performers and leaders.[85]

5. **Customer Experience:** The middle group often has the most direct client interactions, significantly impacting the company's image.[87]

Strategies for Improving Middle Performer Results

To capitalize on this opportunity, sales leaders can:

1. **Identify Best Practices**: Analyze what top performers do differently and teach these skills to middle performers.

2. **Provide Targeted Training**: Offer specific skill development programs tailored to the needs of middle performers.

3. **Use Performance Analytics:** Leverage data to identify areas where middle performers can improve and track progress. We explore this in depth in a later chapter.

4. **Implement Coaching Programs:** Establish mentoring relationships between top and middle performers.

5. **Create Incentives:** Design reward systems that motivate middle performers to strive for excellence.

By shifting focus to the development of middle performers, sales organizations can unlock significant revenue potential and create a more potent, high-performing sales team overall.

Managing the performance of the 80 percent of your sales

team who may not sell as much as the top 20 percent is a critical aspect of your role as a sales leader. Here are some strategies and steps you can implement to help improve the performance of the broader sales team:

Identify Underlying Issues:

Analyze performance data to identify the specific challenges and issues faced by underperforming salespeople. These could include lack of product knowledge, poor sales skills, insufficient training, or inadequate resources.

Provide Training and Development:

Offer targeted training programs and development opportunities to address the identified weaknesses. This might involve sales training, product knowledge sessions, or coaching in specific areas where improvement is needed.

Set Clear Expectations:

Ensure that all members of the sales team understand their roles and responsibilities. Clearly communicate sales targets, quotas, and performance expectations to help them focus on their goals.

Regular Performance Reviews:

Conduct regular one-on-one performance reviews with each salesperson. Provide constructive feedback and set achievable goals for improvement. These reviews should be a two-way conversation, allowing salespeople to voice their concerns and seek support. Make sure that this is a productive and positive conversation and not a verbal beat down.

Mentorship and Coaching:

Implement mentorship programs where top-performing salespeople can mentor and coach their less experienced colleagues. This can facilitate knowledge transfer and skill development. Offer bonuses and other incentives for the mentors willing to help the others on the team.

Sales Tools and Resources:

Ensure that your sales team has access to the necessary sales tools, resources, and technology to support their efforts. This might include CRM software, marketing collateral, and lead generation tools. Help your team optimize the odds of their success by giving them as many tools as possible to help them sell.

Performance Incentives:

Design incentive programs that motivate and reward not only top performers but also those who make meaningful improvements in their performance. Incentives can be financial or non-financial, such as recognition and career advancement opportunities.

Sales Process Optimization:

Review and refine your sales processes to make them more

efficient and effective. This can help all salespeople, especially those who may struggle with complex or inefficient procedures. If you look underneath the hood, you may be amazed at how detrimental your organization's sales process is to your sales team's success.

Continuous Monitoring:

Continuously monitor the progress of your sales team and provide ongoing support. Regularly track key performance metrics and adjust strategies as needed.

Consider Personnel Changes:

While the goal should be to help all salespeople improve, there may come a point where it's necessary to make personnel changes if certain individuals consistently underperform despite support and training efforts. If you've done all the above to help underperformers, get better, and they're still failing, it's time to move them out of your team. Consistent underperformers are a drain on the team.

Team Building and Morale:

Foster a positive and collaborative team environment. Salespeople often thrive in an atmosphere where they feel supported, valued, and part of a cohesive team. This seems like a no brainer, but most sales organizations rule with fear and seldomly praise successful sales team members. The mindset of "the beatings will continue until morale improves," is too prevalent in many sales organizations.

Remember that improving the performance of the 80 percent who may not sell as much as the top 20 percent is an ongoing process. It requires patience, dedication, and a commitment to helping every member of your sales team reach their full potential. Regular communication, feedback, and a focus on skill development are key elements of successful sales team management.

Whether you're building a new sales team from the ground up, backfilling positions or coaching and mentoring existing sales team members, let the 80/20 rule guide you, your efforts and where and with whom you invest your time.

How Do Leaders Create Teams That Consistently Outperform Everyone Else?

Sales leaders can learn a lot about building winning teams from sports dynasties. From the New England Patriots (NFL), the Chicago Bulls (NBA), and Manchester United (soccer/football) to the New Zealand All Blacks (rugby), the Golden State Warriors (NBA), and the Tampa Bay Lightning (NHL) the lessons are there if we pay attention and are open to learning.

Your team must be of 'one mind'.

The legendary Phil Jackson, former head coach of the Chicago Bulls basketball team, calls this the 'Group Mind' and it was the basis of his extraordinary coaching career.[88]

When Jackson first brought Michael Jordan to Chicago, he

---

88   Phil Jackson and Hugh Delehanty, Eleven Rings: The Soul of Success, Illustrated ed. (New York: Penguin Books, 2014)

was the league's top scorer in each of his first six seasons, the best player in the NBA, yet he had never won a title.

Jackson said, "A great player can only do so much on his own. No matter how breathtaking his one-on-one moves, if he is out of sync psychologically with everyone else, the team will never achieve the harmony needed to win a championship."

This is the struggle that every leader faces. "How to get members of the team who are driven by the quest for individual glory to give themselves over wholeheartedly to the group effort."

Jackson would quote Rudyard Kipling: "For the strength of the pack is the wolf, and the strength of the wolf is the pack."

The results of Jackson's egoless approach speak for themselves. When Michael Jordan retired in 2003, he had won six championship rings and was voted Most Valuable Player in all of those finals.

Great leaders turn "ME" into a "WE".

How Do Leaders Quickly Earn Respect?

When you're hiring and training a team, they must respect you. But how do you earn that respect? Sure, your sales team will respect your title, because you're "the boss," but how do you get them to respect YOU?

General George S. Patton once said, "Always do everything you ask of those you command."[18]

Over 2,300 years ago, Xenophon the Greek military leader, mercenary, philosopher, and historian advised us that "Leaders must always set the highest standard. In a summer campaign, leaders must always endure their share of the sun and the heat and, in winter, the cold and the frost. In all labors, leaders must prove tireless if they want to enjoy the trust of their followers." [89]

Be the kind of leader that others WANT to follow. Lead by example and set the standard for others to emulate. Go on sales calls, do some prospecting so you can hear the objections, do "booth duty, etc. If you require your sales team to have certain certifications, make sure you get them too. Be intimately familiar with everything your sales team is up against and must endure daily to succeed. Your team needs to know you are shoulder to shoulder with them in the fight, day in and day out.

How Salesforce Hires Top Performers

Salesforce, a leading CRM platform provider, is known for building high-performing sales teams. They prioritize hiring individuals who align with their company culture, values, and strategic goals. By nurturing a supportive and collaborative environment, Salesforce empowers its sales teams to achieve exceptional results.[90]

Salesforce has successfully carved out its position as a leader not just through its innovative software solutions, but also through its deliberate and strategic approach to building high-performing sales teams. These teams are at the forefront of the company's client interactions, driving growth and ensuring

89   Xenophon, The Education of Cyrus, trans. Wayne Ambler (Ithaca, NY: Cornell University Press, 2001)

90   Marc Benioff and Carlye Adler, *Behind the Cloud: The Untold Story of How Salesforce. com Went from Idea to Billion-Dollar Company—and Revolutionized an Industry*, 1st ed. (San Francisco: Jossey-Bass, 2009)

the ongoing success of the business. At the core of Salesforce's strategy is a meticulous hiring process, aimed at recruiting individuals who are not just skilled and experienced, but also align with the company's culture, values, and strategic goals. Don't blow this part off. Hiring a potential sales superstar won't do your team much good if they're abrasive and rub everyone the wrong way. Among other things, being a cultural fit means that a new team member will get along with others. Seems simple enough, but this is often overlooked.

Salesforce understands that the right people are the linchpin of a high-performing sales team. They prioritize candidates who exhibit a passion for client success, a collaborative spirit, and an innate drive to achieve excellence. By bringing together individuals who share these attributes, Salesforce ensures that its sales teams are cohesive, motivated, and aligned with the company's mission.

Once on board, Salesforce takes a proactive approach to nurture and develop its sales talent. The company invests heavily in training and development programs, ensuring that every salesperson has the knowledge and skills needed to excel in their role. This includes comprehensive onboarding programs, ongoing training sessions, and access to a wealth of resources and tools. Salesforce's CRM platform itself serves as a powerful training tool, providing sales teams with real-time data, insights, and automation that enhance their efficiency and effectiveness.

In addition to training, Salesforce fosters a supportive and collaborative environment that empowers its sales teams to thrive. The company's culture is characterized by open communication, transparency, and a strong sense of community. Sales teams are encouraged to share knowledge, collaborate on deals, and support each other in achieving their goals. This collaborative ethos extends beyond the sales department, with strong alignment and cooperation between sales, marketing, product development, and client support teams. This ensures that the sales teams have the backing and resources they need to succeed, and that the entire organization is working in concert towards common objectives.

Salesforce also places a strong emphasis on performance measurement and recognition. The company has established clear performance metrics and Key Performance Indicators (KPIs) that provide visibility into individual and team performance. These metrics are not just focused on sales outcomes, but also on client satisfaction and long-term relationship building. Salesforce's CRM platform plays a crucial role in tracking and analyzing performance data, enabling sales leaders to identify areas of strength and opportunities for improvement.

Recognition and rewards are integral to Salesforce's strategy for building winning sales teams. The company is known for its generous compensation packages, performance bonuses, and incentives. Beyond financial rewards, Salesforce also places a strong emphasis on recognizing and celebrating achievements, both big and small. This culture of recognition serves to motivate the sales teams, boost morale, and foster a sense of pride and ownership in their work.

Salesforce's emphasis on work-life balance and employee well-being further contributes to the success of its sales teams. The company recognizes that the demands of sales can be intense, and it takes active steps to ensure that its employees have the support and resources they need to maintain a healthy work-life balance. This includes flexible working arrangements, wellness programs, and initiatives aimed at fostering a positive and inclusive work environment. Top performers don't have to be badgered or micro-managed to get their job done. The best are obsessed with winning deals.

Continuous innovation is another hallmark of Salesforce's approach to building high-performing sales teams. The company is constantly looking for ways to enhance its CRM platform, tools, and processes to stay ahead of the curve and empower its sales teams to be more efficient and effective. This commitment to innovation ensures that Salesforce's sales teams have access to the latest technologies and best practices, keeping them at the forefront of the industry.

Salesforce's approach to building winning sales teams is multi-faceted and comprehensive, encompassing recruitment, training and development, performance measurement, recognition, work-life balance, and continuous innovation. Yes, I know, this sounds like some sort of Infomercial for Salesforce, but it's not. They are just exceptionally good at what they do.

By prioritizing individuals who align with the company's culture and values, and by fostering a supportive and collaborative environment, Salesforce empowers its sales teams to achieve exceptional results. The company's investment in training and development, performance measurement, and recognition ensures that the sales teams have the skills, motivation, and support they need to excel. Salesforce's commitment to work-life balance and employee well-being further contributes to the success and sustainability of its sales teams. Finally, the company's relentless pursuit of innovation ensures that its sales teams have access to the best tools and resources available, keeping them at the forefront of the industry. Together, these elements create a winning formula that has propelled Salesforce to industry leadership and continues to drive its ongoing success.

As I write this, Salesforces' market cap is just over $254 Billion. Not bad for a company that was founded in 1999 just a couple of years before the Dot Bomb implosion, and 9/11 brought us a recession.

How to Recruit a World Class Sales Team

Recruiting is always going to be part of a sales leader's job. While HR and a recruiter can help you, ultimately, the responsibility is yours.[91] Generally speaking, you can expect to lose about 10% of your staff per year unless you're in a rebuilding phase. You will also lose some to attrition. Maybe someone leaves because they're not happy with their compensation plan or they get a great offer from a competitor. You will lose some because you'll have to fire them for non-performance. If you're losing more than ten percent of your team per year, it's time to take a hard look internally.

As you add new product lines or expand your geographic territories you will be looking for new talented sales professionals. Depending on the product or products that you sell, whether

---

91   Mike Weinberg, *Sales Management. Simplified.: The Straight Truth About Getting Exceptional Results from Your Sales Team* (New York: AMACOM, 2015)

they be hardware, software, technology related, or non-technology related, it usually takes about six months for a sales professional to get up to speed, and one year for them to truly hit their stride. We're assuming that you're in a complex sale that requires a long timeline.

If you have a key salesperson leave your team because they got a better offer somewhere else, you're going to take a big hit on your revenue for between six months and a year. That's not factoring in how many months it will take you to find someone to backfill that position. That's why it's important for you to maintain your own personal database of talent should one of your sales team quit.

It goes without saying that you need to be aware of any disgruntled sales team members. Especially if they're part of your top 20 percent who bring in a large share of your revenue. Top salespeople will always be in demand and constantly be approached by recruiters to jump ship.

If you have a good relationship with each member of your sales team, they will give you a warning that they're thinking of leaving, or that they've gotten a great offer from a competitor. Fight like a tiger to ensure they stay with you. If they're an underperformer, let them go. They're doing you a favor.

When you start seeing some signs that either you might be needing to let go of a salesperson or upper management is letting you know that there's going to be some new product launches, new geographic expansions, etc., you're going to immediately need to pivot from soft recruiting to hard recruiting.

In the context of hiring top talent, especially from a sales leader's perspective, understanding the difference between "soft recruiting" and "hard recruiting" is essential.

Soft Recruiting: Soft recruiting focuses on building relationships and networks that can lead to future hires. It's a more passive approach where the emphasis is not directly on filling a position but rather on creating a talent pipeline and employer brand that attracts top candidates organically. Here are some key elements of soft recruiting:

Networking: Engaging with potential candidates at industry events, seminars, or through professional networking platforms like LinkedIn. Get to know your competitor's top salespeople. Trade shows are a fantastic way to begin the soft recruiting process.

Employer Branding: Creating a positive perception of the company culture and values through marketing and public relations efforts. A strong employer brand makes people want to work for you. Your vendor partners will know what your company culture is and can help you with your soft recruiting efforts.

Employee Referrals: Encourage current employees to refer people from their network who might fit well with the organization. Be cautious here. It's one thing to begin conversations with an employee referral because the candidate is strong versus they're an old friend of the employee. Great teams aren't built through nepotism. Be willing to push back hard if an employee argues with you to recruit someone who is clearly not a good fit. Hiring someone because they're an old fraternity brother of a current employee is a lousy excuse for giving them the job.

Content Marketing: Sharing valuable content that positions the company as a thought leader and an attractive place to work. This is where YouTube, LinkedIn and other relevant platforms come into play. The goal is to put out content that magnetizes the most talented salespeople to you.

Relationship Building: Maintaining long-term relationships with potential candidates and nurturing them until the right opportunity arises. If you're in a sales leadership position, it should mean that you've been in the industry long enough to have a clear understanding of who the sales movers and shakers are. Periodically meet them for coffee or lunch.

Soft recruiting is about creating a compelling and attractive work environment that naturally draws in top talent. It's less aggressive but requires consistent effort and a strategic approach to branding and network building. The importance of soft recruiting only becomes clear when you suddenly don't have adequate sales territory coverage. Expect to be soft recruiting year-round.

Hard Recruiting: Hard recruiting, on the other hand, is a more aggressive and direct approach to filling specific positions. It's about actively seeking out candidates and persuading them to consider the opportunity. Once you've been approved for the additional headcount, it's time to get to work. If you've done a solid job with your soft recruiting efforts, you should be able to attract top talent quickly.

Here are some key elements of hard recruiting:

Direct Outreach: Contacting potential candidates directly through recruitment platforms, emails, or phone calls. If you have in-house recruiters, make sure they're crystal clear on who and what you're looking for.

Job Postings and Advertisements: Placing ads on job boards, social media, or industry publications. Make sure you help write the job posting. HR/your internal recruiter won't always understand exactly what you need.

Recruitment Events: Participating in or hosting job fairs and recruitment drives.

Headhunting: Engaging the services of a headhunter or a recruiting agency to find and approach candidates with specific skill sets or in specific roles. While some may balk at paying the fees recruiters command, I've always found that it's money well spent.

Incentive-Based Recruiting: Offering bonuses, higher salaries, or other benefits to attract candidates, especially for hard-to-fill sales roles. This is not the time to be cheap. Think of how much revenue you're losing for every month the sales position is vacant.

Hard recruiting is typically faster and more focused on filling immediate vacancies. It is proactive and often involves more direct selling of the position to the candidate.

In practice, you may use a combination of both approaches, depending on your immediate and long-term hiring needs. While hard recruiting might fill an urgent vacancy, soft recruiting is essential for building a sustainable talent pipeline and reducing the need for hard recruiting in the future. The best approach often depends on factors such as the industry, the roles being filled, the company's brand, and the current job market.

The Interview Process

Most organizations are horrible when it comes to hiring the best candidate. Hiring the best candidate is always important, but in sales, it's critical.

Laszlo Bock, former SVP of People Operations at Google, revealed in his book "Work Rules! Insights from Inside Google That Will Transform How You Live and Lead," that interviews are only slightly more predictive than rolling dice when it comes to hiring. Google's extensive data analysis found that the typical interview process was a poor predictor of job performance.[92] Take a moment to think about what that means for you as a sales leader.

It gets even worse. According to a meta-analysis by Schmidt and Hunter, the typical unstructured job interview increases the likelihood of choosing the best candidate by only 2% compared to a random selection.[93] This analysis illustrates the limited predictive power of traditional interviewing techniques. You could literally throw darts at a wall pasted with resumes of your candidates and have the same predictive ability as the average interviewing "process."

Thankfully, there is a bit of good news. The same study by Schmidt and Hunter found that structured interviews, where each candidate is asked the same set of defined questions,

---

92   Laszlo Bock, *Work Rules!: Insights from Inside Google That Will Transform How You Live and Lead*, Illustrated ed. (New York: Twelve, 2015)

93   Schmidt, F. L., & Hunter, J. E. (1998). The Validity and Utility of Selection Methods in Personnel Psychology: Practical and Theoretical Implications of 85 Years of Research Findings. Psychological Bulletin, 124(2), 262-274. https://www.researchgate.net/publication/283803351_The_Validity_and_Utility_of_Selection_Methods_in_Personnel_Psychology_Practical_and_Theoretical_Implications_of_85_Years_of_Research_Findings

were much more effective. The predictive validity of structured interviews was found to be about 0.51 (on a scale where 0 is no predictive validity and 1 is perfect prediction), which is significantly better than unstructured interviews. In other words, it's just slightly better than a coin toss. Yes, that sounds bad, but it's still significantly better than 2%.

The same research also indicated that general mental ability tests are among the best predictors of job performance, with a validity of around 0.65. When combined with structured interviews, the predictive validity can be even higher. If they're not already doing so, ask your HR team to add performance and cognitive tests to the hiring process.

For those of you who hire new salespeople straight out of college based on their GPA's, you may want to reconsider your approach. Or you require an MBA. A study by Ernst & Young found that there was no correlation between academic success and career success in their hiring.[94] As a result, they decided to remove degree classification from entry criteria, recognizing that academic performance wasn't a reliable indicator of future job performance.

You may be thinking "So what am I supposed to do?" There will be some specific sales-related interview questions at the end of this section. Let's explore the thinking behind those questions now.

When it comes to the interview process, focus on questions that are often called behavioral interviewing questions.

---

94   Lucas, S. (2015, September 22). Ernst & Young Stopped Requiring Degrees. Should You? Inc. Magazine. https://www.inc.com/suzanne-lucas/ernst-amp-young-stopped-requiring-degrees-should-you.html

For example, interviewers ask candidates to describe past experiences and how they managed specific situations. These questions often start with phrases like, "Tell me about a time when..." or "Give an example of how you..."

For example, always ask sales professionals to walk you through the largest deal they have ever closed from start to finish, meaning from the initial lead to a closed sale. It's easy to lie about large sales numbers and name marquee accounts, but it's extremely hard to give a detailed explanation of an opportunity from start to close if you weren't actually involved in the process. Have them explain in painful detail the complete process from how the lead was generated, what the proof of concept was like, what obstacles came their way, how they overcame the obstacles, and what was the timeline of the deal.

What you're looking for is someone who understands the entire process from start to finish. You're also looking for some con artist who might be trying to lie their way into the job. The only thing worse than having an open position is filling a position with someone who can't do the job.

Then ask them to explain the largest deal they ever lost. How they answer this question will inform you of how they handle loss, how they course correct and whether they learn from their mistakes. You'll also learn whether they're a team player or not. Will they point the finger at someone else or admit that they made a catastrophic mistake? Once they've shared their explanation, ask "Knowing what you know now, if you could go back in time, what would you have done differently?" Then shut up and listen. You'll quickly know if they learn from their mistakes and can adjust their sales methodology as needed.

Great sales success requires an individual who can think through their mistakes, adapt, and set out in a new direction to success. Some sales professionals are very hard-headed and will just keep doing the same thing repeatedly knowing (thinking?) that it's a numbers game. At some point they will win the deal but that's a brute force way of selling. It's not an intelligent way of selling. Brute force selling only works when the economy is great, or you have enough leads, or your marketplace is large enough that salespeople can fail and move on to another prospect over and over again until they win a deal. That's a numbers game based on volume. That "method" will fail in a spectacular way when the economy turns bad.

When it comes to sales, we have Hunters and Farmers. A Hunter is someone that can go out and get brand new clients, and Farmers are sales professionals who excel at maintaining and growing an existing client base. Each requires unique skill sets. Few salespeople are adept at doing both. It's critical you're clear on what the role you're hiring for requires. Do you need a Hunter, or do you need a Farmer? Do you need a blend of someone who can do both as needed?

One of the mistakes that sales leaders make is hiring what they thought was a superstar, and then finding out that the person was just basically a farmer who had a fantastic territory. So it's critical during the interview process to find out how long they have been working with any account.

Ask questions such as:

- How did you get the account?
- Did you inherit it, or were you the one who pursued it and closed it?

- Help me to understand how you interact with this company.

- How often do you close an opportunity?

- Is your territory geographic, vertical, or product based?

- Which accounts did you earn most of your commissions from?

- Please elaborate?

Be aware that there are some salespeople who have sold for Fortune 500 (Tier 1) companies and were extremely successful, then they get recruited either into a smaller (Tier 2, 3 or 4), less known company or perhaps a startup with no brand name recognition, little to no market share, and/or a new product line. These so-called sales superstars foundered because they didn't know the first thing about prospecting, messaging, understanding who to talk to in the organization, what to say to each person if or when they got them on the phone, or in a face-to-face meeting. They had been successful based on the brand of the company they sold for. They may have inherited some massive legacy accounts. But when it came time to start from nothing, they didn't have a clue how to succeed.

In other cases, the salesperson was smashing quotas year after year, but the reality was that they were just in good territories with little competition, and they were not up to the task or challenge of opening brand new territories with a brand-new product line.

Nothing will implode your sales efforts faster than hiring a person you think is a sales superstar and they turn out to be a dud.

During the interview process, ask the candidate, "When was the last time you learned something new?" [95] What they respond with doesn't matter. You're trying to understand if the candidate has the capability to learn new things and how they do so.

It could be how to play guitar, learn a new language, or new technology. Have them walk you through their process of learning something. Our world changes so quickly that if you end up with an employee who can't course correct and learn new things quickly on the fly, you're going to have an employee that's going to stagnate quickly. Futurist Alvin Toffler once said, "The illiterate of the 21st century will not be those who cannot read and write, but those who cannot learn, unlearn, and relearn."

Finally, you're going to have to get into their mind. Understand their belief systems especially pertaining to success. Sales is a hard profession, and you must have thick skin and have a positive mindset almost to the point of being fanatically optimistic. Otherwise, this profession can grind you into dust.

Asking your candidate about their goals, and how they plan to accomplish them will give you a good understanding of their mindset and their belief systems. If they have a poverty mindset, or seem to be focused on mediocrity, they won't last. Someone with a good blend of realism and optimism makes the perfect salesperson. They must be optimistic, however they also need to be able to see things as they are without seeing them through

95   Trish Bertuzzi, *The Sales Development Playbook: Build Repeatable Pipeline and Accelerate Growth with Inside Sales* (Boston: The Bridge Group, 2016)

rose colored glasses. You can have the best product in the world in a terrific marketplace but if you have a sales professional who has low self-esteem, and doesn't believe in their ability to succeed and achieve excellence, you're going to have a member of your team who will be pulling everyone else down.

As you begin the interview process, ensure that you and the rest of your hiring team keep the following in mind throughout the interview process:

The Cruciality of Cultural Fit

Equally important is ensuring alignment between the candidate's values and the organizational culture. A cohesive team, unified in its values and goals, fosters a productive and positive working environment. Conversely, a misaligned hire can disrupt team dynamics and impede performance.[96] Sales leaders must, therefore, prioritize cultural fit, assessing how well a candidate's values, work ethic, and personality align with those of the organization. If you've ever had two members of your sales team hate each other, then you understand how quickly things can go from bad to toxic. I once had an account manager and a sales engineer who despised each other. The account manager was a hard charger who always wanted to be on the road, and the sales engineer tried to avoid being on the road as much as possible. As you can imagine the two began to detest one another. Eventually, I was forced to make changes to the sales team so they could be paired with colleagues who were a better

---

96   Daniel Coyle, *The Culture Code: The Secrets of Highly Successful Groups* (New York: Bantam Books, 2018)

fit. Thankfully the switch worked, and the sales team began humming again with no more ill will and rancor poisoning the rest of the team. Needless to say, it's better to hire people who will fit well into your corporate culture as well as your sales team's culture.

Assessing Adaptability and Continuous Learning

The rapid evolution of markets and technologies necessitates a sales team that is adaptable and committed to continuous learning. Sales leaders should seek candidates who demonstrate a proactive approach to learning and development, highlighting their ability to stay current and adapt to change.

Balancing Hard and Soft Skills

While technical expertise and product knowledge are critical, the importance of soft skills such as communication, empathy, and emotional intelligence cannot be overstated. These skills play a pivotal role in building client relationships, navigating complex negotiations, and understanding client needs. A balanced assessment of both hard and soft skills is essential in identifying candidates who are well-rounded and poised for success.

Providing Clear Job Previews

Transparency during the recruitment process ensures that candidates have a realistic understanding of the role and its expectations. Is the job for outside sales or inside sales? If it's an outside sales job, how often do you expect them to be on the road? Will they be traveling locally, throughout the state, nationally or internationally? If it's an inside sales job, will they be remote or expected to be in an office? If they're expected to come into an office, how many days per week?

How many sales calls, meetings, and opportunities will they be expected to do and win? What is the quota? How much is the quota over the previous year? Is this a fresh territory, a new product launch, or established territory with an established market share?

Clear communication regarding the challenges and demands of the position helps in setting accurate expectations, leading to better job satisfaction and retention. If you hire someone and mislead them about the job, and performance expectations, it will end badly.

We once hired a sales engineer for what was a new, undeveloped territory. There was no run rate, and no commissions were coming out of the territory. For reasons I still don't understand, the sales engineering manager neglected to tell the new employee this especially important fact. Nor did they offer the new employee a draw of any kind to help him get by until the territory began producing. He quit after six months of being constantly angry that he couldn't make ends meet.

The Interview Process: A Deep Dive

The interview process is a critical component of recruitment, providing an opportunity to assess a candidate's suitability for the sales role. While I addressed a few interview questions above, the additional 15 questions below will give you a well-rounded overview of your candidate and how well they could do in your sales organization.

Sample Interview Questions:

(Since my background is in technology sales and technology sales leadership, the questions will be focused on that, but substitute your own product type and category related questions)

1. Can you explain a complex technology product that you've sold in the past?

- *Purpose:* This question assesses the candidate's ability to understand and articulate complex technical concepts, which is crucial for selling products like routers, firewalls, or cybersecurity solutions.

2. Describe a time when you had to educate a prospect about a technology solution they were unfamiliar with. How did you ensure they understood the value?

- *Purpose:* This question evaluates the candidate's educational and communication skills, important for guiding prospects through complex technology solutions and ensuring they grasp the product's value.

3. Walk me through how you manage long sales cycles and maintain engagement with prospects.

- *Purpose:* Sales of technology solutions like routers and

firewalls often involve lengthy sales cycles. This question aims to understand the candidate's strategies for keeping prospects engaged over time.

4. Can you share an experience where you had to overcome significant objections from a technical decision-maker? How did you handle it?

- *Purpose:* This question assesses the candidate's ability to navigate objections and influence key decision-makers, particularly those with technical expertise.

5. Describe a deal you lost. What went wrong and what did you learn from it?

- *Purpose:* Understanding how a candidate deals with failure and what they take away from such experiences provides insight into their resilience and capacity for growth.

6. How do you stay updated on industry trends and technological advancements?

- *Purpose:* Given the rapidly evolving nature of technology, this question gauges the candidate's commitment to continuous learning and staying current in their field.

7. Tell me about a time when you had to coordinate with multiple stakeholders, both internal and external, to close a deal.

- *Purpose:* Sales of complex technology solutions often

require collaboration with various stakeholders. This question assesses the candidate's ability to navigate these dynamics effectively.

8. How would you differentiate our products from competitors when talking to a potential client?

- *Purpose:* This question evaluates the candidate's knowledge of your products and their ability to articulate unique selling points effectively.

9. Can you give an example of how you've managed a prospect who was already leaning towards a competitor's product?

- *Purpose:* This question evaluates the candidate's ability to sway prospects and position your products more favorably than the competition.

10. Describe your approach to prospecting and generating new leads in the technology sector.

- *Purpose:* For roles that require 'hunter' skills, this question assesses the candidate's initiative-taking approach to identifying and pursuing new business opportunities.

11. Explain a complex sale you closed. What were the challenges and how did you overcome them?

- *Purpose:* This question delves deeper into the candidate's experience with complex sales, assessing their critical thinking skills and perseverance.

12. How do you tailor your communication style when dealing with technical vs. non-technical stakeholders?

- *Purpose:* The candidate's ability to adjust their communication style is crucial for effectively engaging with diverse stakeholders in the sales process.

13. Can you discuss a time when you had to negotiate terms and conditions of a sale? What was your approach?

- *Purpose:* This question evaluates the candidate's negotiation skills, essential for closing deals and ensuring favorable terms.

14. What strategies do you use to maintain positive relationships with existing clients and ensure repeat business?

- *Purpose:* For roles that require 'farmer' skills, this question assesses the candidate's ability to nurture and expand existing client relationships.

15. How do you manage high-pressure situations, such as meeting ambitious sales targets or dealing with challenging clients?

- *Purpose:* This question assesses the candidate's resilience and stress management skills, important for maintaining performance under pressure.

These questions are tailored to gauge the candidate's technical understanding, communication skills, and ability to navigate the complex sales process. They will also help you weed out any liars or underperformers.

To Poach or Not to Poach: Should You Try to Recruit from Your Competitors

When considering whether to lure away a competitor's top salesperson, you're going to have to carefully weigh the potential benefits against the risks and ethical considerations.[97] This is a complicated issue with a few factors to consider:

Potential Benefits

1. **Gaining Industry Expertise:** A top salesperson from a competitor has deep industry knowledge and relationships that could benefit your organization. They may bring valuable insights into competitor strategies and client needs.

2. **Immediate Revenue Impact:** In theory, an experienced salesperson could "hit the ground running" and start generating revenue quickly, though this is not guaranteed.

Risks and Drawbacks

1. **Cultural Mismatch:** There's no guarantee that a salesperson who crushed it at a competitor will fit well within your company's culture and processes. Different organizations have unique sales environments.

---

97   The Alternative Board. (2016, November 2). *How to Take an Ethical Approach to Poaching Employees*. https://www.thealternativeboard.com/blog/taking-an-ethical-approach-to-poaching-employees

2. **Ethical and Legal Concerns:** Poaching employees can lead to legal issues, especially if the salesperson has a non-compete agreement or tries to bring clients with them. This could damage your company's reputation.

3. **Reliability Questions:** A salesperson willing to leave their current employer may do the same to you in the future. Their loyalty may be questionable.

4. **Hidden Costs:** While it may seem like a quick win, hiring from a competitor often still requires significant training and onboarding investment.

Cost of Not Pursuing Top Talent

1. Missed opportunities to gain market share.

2. Slower growth compared to more aggressive competitors.

3. Potential loss of your own top performers to competitors who are actively recruiting. Remember, your competitors may try to steal your talent.

Alternative Approaches

Instead of directly poaching your competitors' employees, you can focus on:

1. Developing your internal talent through well thought out training programs.

2. Creating a strong company culture that attracts top talent naturally.

3. Improving compensation and benefits packages to retain and attract the best salespeople.

4. Investing in innovative sales tools and processes to give your team a competitive edge.

While luring away a competitor's top salesperson may seem tempting, it's often not the silver bullet companies hope for. The risks, both legal and ethical, often outweigh the potential benefits. A more sustainable approach is to focus on building and nurturing your own sales talent while creating an environment that naturally attracts high performers.

As the ancient Chinese proverb says, "Dig your well before you are thirsty." Always be on the lookout for extraordinary talent. Keep a list of potential candidates for each of your sales positions and team members. You do not want to be caught by surprise when a member of your team suddenly quits.

Before You Make the Offer:

> "You don't hire for skills; you hire for attitude.
> You can always teach skills."
>
> **—Southwest Airlines founder Herb Kelleher**

Once you've recruited what you feel is a satisfactory number of candidates for the position, ensure they're scheduled for interviews with the people they're going to be working with every day. While a candidate may look great on paper and interview well, they may rub your team the wrong way. For example, if you're hiring a sales engineer, it's imperative that the actual account manager/account executive who's going to be paired up with that sales engineer gets a chance to interview them. You don't want colleagues who are incompatible working together being forced to work together. The revenue in that territory will inevitably fall. Sometimes what you think is the "perfect" candidate might not be the "perfect" candidate because they're just not going to collaborate well with other people within the organization.

While it's great to have your upper management involved in the interview process, they're not the ones that will be collaborating with them. If possible, do those peer-to-peer interviews face to face. It's too easy for someone to do video interviews and keep it together just long enough to win their way into an organization and then when you end up having to meet them or travel with them, you find out that they're just culturally not a good fit. Being forced to fire the new hire four to six months later is a massive setback.

How to Train a Quota Crushing Sales Team

> "Without training, they lacked knowledge.
> Without knowledge, they lacked confidence.
> Without confidence, they lacked victory"
>
> —Julius Caesar

> "We don't rise to the level of our expectations;
> we fall to the level of our training."
>
> —Archilochus

While the prevailing conventional wisdom is that great sales professionals are born not made, the research shows that's not the case. "Consistently and overwhelmingly, the evidence showed that experts are made, not born. These conclusions are based on rigorous research that looked at exceptional performance using scientific methods that are verifiable and reproducible." In a long term study that included over 100 researchers who looked at experts in every field imaginable from chess masters, neurosurgeons and computer programmers to top ranked fighter pilots, to golfers and firefighters, they discovered that, "The journey to truly superior performance is neither for the faint of heart nor for the impatient. The development of genuine expertise requires struggle, sacrifice, and honest, often painful self-assessment. There are no shortcuts. It will take you at least a decade to achieve expertise, and you will need to invest that time wisely, by engaging in "deliberate" practice—practice that focuses on tasks beyond your current level of competence and comfort. You will need a well-informed coach not only to guide you through deliberate practice but also to help you learn how to coach yourself."[98]

The onus is on us as sales leaders to help create the next generation of sales experts. If you're lucky, you may stumble across a gifted person who picks up the sales profession and succeeds almost immediately. However, we don't want to depend on luck, so we create our own luck.

Most companies drop the ball when it comes to training their salespeople. I've been in sales organizations where I was never given any training on any of the products we sold. Everything I knew about the products, the problems they solved, and the

98   Ericsson, K. A., Prietula, M. J., & Cokely, E. T. (2007, July–August). The Making of an Expert. Harvard Business Review. https://hbr.org/2007/07/the-making-of-an-expert

best vertical to sell to was based on the research I had done in preparation for the interviewing process. Rather than having a structured sales onboarding process in which I was able to quickly get to speed, I had to stumble around through the process of trial and error before I found the right answers. I also spoke with our team's top salespeople for some guidance.

Have a process in place for onboarding. Have a schedule in place for onboarding for the first two to three weeks, or however long your process takes. Make sure that you work through the entire sales process from A to Z. You do have a process and sales methodology, right?

If possible, have your new salesperson shadow your top salesperson. Many companies will just pair a new salesperson with a veteran salesperson who is geographically close to them regardless of their sales success or lack of it. In other words, if you're trying to train a new person to be a top sales professional, don't pair them up with a mediocre salesperson just because it's convenient.

To accelerate the onboarding process and significantly reduce frustration, have your new hire shadow your top salesperson (or at the very least, your second best) during both virtual and in-person meetings for a few weeks. This exposure will familiarize them with the sales cadence, typical conversations, and common objections they'll encounter, even if they have previous experience in comparable sales roles. It's important to remember that the level of excellence at their previous organization may vary, and your products and solutions could require a different sales approach. This firsthand experience can save them months of struggle.

Once the onboarding process is completed, don't stop there.

Sales is an ongoing thing. The sales process changes and continuously evolves. Especially now in the Internet age. Before the Internet, people had to go to salespeople to get all the information they needed. Not anymore. Now, on average your prospect is about 70 percent of the way through their buying process by the time you ever talk to them.[99] It's a different world. Because times are changing, you must change with the times, and your sales team has to be constantly aware of those changes. Ongoing sales training is the key. It must be done regularly. We'll discuss how later.

See to it that your product managers (or product experts) spend time with your salespeople. Their job is to train them on your products, so that the salespeople can internalize the key features and benefits of each product and/or solution in your portfolio.

Your product managers, engineering team, or whoever's on the technical side must have a basic understanding of sales psychology, why people buy, and how persuasion works. The best organizations will put people from non-sales roles through sales training so that they understand what the sales professionals are up against. If you're in the B2B space, people are looking for solutions to business problems. In most cases, that's going to involve technology or software depending on the business you're in. What you do for a living is predicated on your ability and your sales team's ability to solve complex business problems. If the cost of your solution to the client's problem is significantly less than the cost of the problem, you will make a sale.

---

99   6sense. (2024, January 8). Don't Call Us, We'll Call You: What Research Says About When B2B Buyers Reach Out to Sellers. https://6sense.com/blog/dont-call-us-well-call-you-what-research-says-about-when-b2b-buyers-reach-out-to-sellers/

Too often we fall in love with our products and their features, and we lose sight of the benefits they bring to our clients. For example, in the networking technology world we often get lost in "speeds and feeds," while losing track of what the client is trying to accomplish. We lose sight of the pain they are dealing with and become obsessed with just selling them something.

If possible, have either weekly or twice monthly sales meetings with your team. If you can get your team together for 30 minutes every week to discuss recent large opportunity wins, sales training, and having product managers regularly attend as guest speakers, you will create a cadence that helps ensure your sales team is always in a learning mode that is psychologically powerful.

The better training your sales team receives, the more capable they will be of achieving their sales revenue goals. Capability precedes motivation and inspiration. The more capable your team feels, the more motivated they're going to be to tackle those steep revenue goals.

Sales Process and Tools

Train your new salespeople on whatever sales processes and tools you have. For example, CRM software are not all created the same. A salesperson moving from a highly customized Salesforce CRM is going to need to be trained in Microsoft Dynamics 365 CRM. Quoting tools and such are also going to be different and require training. Some organizations will record training sessions so that new people can watch them during their onboarding process. Once they've watched the training sessions, a separate individualized training session is scheduled to help clear up any confusion and answer any remaining questions.

Ensure your new team member is well-versed in using these tools. Conduct regular training sessions and provide support to help them use these tools effectively. Doing so will shorten not only their ramp up time but increase their odds of being successful. We'll discuss using technology in a later chapter.

When Things Go Bad: How to Fire a Member of Your Sales Team

> "It is my practice to try to understand how valuable something is by trying to imagine myself without it."
>
> **- Southwest Airlines Founder Herb Kelleher**

> "Don't water your weeds"
>
> **- Harvey MacKay**

Firing is another subject that sales leaders need to be well versed in. It's always best to fire sooner than later for a few reasons. If you're dealing with an underperforming salesperson, and the rest of the team sees that they can keep getting their base pay without getting fired, it demoralizes the rest of the team who are busy working hard and winning deals.

Another reason you should be fast to fire is when you have a toxic member of your team. Toxicity is like cancer, and it spreads fast. It also is bad for morale. Perhaps you've heard the saying "people don't quit their jobs they quit their bosses." While it's true that many people will quit a job they mostly like because they have a horrible boss, they will also quit when they dislike who they're working with. Be wary of the super star salesperson who despite bringing in record breaking sales revenue also becomes toxic to the rest of the organization. In most cases, it begins when they become pushy, aggressive, and disrespectful to other members of your organization. That includes but is not limited to your inside sales, sales operations, customer service and other people in your organization.

Bring in HR and make sure to get it on record that you're going to counsel the person in question. If you don't, like cancer, it will metastasize and get much worse. If you don't handle it sooner than later, eventually you will be dealing with a team who refuse to work with the salesperson.

Make sure everyone on your team knows what will get you fired. This isn't a fear tactic, it's a way of looking out for them. I once worked at a billion-dollar company where an executive was fired because he used his company-provided laptop to access pornography while traveling on business. Despite having been with the company for many years as a great employee, he was immediately fired. Work with HR to ensure you are clear on what behavior will get an employee fired.

If for example, you have a policy where someone gets put on a Productivity Improvement Plan (PIP) after being well below quota for two of the last four quarters for example, make sure your team is aware of this policy.

Also make sure that you work with your HR team to understand what the legal boundaries are of when you can fire someone and for what reasons. Every state has different laws. If your company is based in one state with one set of laws, the state in which an employee lives and works may have different laws in place. Make sure you're clear on them. Even though most of us work in what are called "At will" states, the legal departments of most organizations will not just let you randomly fire someone. There must be a paper trail. Consult with both your organization's legal team and HR. Be clear on the laws. Too many organizations have dealt with unlawful termination lawsuits because a leader wasn't clear on the employment laws of their respective state.

The key part of maintaining morale and discipline on your sales team is rewarding excellence and punishing mediocrity. As a sales leader, you must decide if an individual on your team either needs more training, more support, or lacks the drive and/or intellectual capacity to do the job well.

One final caveat when firing someone is to make sure you err on the side of fairness. I've seen people struggle in certain territories because the territory was horrible. For whatever reason, it didn't have the support that was necessary to make it thrive. Perhaps a competitor had a foothold that was unbreakable. Or perhaps it is a territory that your organization has neglected, and you've finally put a salesperson in the territory. If revenue expectations aren't realistic, you may have set up a salesperson to fail. If this is the case, it didn't mean they were a bad salesperson, maybe it meant that they never had a chance to succeed.

Your responsibility among others, is to make sure that you set up your team to succeed. You must be fair to your team across the board in each of the territories. Whether they're in one state, or one city, or spread out globally, you have to acknowledge whether a salesperson has a realistic chance of succeeding. If not, determine what it's going to take to turn the territory around so that a salesperson can succeed.

If the territory requires a longer time frame to get it where you need it to be, try to give the salesperson a larger than normal base pay. Or perhaps a larger than normal base pay and a non-refundable draw for the first year. Starving salespeople become desperate salespeople which in turn adversely impacts their ability to sell well. Prospective clients can smell a desperate salesperson from a mile away. If maintaining margin is important to your organization, you've just incentivized a starving salesperson to give away margin.

Sadly, most companies won't do this. Instead, they'll hire a salesperson, knowing the territory needs time to grow, and watch them get destroyed despite giving it their everything. Twelve months later (if they last that long), the salesperson is fired and then the company hires a new salesperson. The new salesperson will then take over the fired salesperson's pipeline and push to get those opportunities won and closed. Depending on how bad the territory is, and how good the salesperson is, they may win enough deals to remain employed. In many cases they won't. The process will keep being repeated until the third or fourth salesperson has inherited enough of a pipeline that enables them to finally start consistently closing enough business to ensure their position with the company.

Not only is this process sadistic and nonsensical, but it's also detrimental to your sales growth and will damage your organization's brand. If your most desired prospects experience a revolving door of salespeople, they're going to see a lot of red flags pop up. The more red flags a prospective new client sees, the less likely they are to buy from you.

What if you're on the fence about firing someone? Like the old saying goes, "You fight with the army you have, not with the army you want." In most cases, you "inherited" your sales team. Assuming you're not in a rebuilding stage, you're going to have to determine just how bad a salesperson is, and whether they should be fired. Determine if they do more harm than good in your organization? For example, if you have an underperforming salesperson who is consistently coming in at 50%-60% of quota, you have to decide if they're just bad at sales or if that territory is too competitive for you. I knew a ferocious salesperson in Las Vegas, Nevada who sold for a tier one networking hardware vendor. Not only was he a great salesperson with deep technical knowledge, he also grew up there. He literally went to high school and college with the people who eventually went on to become the CIO's, CTO's, VPs of IT and such at every major casino in Las Vegas. For almost 20 years, he demolished any competitor who stepped foot in town. He owned the town. Every single competitor salesperson who came into town was crushed by him. He vacuumed up all the noteworthy large deals and left crumbs for everyone else.

If your underperforming salesperson is dealing with that type of situation, you're going to have to develop a unique strategy for them. If that isn't the case, then you need to investigate why they're underperforming. Once you've accurately diagnosed the issue, then and only then can you move on to the next step. Triage. Half of something is better than all of nothing. If your underperformer isn't actively harming your company's brand, nor representing you badly, then you may want to keep them on for a while longer. During this time, give them extra coaching and see if you can get them from an F or D up to a C+ or B. You're going to need to be patient. Depending on your sales cycle, this could take a minimum of 6 months. During this time, you should be doing some soft recruiting.

As a sales leader, you can't be caught flat footed if the underperformer suddenly quits. Remember, the underperformer isn't making the money they expected to. And whether the territory is bad, the product isn't compelling, or they're horrible salespeople, they will begin to actively interview with other companies. A gap in your team means a gap in your potential revenue.

If the underperformer is both bad at sales and has been hurting your company brand, or are actively toxic both internally and externally, then get them on a PIP (Productivity Improvement Plan), cover your bases with HR and legal, and start aggressively recruiting for a new sales representative in that territory. The longer you have no salesperson in that territory the harder it's going to be to regain your footing there.

You may want to have a hard conversation with your leadership about abandoning a territory altogether so you can focus your sales resources on other territories that can bring about a better ROI. As Brian Halligan, the co-founder and CEO of HubSpot, a marketing and sales software company once said, "The art of strategy is knowing when to say no."

Building a high-performing sales team is an essential component for the success of any business. A team that's aligned, motivated, and skilled can significantly drive revenue and contribute to business growth. However, creating such a team isn't an easy task; it involves careful selection, proper training, effective management, and continuous motivation.

Your Checklist for Sales Success: Strategies for Elevating Team Performance

Elevating the performance of your sales team is essential for achieving and surpassing organizational sales targets. It requires a combination of strategic planning, effective management practices, and a deep understanding of the dynamics within the sales team.[100] This section provides you with a checklist and strategies that you can employ to boost your team's performance, build a culture of success, and ensure sustained improvements over time. As you go through the list, note which things you're already doing, which things you're not and how to bridge the gap.

1. Clear Goal Setting and Communication

- **Purpose**: Establish clear, achievable goals for the team and individual members, ensuring everyone understands the targets and what is expected of them.

- **Action Steps**:
  - Use SMART (Specific, Measurable, Achievable, Relevant, Time-bound) criteria to set goals.

---

100   Steve W. Martin, Sales Strategy Playbook: The Ultimate Reference Guide to Solve Your Toughest Sales Challenges (Laguna Hills, CA: Tilis Publishers, 2018)

- Regularly communicate these goals through meetings, digital dashboards, and one-on-one sessions to keep them at the forefront of team activities.

2. Customized Training Programs

- **Purpose**: Tailor training programs to meet the specific needs of the team and individual salespeople, focusing on areas that will maximize their potential and address any skill gaps. Your team will have a remarkably diverse background of training and past selling experience. You need to get them up to the same standard of excellence.

- **Action Steps**:
  - Conduct skills assessments to identify areas for improvement.
  - Develop or source training programs that address these specific needs, such as negotiation skills, product knowledge, or advanced sales techniques.
  - Implement regular training sessions and follow-up to ensure skills are applied.

3. Performance Monitoring and Feedback Loops

- **Purpose**: Continuously monitor performance and provide timely, constructive feedback to help team members improve and stay aligned with company goals. No feedback equals no improvement.

- **Action Steps**:

  - Use CRM and sales management tools to track performance metrics like sales volume, conversion rates, and client engagement.

  - Schedule regular review meetings to discuss these metrics with team members, offer feedback, and adjust strategies, as necessary.

  - Remember, these are tools not the entire process. Don't become a dashboard junky addicted to the data, while forgetting the point of sales.

4. Motivational Incentives and Rewards

- **Purpose**: Motivate the sales team by aligning personal rewards and incentives with performance achievements. If you're not familiar with it, read up on Maslow's Hierarchy of Needs. It will give you a deeper understanding of what motivates people.

- **Action Steps**:

  - Design incentive programs that reward not only the top performers but also those who show significant improvement.

  - Offer a mix of financial incentives, recognition awards, and career development opportunities to cater to different motivational needs.

5. Encouraging Team Collaboration and Communication

- **Purpose**: Foster a collaborative environment where sales team members feel comfortable sharing insights, challenges, and successes. Most companies say they do this, but they don't. Don't BS yourself. Commit to this.

- **Action Steps**:
  - Implement team-building activities that enhance trust and communication.
  - Use collaborative tools and platforms that encourage sharing of strategies and client feedback within the team.
  - Encourage mentorship by pairing less experienced salespeople with veterans.

6. Leadership Development and Empowerment

- **Purpose**: Develop leadership skills within the team to foster a sense of ownership and responsibility and prepare team members for future leadership roles.

- **Action Steps**:
  - Identify potential leaders and provide them with leadership training and responsibilities.
  - Encourage initiative and allow team members to lead projects or mentor others.
  - Create a leadership track for high performers, offering them opportunities to engage in decision-making processes.

7. Adapting to Market Changes and Innovations

■ **Purpose**: Keep the sales team agile and responsive to market conditions and technological advancements. You should never be surprised or caught off guard by anything that happens in your ecosystem.

■ **Action Steps**:

- Stay informed about industry trends and emerging technologies that could impact your sales strategies.

- Regularly update the team on these trends and integrate new tools and approaches into the sales process.

- Encourage a culture of innovation where team members can suggest and trial new strategies.

8. Strengthening Emotional Resilience

- **Purpose**: Equip the team to manage the pressures and challenges of sales roles effectively, enhancing overall team stamina and morale. Sales is a tough business and it's not getting easier.

- **Action Steps**:

- Provide training and resources on stress management and resilience building.

- Encourage a healthy work-life balance and support initiatives that reduce burnout.

- Create a supportive work environment where team members feel valued and supported. Make sure they have each other's back. And of course, make sure (with actions) that your team KNOWS that you have their backs.

By implementing these strategies, you can create an environment that not only drives high performance but also nurtures the professional growth and well-being of each team member. Sales is hard in a good economy, but when the economy is bad, it can be downright soul crushing.

CHAPTER 9

Effective Sales Planning and Execution

"Begin with the end in mind."

—Stephen Covey

"Let your plans be dark and impenetrable as night, and when you move, fall like a thunderbolt."

—Sun Tzu, The Art of War

"If you know the enemy and know yourself, you need not fear the result of a hundred battles."

—Sun Tzu, The Art of War

Sales planning and execution are the bridges that connect your strategic goals with the tangible outcomes you're striving for. A well-crafted sales plan ensures that resources are allocated effectively, goals are set, and strategies are executed efficiently to achieve desired results.

We will begin by exploring the importance of aligning sales plans with the strategic vision and objectives of the organization. By understanding the larger context and strategic direction, sales leaders can develop plans that are focused, purposeful, and synchronized with broader business goals.

You'll notice that this chapter is very regimented and detailed. There's a reason for that. Strategic execution is where most organizations fall apart. We've already discussed the failure rate. It's embarrassingly bad. The steps we're going to go over below are detailed because competent execution needs to be structured. If it's not structured, things won't be done the way they need to be done, or in the time frame they need to be done. Try to stay as close to what I've outlined below as possible.

Execution is where strategy meets action, and effective execution is key to turning plans into tangible outcomes. We will delve into the process of implementing sales processes, systems, and workflows that enable efficient and streamlined execution later. From territory management to pipeline management, we will also explore best practices and tools that help sales leaders, and their teams execute their plans effectively.

We will also discuss the role of sales leadership in providing guidance, support, and motivation to the sales team during the execution phase. As we discussed earlier, change is hard, even when you want to make the change, and even when the chance will be good for you. It's still hard. We will explore strategies for effective communication, delegation, and accountability that ensure the team is aligned, empowered, and equipped to deliver exceptional results. It's simple, but it's not easy.

By the end of this chapter, you will have a comprehensive understanding of effective sales planning and execution. Armed with this knowledge, you will be equipped to develop realistic sales plans, set clear goals, implement efficient processes, and lead your sales team to execute with precision.

Sales planning and execution is the lifeblood of any organization aiming to be profitable. It is a strategic approach that allows sales teams to focus their efforts and resources effectively to maximize sales. Effective sales planning and execution requires understanding your target market, setting clear objectives, creating a detailed sales plan, and following through with meticulous execution.[101] Let's distill some of the concepts we've already discussed and break them down into actionable steps.

A. Understand Business Priorities

Business Vision and Mission: Start by aligning your sales objectives with the overall vision and mission of your company. This ensures that your sales goals contribute to broader business ambitions. Too many sales leaders think they can create a strategy that is at odds with their organization's strategy. The more aligned they are, the easier it will be to get the buy-in from other department leaders. If they're not perfectly aligned, start your efforts where they are and achieve some early successes. Doing so will give you the political capital you'll need to get the buy-in from other departments later in the process.

Strategic Business Objectives: Identify key business objectives for the period. These could range from market expansion, client acquisition, increasing market share, improving

---

101   Robert S. Kaplan and David P. Norton, *The Execution Premium: Linking Strategy to Operations for Competitive Advantage* (Boston: Harvard Business Press, 2008)

client satisfaction, or launching new products and/or services. As famed business strategist Michael Porter once said, "Strategy is choice. Strategy means saying no to certain kinds of things." Pick one main thing to focus on. Do not dilute your efforts.

B. Set SMART Goals

Specific: Goals should be clear and specific enough to focus your efforts and feel real and attainable. For example, instead of setting a goal to "increase sales," specify "increase sales of Product X by 15% in the next quarter."

Measurable: Establish concrete criteria for measuring progress toward the attainment of each goal. Measurable goals help keep the team on track and motivated.

Achievable: Goals should be realistic and attainable to be successful. This means setting goals that are challenging yet possible with the resources and time available. It's okay to make your team stretch, but make sure the goal is within the realm of reality.

Relevant: Ensure that each goal matters to the business and contributes to its overall objectives. Each goal should align with other relevant goals and fit within the immediate and long-term plans. Think of it as Legos. Make sure that each piece snaps tightly into other pieces of whatever you're building.

Time-bound: Every goal needs a deadline, so you have a clear endpoint to focus on. This helps to prevent everyday tasks from taking priority over your longer-term goals. A goal without a definitive timeline is merely a dream.

C. Break Down Goals into Actionable Steps

Action Plans: Once you've set your SMART goals, break them down into smaller, manageable tasks or steps. This could involve identifying key activities, assigning responsibilities, and setting shorter timelines.

Resource Allocation: Determine what resources (budget, personnel, technology) are necessary to achieve these goals and plan how to allocate them effectively. Chances are, you won't get all the resources you need, so be prudent on how you place and use whatever you have at your disposal. Remember, you fight with the army you have, not the army you want. Do the best you can, with what you have right now.

D. Ensure Alignment Across the Organization

Cross-Functional Collaboration: Engage with other departments (marketing, product development, customer service) to ensure that sales goals are aligned with their plans and objectives. This fosters a unified approach towards achieving common business goals. Appeal to the self-interest of the leadership in each department. Also know who in those departments makes things happen. Knowing the official org chart is one thing, but knowing how the organization works is often radically different. Appeal to the self-interest of the organization's true shot callers.

Communication: Clearly communicate these goals and their importance to the sales team and the wider organization. Everyone should understand how their work contributes to the achievement of these goals. This step is often ignored, and too many people aren't clear on how they fit into the big picture.

E. Establish Feedback Loops

Regular Check-ins: Set up regular review sessions to assess progress towards goals, identify any roadblocks, and adjust plans as necessary. Course correction is a normal part of the process, however if you're not regularly stopping to check, you're heading into a world of problems. As Winston Churchill eloquently said, "However beautiful the strategy, you should occasionally look at the results."

Adaptability: Be prepared to revise goals as market conditions, competitive landscapes, and internal capabilities evolve. Covid-19 should be a good reminder of how fast our current situation can be flipped on its head.

F. Celebrate Achievements

Recognition: Acknowledge and celebrate when goals are met. This boosts morale and motivates the team for future challenges. Though it's a cynical statement, Napoleon Bonaparte had a point when he quipped, "A soldier will fight long and hard for a bit of colored ribbon."

Learn from the Process: Analyze completed goals to understand what worked, what didn't, and how processes can be improved for future goal-setting exercises. As futurist Alvin Toffler once wrote, "The illiterate of the 21st century will not be those who cannot read and write, but those who cannot learn, unlearn, and relearn."

By leading the charge on defining clear and well-structured objectives and goals, you can create a focused, motivated, and aligned team that is equipped to drive towards achieving business success. This step not only sets the direction but also energizes and guides your entire sales force towards common achievements. As you move forward, ensure you keep your finger on the pulse of your organization's politics.

Now let's unpack things more and get granular.

Aligning Sales plans with the Strategic Vision and Objectives of the Organization

Let's dig deeper into a point we just discussed above. As sales leaders, we all get our marching orders from either upper management, the board of directors, venture capitalists or the private equity firm that acquired your company. Therefore, our sales strategy must be coordinated with their overarching vision and objectives. While you may not get the orders you want, or necessarily agree with, it is your responsibility to figure out how to succeed. Period.

You may be tasked with a new product launch, expanding into a new geographic territory, taking market share from a competitor or simply growing revenue by 20 percent or more. Once you've been told what your organization's strategic vision and key objectives are, you can get to work and create a strategic framework followed by a tactical plan. Don't jump the gun and create your strategy and tactical plan of execution before you get your orders. It would be a waste of your time and energy to do so and then must scrap the plan and begin all over again.

Be patient. What if your leadership takes too long to get you the orders you can execute? Then and only then you can create a skeleton of your strategy. Take note of your resources. How many people do you have on your outside sales team? How many are on your inside sales team? What kind of pre and post sales technical resources do you have available? Which trade shows (if any) do you want to make sure are budgeted? Most often, trade show budgets come from the marketing department not sales, so you may need to discuss your ideas and needs with whomever leads your marketing and trade show efforts.

Also take this time to determine what kind of training your team is going to require. Do they need more sales training? Every sales professional needs ongoing sales training. Do they need extra technical training? Get that lined up.

Even if your leadership team is slow to get you the information you need, you can still put in place a few key pieces of your strategy and tactical plan.

Setting Clear Goals and Targets

Once you've been given your orders of what you and our sales team are expected to accomplish, you can flesh out your plan.

Determine Your Goals

If everything is a priority, then nothing is. Prioritizing your sales team's activities so they manage their selling time wisely is a foundational aspect to a good strategy. Make sure that the goals you set for your team members are achievable. Nothing is more demoralizing to a sales pro than a quota or goal they know they have next to zero probability of achieving. We want to challenge our sales team, not crush them under the weight of a goal or quota so large that they'd rather quit and start over again somewhere else. I've seen this happen many times.

Chances are, you will get little to no voice in helping set your team's overall quota. That doesn't mean you should just roll over and accept whatever is given. If you disagree with the team goal/quota, make yourself heard. Explain with data and as many facts as you have why this quota isn't realistic. If you don't voice your opposition as soon as you hear The Number, your silence will be seen as tacit approval. Tacit approval means that you're in agreement and feel that the quota is indeed achievable. Remember, it's your job on the line, and if you and your team miss the quota, the leadership will be coming after you. The larger the amount you miss the quota, the greater the chance you will be fired.

Once you've shared your concerns and the data behind your concerns, your leadership should back off the number a bit. If they don't, at least you're on record for having pushed back. One of two things will happen:

1. You will hit your quota and now you are seen as a sales leadership superstar!

2. You miss your quota and now you can tell your leadership team, "I tried to warn you, but you wouldn't listen."

Either way you've created a narrative that will benefit you. There's a reason that the average tenure for a VP of Sales is down to 19 months.

If, however, the goal/quota you're given makes sense and is achievable, then you're ready for the next step.

Determine Your Key Results

As the saying goes, "Not everything that counts can be counted, and not everything that can be counted counts." We are awash in a relentless flood of data. While having good data at your fingertips can be of great benefit, having too much, or the wrong data can and is detrimental to your efforts.

Monitoring performance and iterating on strategies are essential components of a successful sales framework. This process involves continuously assessing sales activities against set objectives and using insights gained to refine and improve strategies. Integrating sales best practices with psychological insights can enhance the effectiveness of this iterative process.[102]

Here's a detailed approach:

Key Performance Indicators (KPIs): Establish clear, measurable KPIs that align with your sales objectives. These should cover a range of areas including sales volume, revenue, client acquisition and retention rates, lead conversion rates, and sales cycle length. It's critical that the KPIs that you pick are the ones that truly do impact and matter to your sales efforts. Many organizations use KPIs that are disconnected from the reality of what profoundly affects their sales.

Regular Reporting and Analysis: Implement a system for regular reporting and analysis of sales data. This should involve both quantitative metrics and qualitative insights, enabling a comprehensive view of performance. It should be often enough that you get a clear picture of trend lines but not so often that

---

102   Jason Jordan and Michelle Vazzana, *Cracking the Sales Management Code: The Secrets to Measuring and Managing Sales Performance* (New York: McGraw-Hill, 2011)

you're buried in data that doesn't change much.

Sales Technology Utilization: Leverage advanced sales technologies, such as CRM and analytics platforms, to gather and analyze sales data in real-time. These tools can provide valuable insights into client behaviors, sales trends, and team performance. There are now some phenomenal SaaS products created just for sales leaders that are game changers.

Continuous Improvement Process: Adopt a continuous improvement mindset, using the Plan-Do-Check-Act (PDCA) cycle or similar methodologies to systematically review and refine sales processes and strategies based on performance data.

While you've probably heard of KPI's (and are tired of hearing about them), the PDCA cycle may be new to you. I have found it a great tool to get more value from using KPIs.

The Plan-Do-Check-Act (PDCA) cycle, also known as the Deming Wheel, was created by W. Edwards Deming. He was an American engineer, statistician, professor, author, lecturer, and management consultant known for his work in the field of quality management and for his significant contribution to Japan's remarkable post-World War II industrial recovery.

The PDCA cycle is a continuous loop of planning, doing, checking (or studying), and acting. It's a method used to achieve continuous improvement in processes and products. The PDCA cycle is widely applied in various industries and functions, including sales, manufacturing, and service delivery, to enhance efficiency, effectiveness, and adaptability. Here's a brief overview of each phase:

Plan

Identify the Problem or Opportunity: Begin by clearly defining the problem you're trying to solve or the opportunity you want to capitalize on. This involves gathering relevant data and insights to understand the current state and identifying the gap between the current and desired state.

Analyze the Situation: Use tools like SWOT analysis (Strengths, Weaknesses, Opportunities, Threats), root cause analysis, or the 5 Whys technique to deeply understand the problem or opportunity.[103] This phase should involve stakeholders to get a comprehensive view.

Set Objectives: Define clear, measurable objectives that you aim to achieve through your improvement efforts. These objectives should be SMART (Specific, Measurable, Achievable, Relevant, Time-bound).

Develop Hypotheses: Based on your analysis, develop hypotheses about what changes could lead to improvement. These are educated guesses that you will assess during the Do phase.

Plan Actions: Design and plan the actions needed to evaluate your hypotheses. This includes detailing the steps, assigning responsibilities, setting timelines, and determining the resources required.

---

103   Eric Ries, The Lean Startup: How Today's Entrepreneurs Use Continuous Innovation to Create Radically Successful Businesses (New York: Crown Business, 2011)

Do

Implement the Plan: Execute the planned actions on a small scale, if possible, to minimize risk (I'm looking at you unnamed cybersecurity company that caused a global IT meltdown). This phase is about testing the change and collecting data on the outcome. It's crucial to document the process and any deviations from the plan.

Monitor and Document: Carefully monitor the implementation process and document everything. This data will be crucial for the Check phase to evaluate whether the changes are moving you towards your objectives.

Check (Study)

Analyze the Results: With the data collected during the Do phase, analyze the outcomes of your test. Compare the results against your objectives to see if the changes led to improvement.

Learn from the Data: This step involves learning from the results. Did you achieve the desired outcomes? What worked well, and what didn't? This phase may involve revisiting your initial analysis and understanding if any new insights have emerged.

Decide on Next Steps: Based on your analysis, decide whether the changes should be adopted, adapted, or abandoned. If the results were positive, you might move to the Act phase to implement the changes on a larger scale. If not, you might need to go through another Plan-Do-Check cycle with different hypotheses.

Act

Standardize the Improvement: If the changes have proven successful, standardize these improvements. This involves updating procedures, training materials, and processes to incorporate the new method.

Implement on a Larger Scale: Roll out the successful changes across the relevant parts of the organization. Ensure that all stakeholders are informed and trained, as necessary.

Plan for Continuous Improvement: The Act phase also involves planning for continuous improvement. Even after implementing changes, the PDCA cycle encourages you to start again, looking for further improvements. This might involve setting new objectives or tackling other areas of opportunity.

Continuous Improvement

The PDCA cycle is iterative, with the conclusion of one cycle leading into the beginning of another. This continuous loop ensures that organizations can adapt to changes, respond to new challenges, and constantly enhance their processes and products. The key to successfully implementing the PDCA cycle is a commitment to ongoing learning and adaptation, supported by a culture that encourages experimentation, recognizes the value of failure as a learning opportunity, and strives for excellence. For us in sales, it allows us to test out new ideas without having to do a forklift upgrade of our sales team and all of the current sales processes.

Let's tie the PDCA cycle to KPI's.

The Plan-Do-Check-Act (PDCA) cycle, combined with

Key Performance Indicators (KPIs), will provide you with a framework for continuous improvement in your sales team's performance. By integrating these two approaches, sales teams can systematically identify areas for enhancement, implement changes, measure outcomes, and make informed adjustments to their sales strategies. Here's how these concepts can be tied together effectively:

Plan

Identify Objectives: Start by defining clear sales objectives that align with broader business goals. These might include increasing revenue, improving client retention rates, or expanding into new markets.

Select Relevant KPIs: Choose KPIs that will effectively measure progress towards these objectives. For your sales team, relevant KPIs might include sales growth, conversion rate, average deal size, customer lifetime value (CLV), and customer acquisition cost (CAC).

Set Targets: For each KPI, set specific, measurable targets based on historical data, industry benchmarks, or strategic goals. These targets will guide the sales team's efforts and provide a clear measure of success.

Do

Implement Strategies: Execute the sales strategies designed to achieve the set targets. This might involve training sessions to improve sales skills, new marketing campaigns to generate leads, or the introduction of sales enablement tools.

Monitor Progress: Keep track of KPIs in real-time using CRM tools and dashboards. This ongoing monitoring allows the sales team to stay aligned with their targets and make immediate adjustments as needed.

Check

Review KPIs: At the end of the cycle, review the outcomes by comparing the actual performance against the set targets for each KPI. Analyze both successes and areas where performance did not meet expectations.

Identify Insights: Look for trends, patterns, and insights that explain the results. Understand why certain strategies worked well and why others did not. This step is crucial for learning from experience and making data-driven decisions.

Act

Implement Improvements: Based on the review, decide on actions to improve sales performance. This might involve refining sales processes, offering additional training, or revising sales strategies.

Adjust Targets and Strategies: If necessary, adjust your KPI targets to more realistic levels based on the insights gained. Similarly, update your sales strategies to incorporate the lessons learned during the cycle.

Prepare for the Next Cycle: With improvements in place, the sales team is ready to begin a new PDCA cycle. This iterative process ensures continuous refinement and optimization of sales strategies.

Continuous Improvement through PDCA and KPIs

By using the PDCA cycle in conjunction with KPIs, your sales team can create a dynamic environment of continuous improvement. This approach allows for:

- **Strategic Alignment:** Ensuring sales efforts are consistently aligned with broader business goals.

- **Data-Driven Decision Making:** Making informed decisions based on actual performance data, leading to more effective sales strategies.

- **Agility**: Quickly responding to changes in the market or within the organization, allowing the sales team to stay competitive and meet evolving client needs.

In practice, this might look like you noticing that your sales team's client acquisition cost (CAC) is higher than the industry average. You could plan to implement new lead generation tactics, do so while monitoring lead quality and cost, check the impact of these tactics on CAC, and then act by standardizing the most effective tactics across the team. By continually cycling through PDCA, you not only aim to reduce CAC but also enhance overall sales efficiency and effectiveness.

The Midway Method: Strategic Sales Execution Wins Through Precision and Insight

The Battle of Midway in June 1942 stands as a historical landmark of strategic brilliance, much like a landmark success in the high-pressure world of sales.[104] This battle not only changed the course of the Pacific Theater in World War II but also shows us how in-depth planning and precise execution can lead to monumental achievements against formidable odds.

Initial Assessment: Leveraging Intelligence

Admiral Chester W. Nimitz, much like a visionary sales leader, recognized the importance of actionable intelligence. In the months leading up to the battle, American cryptographers made a breakthrough in decoding Japanese naval communications. This intelligence coup provided insights comparable to a sales team gaining access to crucial data about a competitor's next big move or a potential client's buying intentions.

With this information, Nimitz, akin to a strategic sales leader, meticulously prepared to counter the Japanese plan, which aimed to lure American forces into a trap at Midway Atoll. This scenario mirrors a high-stakes market where competitors are aggressively vying for dominance, and the right intelligence can shape the battlefield.

Strategic Planning: Coordinating Resources

Nimitz's approach was defined by the strategic allocation and coordination of available resources. He positioned his limited carriers and support vessels in a location that maximized their strategic impact, much like allocating sales resources to

---

104   Trent Hone, Mastering the Art of Command: Admiral Chester W. Nimitz and Victory in the Pacific (Annapolis, MD: Naval Institute Press, 2022)

capitalize on a critical market opportunity. This resource allocation ensured that when the battle commenced, his forces could strike with the element of surprise, leveraging their position to maximum effect.

This level of coordination is symbolic of a well-oiled sales operation where timing, positioning, and resource deployment are synchronized to capture a key account or dominate a market segment.

Execution: The Decisive Strike

The execution of Nimitz's plan at Midway was akin to the flawless rollout of a major sales campaign. On June 4, 1942, as the Japanese fleet advanced, believing they had the upper hand, American forces launched a series of attacks. The initial waves were risky and costly, similar to the early phases of a market penetration strategy that might involve significant investment without immediate returns.

However, these efforts set the stage for a decisive strike, much like a sales team positioning itself through preliminary engagements and then capitalizing on a sudden opportunity to close a major deal. The American dive bombers' timely arrival on the scene, finding the Japanese carriers at their most vulnerable, turned the tide—akin to a sales team exploiting a competitor's momentary weakness at a critical juncture.

Aftermath and Reflection: Lessons for Sales Leaders

The victory at Midway is credited with significantly altering the balance of power in the Pacific, demonstrating how well-executed plans based on solid intelligence and resource coordination can yield spectacular results. For sales leaders, Midway underscores the value of:

1. **Insight-Driven Strategy:** Understanding the competitive landscape through rigorous intelligence gathering.

2. **Resource Alignment:** Efficiently deploying resources where they can make the most significant impact.

3. **Execution Excellence:** Executing plans with precision, ensuring that every team member understands their role and the timing of their actions.

The Battle of Midway teaches that even under extreme pressure and against formidable odds, a well-planned and expertly executed strategy can lead to overwhelming success. For those in sales, it's a compelling reminder that the right mix of insight, planning, and execution can turn potential defeat into historic victory.

ServiceNow's Execution Excellence

If you're in enterprise IT, you've probably encountered ServiceNow. If you're not familiar with them, ServiceNow is a global leader in IT service management (ITSM) and workflow automation, renowned not only for its innovative products but also for its execution excellence. The company's remarkable growth trajectory and sustained market leadership offers valuable insights into how strategic planning and flawless execution can drive business success. Let's look at the key factors behind ServiceNow's execution excellence and the lessons that can be applied by sales leaders in any industry.

Background

Founded in 2004 by Fred Luddy, ServiceNow revolutionized the IT industry by introducing a cloud-based platform that enables organizations to manage digital workflows.[105] Luddy founded ServiceNow in 2004, just two weeks before his 50th birthday. This came after he lost his $35 million fortune overnight due to accounting fraud at his previous company, Peregrine Systems, where he was the CTO. Most people would resign themselves to defeat, not Luddy.[106]

Over the years, ServiceNow has grown from a niche ITSM provider to a Fortune 500 company, with a market capitalization exceeding $169 billion at this writing. The company's success is attributed not only to its innovative products but also to its rigorous execution strategy.

Strategic Planning and Vision Alignment

ServiceNow's execution excellence begins with its disciplined strategic planning and alignment with a clear vision. Fred Luddy envisioned a platform that could streamline and automate the myriad processes that run businesses, thereby improving efficiency and productivity. This vision was meticulously translated into actionable strategies that guided the company's exponential growth.

Insight: ServiceNow's strategic planning involves setting clear,

105   Horatio Alger Association. (2023). Frederic B. Luddy: Horatio Alger Award Recipient, Class of 2023. Retrieved from https://horatioalger.org/members/detail/frederic-b-luddy/

106   Gordon, J. (2024, March 3). Fred Luddy's Remarkable Comeback. Just Go Grind. https://www.justgogrind.com/p/fred-luddy

ambitious, yet achievable goals. The company ensures that every department and team understand how their efforts contribute to the overall vision.[107] This alignment fosters a unified approach toward common objectives, enhancing execution effectiveness.

Customer-Centric Approach

A cornerstone of ServiceNow's success is its unwavering focus on customer success, which drives its execution strategies.

Execution Excellence: ServiceNow has established an effective Customer Success Management (CSM) program, where dedicated teams work closely with clients to ensure they derive maximum value from the platform. This proactive approach not only enhances customer satisfaction but also drives customer loyalty and retention.

Insight: By investing in customer success, ServiceNow ensures that its customers are not only satisfied but also advocates for the brand. This focus on customer outcomes fosters long-term relationships and repeat business, transforming relationships from transactional to transformational.

Innovative Use of Technology

ServiceNow leverages innovative technology to streamline its execution processes. The company's platform integrates advanced analytics, artificial intelligence (AI), and automation to enhance efficiency and decision-making.[108]

---

107   GuideVision. (n.d.). What is ServiceNow's strategy for 2021? Retrieved from https://www. guidevision.eu/insights/what-is-servicenow%27s-strategy-for-2021

108   Willem. (2023, December 29). ServiceNow Gen AI: An Introduction. ServiceNow. https://www.servicenow.com/community/intelligence-ml-articles/ servicenow-gen-ai-an-introduction/ta-p/2776240

Execution Excellence: ServiceNow's AI-driven solutions, such as predictive analytics and automated workflows, empower organizations to operate more efficiently. These technologies enable ServiceNow to execute its sales strategies with precision and speed, providing customers with tools that drive their digital transformation efforts.

Insight: Embracing technology to automate routine tasks and provide data-driven insights can significantly enhance execution efficiency. As sales leaders, investing in tools that enable teams to focus on high-value activities while leveraging AI for smarter decision-making is essential.

Agile and Iterative Approach

ServiceNow adopts an agile and iterative approach to its execution strategies.[109] This flexibility allows the company to quickly adapt to changing market conditions and customer needs.

Execution Excellence: ServiceNow regularly reviews and refines its strategies through iterative processes. The company conducts quarterly business reviews (QBRs), where teams assess performance, identify challenges, and adjust tactics accordingly.

Insight: An agile approach to execution enables organizations to remain responsive and adaptive. Regular reviews and iterative adjustments ensure that strategies remain relevant and effective in dynamic environments.

---

109   Fugere, T. (2023, November 13). Navigating the Path to ServiceNow Excellence in 2024. Thirdera. https://www.thirdera.com/insights/navigating-the-path-to-servicenow-excellence-in-2024

Strong Organizational Culture

ServiceNow's organizational culture plays a pivotal role in its execution excellence.[110] The company fosters a culture of innovation, collaboration, and customer-centricity.

Execution Excellence: ServiceNow's culture emphasizes customer focus, innovation, and employee empowerment.[111] This culture promotes open communication, cross-functional collaboration, and a shared commitment to the company's goals.

Insight: Cultivating a strong organizational culture that aligns with strategic objectives can enhance execution by fostering teamwork, employee engagement, and a shared sense of purpose.

Performance Metrics and Accountability

ServiceNow employs meaningful performance metrics to track progress and ensure accountability. Key performance indicators (KPIs) are used to measure success and guide decision-making.[112]

Execution Excellence: ServiceNow's performance metrics encompass various aspects, including sales performance, customer satisfaction, and platform adoption rates. Regular

---

110   Thomas, S. (2023, April 6). Inside ServiceNow's Award Winning Employee Culture. ERP Today. https://erp.today/inside-servicenows-award-winning-employee-culture/

111   Barker, L. (2020, August 17). Driving culture and motivating our people in challenging times. ServiceNow. https://www.servicenow.com/blogs/2020/corporate-culture

112   ServiceNow. (n.d.). Baseline and track performance, usage KPIs, and metrics. Retrieved from https://www.servicenow.com/content/dam/servicenow-assets/public/en-us/doc-type/success/playbook/performance-kpi-metrics-guide.pdf

performance reviews and transparent reporting mechanisms ensure that teams remain accountable for their results.

Insight: Establishing clear KPIs and maintaining account-ability through regular performance reviews can drive consistent execution and continuous improvement.

Final Thoughts on ServiceNow

ServiceNow's execution excellence is a testament to the power of strategic planning, customer-centricity, technological inno-vation, agility, strong culture, and accountability. As sales leaders, we can all learn much by applying what they've done to our own organizations. By integrating these elements into your execution strategies, you can enhance your team's effective-ness and drive sustained success. ServiceNow's journey from a disruptive startup to a global market leader provides valuable lessons for your organization's efforts to excel in execution and achieve your strategic goals. It's simple, but it's not easy.

CHAPTER 10

The Tech Savvy Buyer and Leveraging Technology for Enhanced Sales Performance

"The only constant in the technology industry is change."

—Marc Benioff

"There is no better experience than giving someone a piece of technology that lets them do
something they never thought they could do."

—Fred Luddy

"The fast learn and adapt, the slow seek blame and comfort."

—Reid Hoffman

Before we dive into how you and your sales team can best take advantage of the explosive growth of technology tools, we need to take a brief look at how the buying process has changed for the buyer. Twenty plus years ago, salespeople held the power. What does that mean? It means that back in the "good old days," if a buyer wanted to get information on a new product, they would have to get the information from a salesperson. The balance of power leaned towards the sales organization. But then the Internet happened, YouTube happened, and then social media happened and suddenly, buyers could learn about many possible options to the business problem they had without meeting with a salesperson. The balance of power has now flipped in favor of the buyer.

What does that mean in practical terms?

Let's look at the key ways the process has transformed:

Increased Buyer Independence

Buyers are now far more informed and self-sufficient in their purchasing journey:

> They conduct extensive online research before engaging with salespeople, relying on company websites, third-party reviews, and industry publications.[113] [114]

> Buyers spend only about 13 percent of their time talking to sellers, often split among multiple vendors.

> More than 80 percent of B2B customers have a short-list of vendors in mind before they start researching solutions.

---

113   Petrone, P. (2023, May 2). How B2B Sales Has Changed Over the Last 20 Years – And How to Best Respond. LinkedIn. https://www.linkedin.com/business/sales/blog/strategy/how-b2b-sales-has-changed-in-the-past-20-years

114   The Dock Team. (2023, August 29). The B2B buyer journey has changed. Have you? Updated June 26, 2024. Dock. https://www.dock.us/library/b2b-buyer-journey

Digitalization of the Buying Journey

The buying process has become predominantly digital:

58 percent of buyers start their research by reviewing company websites.

Product demos and trials have become crucial, with nearly 75 percent of buyers basing their final decision on a demo.

E-commerce and digital marketing have replaced traditional methods like trade catalogs and manual sales materials.[115]

Larger, More Complex Buying Committees

Decision-making has become more collaborative and complex:

The average B2B buying journey now involves between 11 to 20 stakeholders, up from just 5 a decade ago.

Buying committees typically consist of three tiers: ultimate approvers, core committee members, and internal influencers.

Changing Buyer Expectations

Modern B2B buyers, often millennials and Gen Z, have new preferences:

---

115   Contentserv. (n.d.). How B2B commerce has changed in the last 20 years. Retrieved from https://www.contentserv.com/infographics/infographic-how-b2b-commerce-has-changed-in-the-last-20-years

They expect personalized experiences and smooth, error-free, and accessible buying processes.

Buyers want sellers to be engaged, personal, and available throughout the journey.

There's an increased focus on values, with sustainability and ESG factors becoming more important than traditional criteria like price or product innovation.[116]

Professionalization of the Purchasing Process

Organizations have formalized their approach to B2B purchases:

Eighty-six percent of companies are "professionalizing" their purchasing process by scrutinizing vendors more thoroughly.

Seventy-seven percent of businesses start the process of re-bidding for an existing contract of major enterprise deals at least every two years, with 44 percent doing so annually.

Emphasis on Thought Leadership

Demonstrating expertise has become crucial in the initial stages of the buying process:

Buyers use thought leadership content to assess a company's innovative thinking, vision for the future, and talent quality.

---

116   Lofthouse, G. (n.d.). The customer journey: How has B2B buying changed? Financial Times. Retrieved from https://longitude.ft.com/the-customer-journey-how-has-b2b-buying-changed-gareth-lofthouse/

Providing valuable insights and ideas has become essential for competing and winning business.

Shift to Virtual Sales

The COVID-19 pandemic accelerated the move towards virtual sales processes:

Buyers now expect virtual options for nearly all purchases, similar to B2C experiences.[117]

Face-to-face meetings have largely been replaced by video calls and digital interactions.

The B2B buying process has evolved from a straightforward, sales-driven model to a complex, buyer-led journey that is heavily influenced by digital resources, involves more stakeholders, and requires vendors to demonstrate expertise and value long before any formal sales interactions occur. It's enough to give sales leaders a case of bad heartburn.

Now let's take a look at how all this has impacted on our ability to sell to this very tech savvy consumer. Leveraging technology for enhanced sales performance is no longer a luxury but a necessity for organizations aiming to stay competitive and achieve sustainable growth.

The Technological Evolution in Sales

Over the past decade, the sales function has undergone a

117   Davidson, M. (2023, July 10). 3 Ways B2B Buying Behavior Has Changed—Forever. Allego. https://www.allego.com/blog/how-b2b-buying-behavior-has-changed-forever/

profound transformation driven by technological advancements. From customer relationship management (CRM) systems to artificial intelligence (AI) and predictive analytics, the sales technology ecosystem has expanded, offering a flood of tools designed to optimize every aspect of the sales cycle. If you and your sales team feel overwhelmed, you're not alone.[118]

Here are some key points that support this:

1. Sales teams are using an average of ten tools to close deals, but 94 percent of sales organizations plan to consolidate their tech stacks in the coming year to boost productivity. This suggests there is a sense of tool overload.[119]

2. Research shows that salespeople who feel overwhelmed by technology are 43 percent less likely to meet quota. This indicates that too much technology can hinder performance.

3. With over 8,000 sales tools available on the market today, it's easy for sales teams to get overwhelmed when trying to choose the right tools.[120]

4. Sales reps are spending only 28 percent of their week selling, with the majority of their time consumed by other tasks like deal management and data entry. This implies

118   Tobias, G., Riley, C., Giblin, C., & Gregory-Hosler, B. (2023, August 22). *Sellers Are Overwhelmed by New Technology.* Harvard Business Review. https://hbr.org/2023/08/new-technology-is-overwhelming-sales-teams

119   Connaughton, B. (2023, October 15). 12 Best Sales Productivity Tools to Empower Your Sales Team. Qwilr. https://qwilr.com/blog/sales-productivity-tools/

120   UserGems. (n.d.). 13 of the best sales tools we recommend for sales reps in 2022. Retrieved from https://www.usergems.com/blog/sales-tools

that the multitude of tools may be adding administrative burden rather than enhancing productivity.

5. Sales leaders have been pursuing a "just one more" strategy - asking sellers to learn one more skill, master one more technology, or adopt one more tool in hopes of closing more deals. However, this has made the salesperson's job more unmanageable.

6. There's a growing trend towards consolidating and streamlining sales tech stacks. Companies are looking to choose tools that integrate well with existing systems and avoid overwhelming reps with multiple tools that do the same thing.

While sales technology tools can boost your sales team's productivity, the sheer number and complexity of available options are simply overwhelming most sales teams. The focus is shifting towards finding the right balance of tools that truly enhance your team's productivity without overwhelming your sales reps. We'll get into some best practices later in this chapter. For now, let's look at some of the technologies that you can use. This evolution has enabled sales teams to move from traditional, intuition-based approaches to data-driven, strategic methodologies that enhance decision-making and performance. And make no mistake, the sales teams who figure out the smartest way to take advantage of the most relevant tools at their disposal will dramatically outperform those who don't.

The Evolution of Technology and Selling

In the ever-evolving landscape of B2B sales, a quiet revolution has been taking place, one that might not seem as dramatic as the dot-com bubble or as publicized as the rise of Silicon Valley, yet its impact is profound. Over the last quarter-century, the domain of B2B sales has undergone a transformation not through one singular invention, but through a convergence of technological advancements that have rewritten the rules of engagement between businesses.

Consider the advent of Customer Relationship Management (CRM) systems. Not long ago, sales data was a cumbersome trove of paper files; today, platforms like Salesforce and HubSpot serve as the nervous systems of sales operations, offering not just storage, but insights and foresight. A salesperson equipped with a top-notch CRM system can predict client behaviors, personalize communications, and manage relationships with a precision that would have seemed like clairvoyance two decades ago.

Then there's the quiet power of data analytics and artificial intelligence. It's a development akin to the leap from telegraph to the telephone. Where once sales strategies were shaped by intuition and experience, now they are sculpted by algorithms capable of digesting enormous amounts of data to predict trends, optimize pricing, and personalize marketing efforts with an accuracy that is almost uncanny.

Social selling has transformed platforms like LinkedIn from mere networking sites into vital sales tools. Here, salespeople do not just connect; they build their personal brand, share insights, and subtly weave their sales narratives into the fabric of daily conversation. It's a new dance of engagement, where knowledge and reputation can be as compelling as the hard sell once was.

The mobility revolution—smartphones and tablets—has untethered the sales force from their desks, allowing them to engage with clients anytime, anywhere. This mobility has made sales a 24/7 endeavor, with the power of an entire office fitting snugly into the pocket of a salesperson's pants.

Automation tools, too, have redefined the notion of productivity. What used to be a grueling task of lead generation and client follow-ups is now streamlined by automated systems that can mimic, and often enhance, human interaction without ever needing to take a coffee break.

And consider the rise of video conferencing and virtual sales technologies. In the face of global disruptions like the COVID-19 pandemic, these tools have not just been convenient; they've been crucial, enabling sales teams to mimic the face-to-face experience with a fidelity that bridges continents.

Lastly, there's the quiet behemoth of e-commerce. Platforms like Alibaba and Amazon Business have not just opened new sales channels but have democratized access to B2B purchasing, allowing smaller businesses the kind of purchasing power and efficiency that was once the sole preserve of giant corporations.

Together, these technologies have not merely changed how businesses sell to each other. They have transformed the very essence of commercial engagement, turning every exchange into a data-driven dance, every interaction into an informed strategy, and every relationship into a well-nurtured journey.

This is the new era of B2B sales—a testament to the quiet power of technological evolution. The question is, are you prepared to take advantage of it?

The Strategic Importance of Technology in Sales

If you're one of those sales leaders who thinks, "Meh, we use CRM and a few other tools. We're all set." You may find yourself being repeatedly outmaneuvered and outsold. While too many tools can bury your team in an administrative hell, too few tools will doom your team to being left behind.

Your being committed to the strategic integration of technology into sales operations is crucial for several reasons:[121]

- **Efficiency and Productivity**: Technology streamlines routine tasks, allowing sales teams to focus on high-value activities such as building relationships and closing deals. The more time your team must focus on building relationships and closing deals, the more money everyone makes. Automation tools, for example, can manage data entry, follow-up emails, and scheduling, significantly reducing administrative burdens. Salespeople already spent too much time on administrative tasks. Anything you can do to help them spend more time selling and less time on administrative tasks helps to give them an edge.

121   Korn Ferry. (n.d.). How does sales technology improve sales productivity? Retrieved from https://www.kornferry.com/insights/featured-topics/sales-transformation/how-does-sales-technology-improve-sales-productivity

- **Data-Driven Decision Making**: Advanced analytics and AI provide insights into client behavior, market trends, and sales performance. These insights enable sales leaders to make informed decisions, predict future trends, and tailor strategies to meet specific objectives. Chances are, you're being reactive, not proactive. Data driven decision making will help guide you to making smarter proactive decisions.

- **Enhanced Customer Engagement**: Technology enables more personalized and timely interactions with clients. CRM systems, chatbots, and social media monitoring tools help sales teams understand and respond to client needs more effectively, fostering deeper engagement and loyalty.

- **Scalability and Flexibility**: Cloud-based solutions and mobile platforms provide sales teams with the flexibility to operate from anywhere, ensuring seamless collaboration and communication. These technologies also allow businesses to scale their operations efficiently as they grow.

Key Technologies That Will Transform Sales Performance

So, what technologies should you be taking advantage of (assuming that you aren't already)? There are several key technologies that are at the forefront of enhancing sales performance. Let's explore each in detail, highlighting their functionalities, benefits, and best practices for implementation.[122] [123]

---

122   Ross, K. (2024, August 24). The future of sales: How technology is revolutionizing sales performance management. AZ Big Media. https://azbigmedia.com/business/the-future-of-sales-how-technology-is-revolutionizing-sales-performance-management/

123   Impact. (2022, August 25). 5 Innovative Technologies That Can Actually Improve Sales Performance. https://www.impactmybiz.com/blog/how-to-improve-sales-performance-with-technology/

1. Customer Relationship Management (CRM) Systems:

- This one is a no brainer. CRMs serve as the backbone of your sales operations, centralizing customer data and interactions. They provide a holistic view of your customer's journey, enabling your sales team to manage relationships more effectively and personalize their approach.

2. Sales Automation Tools:

- Automation tools streamline repetitive tasks such as lead generation, follow-ups, and reporting. Repetitive tasks are mind numbingly boring yet a necessary part of your sales process. Being able to automate these tasks not only boosts your sales team's efficiency, it also ensures that no critical steps are overlooked, leading to more consistent and reliable sales processes.

3. Artificial Intelligence and Machine Learning:

- Every time you turn around, you're hearing AI, AI, AI. How can AI help your sales team crush their quota? AI and machine learning algorithms analyze vast amounts of data to provide predictive insights and recommendations. You may think you or the members of your sales team are up to the task of regularly diving headfirst into massive amounts of data and making informed conclusions, but no one has the mental capacity to do what they can do at the scale that they can. These technologies can identify potential leads, forecast sales trends, and suggest optimal strategies for engagement and conversion. Yes, there's a lot of hype behind all things AI at the moment, but there are tools that will transform the sales process for those agile enough to take advantage of it.

4. Predictive Analytics:

- Predictive analytics leverages historical data to forecast future sales outcomes. This helps you and your sales team allocate resources more effectively, identify high-potential opportunities, and mitigate risks. Think of the hours of your life you'll get back because you're not trying to make sense of all that data on your own. Not to mention, it will help prevent you from coming to the wrong conclusions.

5. Sales Enablement Platforms:

- Sales enablement tools provide your sales team with the resources, content, and training needed to engage buyers effectively. These platforms ensure that your sales reps have access to the latest product information, case studies, and competitive insights. The key word here is enablement. Anything you can do to help enable your team is a good thing.

6. Social Selling Tools:

- Social selling platforms allow sales teams to engage with prospects and clients on social media. These tools help in building relationships, understanding client sentiment, and identifying opportunities for engagement. If you've been in this business long enough to remember a time where there was no such thing as a "Social Media Manager," then you understand how important social selling has become.

7. Mobile Sales Applications:

- Mobile apps enable sales teams to access critical information, collaborate with colleagues, and manage client interactions on the go. This flexibility is crucial for maintaining productivity and responsiveness in a fast-paced sales environment. In sales, speed equals more closed deals.

Implementing Technology for Maximum Impact

While the potential benefits of leveraging technology are massive, successful implementation requires careful planning and execution.[124] Below is a step-by-step guide to integrating technology into sales operations, covering aspects such as selecting the right tools, training the sales team, and measuring the impact on performance.[125]

---

124   Swenson, D. (2024, January 25). Professor's research explores the impact of technology on sales team interactions with clients. Elon University News. https://www.elon.edu/u/news/2024/01/25/professors-research-explores-the-impact-of-technology-on-sales-team-interactions-with-clients/

125   Sasson, M. (2024, May 22). How to Build the Perfect Sales Tech Stack for 2024. Walnut. https://www.walnut.io/blog/sales-tips/sales-tech-stack/

The 8 Steps to Successful Sales Tool Technology Integrations

Step 1: Assessing Needs and Setting Objectives

- **Identify Pain Points**: Engage with your sales team to identify challenges in the current sales process that could be alleviated with technology. Encourage them to be brutally honest in their feedback. If you get this first step wrong, everything else that follows will also be wrong. You can't build a skyscraper on a bad foundation.

- **Define Objectives**: Clearly outline what you aim to achieve with the integration of new technology—be it increasing sales efficiency, reducing the sales cycle, enhancing client relationships, or improving data management. Try to limit your choice to one or two. Anymore and your focus becomes dispersed. Think laser, not lightbulb.

Step 2: Selecting the Right Tools

- **Research Solutions**: Explore various tools that address your identified needs. Consider features, scalability, compatibility with existing systems, user reviews, and cost.

- **Involve Stakeholders**: Include feedback from IT, sales, and other departments affected by the new tools. This can help ensure the chosen technology aligns with everyone's needs and capabilities. If they have "skin" in the game from the beginning, they are more likely to help ensure the integration is successful.

- **Vendor Evaluation**: Shortlist vendors and evaluate their offerings through demos, trials, and detailed discussions about support and upgrades. This can be a chore but the ROI on your investment of time will be massive.

Step 3: Planning the Integration

- **Integration Strategy**: Develop a detailed plan that includes timelines, key milestones, responsibilities, and required resources. As the French writer Antoine de Saint-Exupery once wrote, "A goal without a plan is just a wish."

- **Risk Management**: Identify potential risks associated with the tool integration and develop mitigation strategies.

Step 4: Training the Sales Team

- **Customized Training Programs**: Design training sessions tailored to various levels of tech-savviness within the team. Include hands-on sessions, tutorials, and Q&A sessions. Realize that individual members of your team will not all "get it" at the same time. There's a bell curve to learning new things.

- **Ongoing Support**: Establish a support system with IT helpdesk and super-users who can offer ongoing assistance and troubleshoot issues. The less time your team is trying to troubleshoot issues by themselves, the better.

Step 5: Implementing the Tools

- **Pilot Testing**: Start with a pilot program to evaluate the tool in a controlled environment. This allows you to make necessary adjustments before full-scale implementation. This is a crucial step that cannot be skipped.

- **Rollout**: Based on the feedback from the pilot, roll out the tool to the entire team. Ensure ongoing communication and availability of support to address any immediate issues. Listen to the feedback both good and bad.

Step 6: Measuring Impact

- **Performance Metrics**: Set up metrics to evaluate the technology's impact on sales performance. These might include lead conversion rates, sales cycle length, revenue per sales rep, and overall client satisfaction. Be clear on what a "win" looks like.

- **Regular Feedback**: Collect and analyze feedback from the sales team regarding the usability and effectiveness of the tool. Use this feedback to adjust and improve training. Listen to the feedback both good and bad. Don't take it personally if some of the feedback is bad.

Step 7: Review and Optimize

- **Continuous Improvement**: Regularly review the use and effectiveness of the tools. Look for new needs that arise as your sales process evolves and consider updates or additional tools to address these. Once you go live, you'll discover challenges and issues. That's part of the process. Be comfortable rolling with it.

- **Adapt Training and Support**: As the team grows more familiar with the tools, adapt the training programs to focus on advanced features and deeper integration into daily sales activities. The goal is to get your team from newbie to mastery as quickly as possible.

Step 8: Foster a Culture of Innovation

- **Encourage Exploration**: Encourage the sales team to explore innovative ways to use the technology. This can lead to improved practices and creative strategies. You'll be surprised by some of the ingenious things they come up with.

- **Reward Innovation**: Recognize and reward team members who successfully integrate recent technology into their sales strategies or who contribute ideas for further enhancement. Recognition and cash go a long way to igniting a fire within each member of your team.

By following these steps, you can ensure that the integration of recent technology into your sales operations not only smooths out initial bumps but also sets the stage for sustained improvements in your sales team's performance and client engagement.

The Future of B2B Sales and Technology[126]

We began this chapter on the impact of technology on sales over the past 25 years including the present day. But what about the next few years? What do sales leaders need to be prepared for?[127] As you have already imagined, the trajectory set by the last 25 years is not merely continuing; it is accelerating, propelling us into territories once reserved for science fiction. Just the fact that the entirety of the world's knowledge is accessible to you via a device you can hold in your hand should remind you of how far technology has come. The convergence of advancing technologies promises not just to refine the sales processes but to revolutionize them, foreshadowing a future where sales are more predictive, personalized, and interconnected than ever before.

Predictive Sales and Artificial Intelligence: Imagine a world where AI does not just respond to the market but anticipates it. Salesforce's Einstein AI, for instance, provides predictive insights that forecast client behaviors and sales

---

126   Gervet, E. (n.d.). The Future of B2B Sales. Kearney. Retrieved from https://www.kearney.com/documents/291362523/291368496/ The%2Bfuture%2Bof%2BB2B%2Bsales%2B%281%29. pdf/90f77854-6899-dedb-84d1-12b4aa7c8147

127   Draup. (2023, November 14). Future of B2B Sales: 8 High-Impact Trends to Watch For in 2024. https://draup.com/sales/blog/ future-of-b2b-sales-8-high-impact-trends-to-watch-for-in-2024/

outcomes, allowing companies like Coca-Cola to dynamically adjust marketing strategies in real-time.[128] This evolution of AI from reactive to proactive analytics empowers sales teams to optimize each interaction and maximize opportunities in ways that humans alone could never achieve.

Augmented and Virtual Reality: As AR and VR technologies mature, their integration into B2B sales processes is transforming the sales experience. A real-world example of this in the B2B space is Siemens, which uses AR to help potential clients visualize complex machinery and systems within their own facilities before purchase.[129] This application of AR enables Siemens to provide a highly interactive and detailed view of how their equipment will fit and function in the client's space, enhancing decision-making and client satisfaction. In broader B2B scenarios, these technologies enable sales teams to offer similarly immersive experiences. For instance, companies like Caterpillar use VR to allow potential clients to virtually operate heavy machinery in simulated environments.[130] This not only highlights the product's capabilities in a realistic setting but also enhances buyer engagement and confidence, making the sales process more interactive and impactful. Such immersive experiences can deeply engage decision-makers, offering them a tangible

128   McKevitt, J., & Burt, A. (2017, March 29). Salesforce's Einstein AI wants to count your bottles of Coca-Cola. Supply Chain Dive. https://www.supplychaindive.com/news/einstein-artificial-intelligence-salesforce-ibm-watson-coca-cola-inventory-management/439201/

129   Siemens. (2024, June 10). 5 ways industrial AR transforms work. Siemens Blog. https://blogs.sw.siemens.com/teamcenter/industrial-ar-transforms-work/

130   Cat Simulators https://catsimulators.com/

feel for the products and services, far beyond what tradition-al sales presentations could achieve.

Blockchain for Trust and Transparency: Blockchain technology is set to radically change how trust and transpar-ency are managed in B2B transactions. De Beers, for instance, uses blockchain to trace the origin of diamonds, ensuring they are conflict-free.[131] In B2B sales, smart contracts on platforms like Ethereum can automate agreements and ensure compliance from both parties without the need for intermediaries, thus reducing costs and speeding up the sales cycle while enhancing trust among parties.

IoT and Connected Devices: The Internet of Things (IoT) enables sales teams to monitor and analyze how products are being used in real-time. Companies like Rolls-Royce use IoT sensors to track the performance of their jet engines, offering maintenance and repairs proactively.[132] This approach to sales becomes less about individual purchases and more about man-aging ongoing client relationships, foreseeing needs before the client even identifies them.

Hyper-Personalization Through Big Data:[133] As data collection becomes more pervasive and powerful, hyper-per-sonalization is becoming the norm in B2B sales. Amazon and

131   Jenkinson, G. (2022, May 6). Blockchain technology to power De Beers' diamond production. Cointelegraph. https://cointelegraph.com/news/blockchain-technology-to-power-de-beers-diamond-production

132   RTInsights Team. (2016, October 11). How Rolls-Royce Maintains Jet Engines With the IoT. RTInsights. https://www.rtinsights.com/rolls-royce-jet-engine-maintenance-iot/

133   Avaus. (n.d.). Sales in 2025 – The Future of B2B Sales is all About Data and Hyper Automation. Retrieved from https://www.avaus.com/blog/sales-in-2025-the-future-of-b2b-sales-is-all-about-data-and-hyperautomation/

Netflix excel at using big data for personalizing recommendations at an individual level; similarly, B2B companies can tailor sales pitches and products not just to industries but to individual companies and decision-makers, using vast datasets that include past purchases, interaction history, and even sentiment analysis from social media.

Seamless Integration Across Platforms: Future B2B sales platforms will be characterized by their ability to integrate seamlessly across different channels and tools. HubSpot, for example, integrates with various business systems to provide a unified view of sales, marketing, client service, and inventory management, enhancing every step of the sales funnel from lead generation to post-sales support.[134]

Ethical AI and Privacy: As capabilities expand, so will the ethical considerations surrounding AI and data privacy. Companies will need to navigate the fine line between personalized sales approaches and respect for client privacy, ensuring compliance with global standards and regulations. This will be critical not just for legal compliance but for maintaining public trust.

In this future, the art of sales will be driven by a blend of technological sophistication and strategic insight, where human creativity and relationship-building are enhanced by data-driven intelligence. This evolution will not render the human element obsolete but will elevate the sales profession to new heights, leveraging technology to make every interaction

---

134   Shkurina, E. (2023, April 20). 27 Top HubSpot Integrations for Marketing, Sales, and RevOps. New Breed. https://www.newbreedrevenue.com/blog/5-hubspot-integrations-you-should-be-using

more meaningful and every transaction more efficient. The future of B2B sales, shaped by these technological forces, will be more than a mere exchange of goods and services; it will be a sophisticated symphony of data, analysis, and human engagement. Whether you're ready or not, it's coming.

Reflection Points: Technology's Role in Your Current Strategy

As technology continues to evolve at a rapid pace, its role in your sales strategies becomes increasingly vital.[135] Reflecting on how technology is integrated into your current sales strategy is crucial for identifying areas of improvement, ensuring alignment with overall business objectives, and maximizing the return on technology investments.[136] Now let's take a deep dive into the reflection points to consider when evaluating the role of technology in your sales strategy.[137]

1. Alignment with Your Strategic Objectives

- **Reflection Point**: How well does your current technology stack align with your strategic business objectives? Are the tools and systems you use contributing to the achievement of your long-term goals?

---

135 Accenture. (2023, July 26). Strategy at the Pace of Technology: Reinventing Business Strategy to Harness Technology Acceleration. https://www.accenture.com/us-en/insights/strategy/strategy-pace-technology

136 Nasstar. (n.d.). The Benefits Of A Defined Technology Strategy. Retrieved from https://www.nasstar.com/hub/blog/benefits-defined-technology-strategy

137 OSIbeyond. (2023, June 8). Technology Strategy 101. https://www.osibeyond.com/blog/technology-strategy-101/

- **Advanced Insight**: Assess whether the technologies you have in place support your strategic priorities, such as market expansion, client satisfaction, and revenue growth. Ensure that each tool is not only functional but also strategically aligned with your overall vision.

- **Action**: Conduct a strategic review to map each piece of technology against your business objectives. Identify any gaps where technology might not be fully supporting your goals and consider potential upgrades or novel solutions.

2. Integration and Interoperability

- **Reflection Point**: How seamlessly are your sales technologies integrated? Do they work together to provide a cohesive system, or do they operate in silos?

- **Advanced Insight**: Evaluate the interoperability of your CRM, marketing automation, analytics, and other sales tools. Effective integration minimizes data silos, reduces manual data entry, and enhances the overall efficiency of your sales processes.

- **Action**: Review your technology integration strategy and look for opportunities to enhance connectivity between systems. Consider using middleware solutions or API integrations to ensure data flows smoothly across platforms.

3. User Adoption and Training

- **Reflection Point**: Are your sales team members fully

utilizing the available technologies? Do they have the necessary training to use these tools effectively?

- **Advanced Insight**: User adoption is a critical factor in the success of any technology implementation. Assess whether your sales team understands the benefits of the tools and feels confident in using them. Identify any training gaps that might hinder full utilization.

- **Action**: Implement ongoing training programs and provide resources such as user guides and workshops. Encourage a culture of continuous learning and technology adoption.

4. Impact on Sales Performance[122] [123]

- **Reflection Point**: How is technology impacting your sales performance? Are you seeing measurable improvements in key performance indicators (KPIs) such as lead conversion rates, sales cycle length, and client satisfaction?

- **Advanced Insight**: Use data analytics to evaluate the impact of technology on sales outcomes. Look for trends and correlations between technology usage and performance metrics. This analysis can reveal whether your current tools are driving the expected results or not.

- **Action**: Regularly review sales performance data and adjust your technology strategy based on insights gained. Experiment with new tools or features that could further enhance performance.

5. Client Experience Enhancement

- **Reflection Point**: How does your technology strategy enhance the client experience? Are you using tools that provide personalized, timely, and relevant interactions with your clients? We've already discussed how much easier it is to sell more to an existing client than it is to find a new one.

- **Advanced Insight**: Assess the effectiveness of your CRM, client support systems, and communication platforms in delivering a superior client experience. Personalized interactions, efficient problem resolution, and seamless communication are key drivers of client satisfaction.

- **Action**: Gather client feedback to understand their experience with your sales processes. Use this feedback to refine your technology usage and improve client interactions.

6. Scalability and Flexibility

- **Reflection Point**: Is your technology stack scalable to support future growth? Can it adapt to changing business needs and market conditions?

- **Advanced Insight**: Evaluate the scalability of your current technologies. As your business grows, your technology should be able to manage increased data volumes, more complex processes, and a larger user base without compromising performance.

- **Action**: Plan for scalability by choosing flexible, cloud-based solutions that can grow with your business. Regularly review and update your technology infrastructure to ensure it remains sturdy and adaptable.

7. Cost-Benefit Analysis

- **Reflection Point**: Are you getting a good return on investment (ROI) from your technology expenditures? Do the benefits justify the costs?

- **Advanced Insight**: Conduct a cost-benefit analysis to evaluate the fiscal impact of your technology investments. Consider both direct costs (such as software licenses and maintenance) and indirect costs (such as training and downtime during implementation).

- **Action**: Optimize your technology spending by focusing on tools that deliver the highest ROI. Eliminate or replace underperforming technologies and reinvest in areas that provide significant value.

8. Innovation and Competitive Advantage

- **Reflection Point**: How does your use of technology position you against competitors? Are you leveraging innovative solutions to gain a competitive edge?

- **Advanced Insight**: Stay informed about emerging technologies and industry trends. Assess whether your current technology stack includes innovative solutions that differentiate you from competitors and enhance your market position.

- **Action**: Foster a culture of innovation by encouraging experimentation with recent technologies. Regularly review competitive intelligence to identify technological advancements that can give you a strategic advantage.

Final Thoughts

Reflecting on the role of technology in your current sales strategy is an ongoing process that requires continuous evaluation and adjustment. By considering these reflection points, you and your sales leaders can ensure that your technology investments are aligned with strategic objectives, fully utilized by the team, and deliver measurable improvements in sales performance and client experience. This proactive approach to technology management will help maintain a competitive edge and drive long-term success in an ever-evolving market.

How Technology Helped to End World War II

No, we're not talking about the Manhattan Project, nor the forceful leadership of Major General Leslie Groves of the U.S. Army Corps of Engineers, nor the brilliance of nuclear physicist J. Robert Oppenheimer in the heart of World War II. This is a story about a lesser-known use of technology to help end the war at a place called Bletchley Park[138]. Bletchley Park became the epicenter of one of the most significant technological advancements in military history, the breaking of the Enigma code. The Enigma machine was a complex cipher device used by the Germans to encrypt military communications, believed by many to be unbreakable. The effort was led by Alan Turing, an English mathematician, computer scientist, logician, cryptanalyst, and philosopher.

This feat, achieved through the ingenious use of early computing technology like Alan Turing's Bombe machines, exemplifies the profound impact that technology can have on strategic operations. Just as the Allied forces gained a monumental advantage by decrypting German communications, modern sales teams can harness contemporary technological tools to gain significant competitive edges in their fields.

Strategic Insights Through Data Analytics

The work at Bletchley Park was, fundamentally, about decrypting and interpreting vast amounts of data to extract actionable intelligence. Similarly, sales teams today can use data analytics technologies to decipher vast pools of market and client data. By leveraging tools like CRM systems integrated with AI, sales professionals can gain insights into client behaviors, preferences, and buying patterns. These insights allow for the crafting of highly targeted marketing campaigns and sales pitches, much

---

138   Sinclair McKay, The Secret Life of Bletchley Park: The WWII Codebreaking Centre and the Men and Women Who Worked There (London: Aurum Press, 2011)

like how Allied strategists used decrypted messages to plan military operations.

Enhancing Efficiency with Automation

The Bombe machines at Bletchley Park automated the painstaking process of codebreaking, significantly accelerating the Allies' ability to gather intelligence. In a parallel manner, sales teams can use automation tools to streamline numerous aspects of the sales process, from lead generation to client follow-up. Automation not only speeds up these processes but also reduces the likelihood of human error, freeing up your sales representatives to focus on higher-value activities like relationship building and complex negotiations.

Virtual Collaboration and Communication

Just as Bletchley Park brought together some of the brightest minds from diverse backgrounds to work collaboratively on codebreaking, modern communication technologies enable seamless collaboration among sales teams distributed across the globe. Platforms like Slack, Microsoft Teams, and Zoom allow sales teams to share insights, strategies, and updates in real-time. This capability is particularly critical in a globalized market where teams often work across different time zones and regions.

Predictive Technologies for Forward Planning

The predictive power of Turing's Bombe provided the Allies with foresight into enemy plans. Similarly, predictive sales tools can forecast market trends and client needs before they become apparent. Sales teams can utilize AI-powered tools to predict which products will be in demand next season, which leads are most likely to convert, or even when a client might be ready for an upsell. This foresight allows for proactive rather than reactive strategies, optimizing sales outcomes.

Training and Simulation

The rigorous training of codebreakers at Bletchley Park was critical to their success. Today, VR can simulate real-life sales scenarios for training purposes, providing salespeople with a risk-free environment to hone their skills. From practicing sales pitches to navigating complex client service interactions, VR simulations can prepare sales teams for a variety of challenges they might face in the field.

By embracing these technological tools, sales teams not only enhance their operational efficiency but also gain deeper insights into the competitive landscape, much like the Allies at Bletchley Park. This strategic use of technology, when executed effectively, transforms sales processes, boosts productivity, and drives significant business growth. In this way, the legacy of Bletchley Park lives on, inspiring not only cryptologists but also sales professionals to leverage technology for strategic advantage.

CHAPTER 11

The Execution Framework for the Strategic Sales Leader

"Plans are only good intentions unless they
immediately degenerate into hard work."

—Peter Drucker

"Strategy without tactics is the slowest route to victory.
Tactics without strategy is the noise before defeat."

—Sun Tzu

"Execution is the job of the business leader."

—Larry Bossidy

In our ever-changing world of strategic sales, execution is not just about following through, it's about making the right moves at the right time with precision and adaptability. This chapter is designed to arm you with the methodologies and tools necessary to transform strategic plans into successful outcomes. This chapter delves into the core components of an effective execution framework, offering a detailed roadmap for sales leaders who are committed to driving performance and achieving sales excellence.

Sales Forecasting and Performance Analysis

> "War is essentially a calculation of probabilities."
>
> —Napoleon Bonaparte

Sales leaders live and die by their forecasts. If you get it right and your sales number lands where you predicted, you get to remain employed. If you repeatedly miss it over several quarters, expect to be called to explain why your forecasts were so far off and what your plan is to get back on track.

As you know, sales forecasting is an essential tool for sales leaders, hopefully providing insights into future sales trends, demand patterns, and revenue projections. Accurate sales forecasting and performance analysis are critical elements of effective sales management. They not only impact day-to-day sales activities but also shape long-term strategic decisions made by your organization.

Understanding Sales Forecasting

Sales forecasting is the process of estimating future sales. There's an art and science to it. If you do it right, sales forecasts enable your organization to make informed decisions about managing their workforce, resources, and cash flow. Forecasting can range from predicting short-term individual sales to projecting long-term industry trends.[139] You must be adept at both.

There are several methods of sales forecasting, each with

---

139   John T. Mentzer, Sales Forecasting Management: A Demand Management Approach, 2nd ed. (Thousand Oaks, CA: Sage Publications, 2001)

their strengths and weaknesses. The choice of method depends on factors such as the nature of your business, the availability of historical data, and market conditions.

Qualitative Methods

Qualitative forecasting methods are particularly useful when past data is not available. They rely on market research and expert opinions rather than historical data. If you're leading a startup, or launching a new product, you're not going to have much data to refer to.

Methods include:

1. **Sales Force Composite**: Each salesperson estimates their future sales based on their knowledge of their clients and territory. These individual forecasts are then combined to create a company-wide forecast.

2. **Delphi Method**: A panel of subject matter experts in your organization makes individual forecasts. These forecasts are then discussed and revised until the panel reaches a consensus.

3. **Market Research**: This involves gathering data directly from clients through methods like surveys or interviews. Depending on the scale, they can be immensely helpful. If your sample size is too small, it's anecdotal.

Most sales leaders will use the Sale Force Composite method to help them build accurate forecasts.

Implementing a Sales Forecasting Process[140] [141]

Implementing an accurate sales forecasting process involves several steps:

1. **Define the Time Period**: Determine whether the forecast will be for a month, a quarter, a year, or longer. Your sales cycle will help determine which you use.

2. **Choose a Forecasting Method**: Based on your business needs and the available data, choose the most suitable forecasting method. As mentioned above, most sales teams use the Sales Force Composite method.

3. **Collect and Analyze Data**: Gather historical sales data and other relevant information. Analyze this data to identify trends and patterns. You should have a good CRM in place to help with this along with other analytical tools.

4. **Create the Forecast**: Use your chosen forecasting method to create the sales forecast.

5. **Review and Revise**: Regularly review and update your forecast based on new data or changes in market conditions.

Depending on how long you've been leading your sales team, you will quickly learn to determine which of your salespeople are accurate with their forecasts. Some will be

140   Cameron, C. (2024, March 21). Sales Forecasting Process - Step-by-Step Guide. BoostUp. https://www.boostup.ai/blog/sales-forecasting-process

141   Frost, A. (n.d.). The Ultimate Guide to Sales Forecasting From HubSpot's Senior Director of Global Growth. HubSpot. Retrieved from https://blog.hubspot.com/sales/sales-forecasting

accurate month in and month out. Some will overstate their forecast size. You'll have to figure out how much they overstate their forecast so you can bring it down. For example, if you have a sales team member who consistently overstates their forecast between 25 percent to 35 percent, you know to reduce it by that much in your own forecast. You can do the same with salespeople who understate their forecast because they're nervous about going on record with everything they think they can close.

You will also need to be aware that some salespeople underestimate how long it will take to close an opportunity. If your average sales cycle is five months and you have a salesperson telling you that a particular opportunity is going to close in three months, your ears should perk up. You need to drill into why they think this will close faster than most deals. In most situations, salespeople underestimate how long an opportunity will take to close. For example, a salesperson will forecast that an opportunity will close in five months, but it doesn't close for seven months. This will cause problems for you. Especially if that time frame falls outside of your fiscal quarter or end of your fiscal year.

As you become familiar with the capabilities of your individual sales team members, you'll get more accurate with deciphering the reality versus what they tell you so you can ensure your forecast is spot on. If you're not sure, it's better to under promise and over deliver.

The Role of Performance Analysis

> "Not everything that counts can be counted, and not everything that can be counted counts."
>
> —William Bruce Cameron

Performance analysis complements sales forecasting by evaluating the effectiveness of sales activities and identifying areas for improvement. This involves tracking key performance indicators (KPIs) and analyzing sales data.

Common sales KPIs include the number of new leads, conversion rates, average deal size, sales cycle length, and client churn rate. These KPIs provide valuable insights into sales performance at both the individual and team levels. It's critically important that you choose KPIs that are truly tied to sales results. You'd be amazed at some of the sales leaders who fall in love with endless amounts of KPIs that are tangentially related to how sales are made by their team.

How often do you ask yourself if the KPIs your sales organization uses are relevant?

Choosing the right Key Performance Indicators (KPIs) for creating an accurate sales forecast involves selecting metrics that provide insight into your sales process, your client behavior, and market conditions[142]. Here's a structured approach to selecting these KPIs:

---

142   Bernard Marr, Key Performance Indicators (KPI): The 75 Measures Every Manager Needs to Know, 1st ed. (Harlow, England: Financial Times/Prentice Hall, 2012)

1. Understand Business Objectives

- Align your KPIs with strategic objectives, such as market expansion, client retention, or revenue growth. Knowing what your business aims to achieve helps in focusing on relevant metrics.

2. Identify Sales Funnel Stages

- Map out the sales process from prospecting to closing. Understanding each stage allows you to measure the effectiveness and efficiency of each part of the sales cycle. Make sure that everyone is clear what each stage of the funnel means. If you were to ask each member of your sales team to describe to you every stage of the sales funnel and what it means, you may be surprised with the disparate answers you get. Spell it out for them.

3. Choose Leading and Lagging Indicators

- **Leading indicators** predict future sales activities and help adjust strategies proactively. Examples include:
  - **Sales Pipeline Growth**: Measures the increase in the number of opportunities.
  - **Lead Conversion Rates**: Tracks how well leads are converted into opportunities.
  - **Average Deal Size**: Helps forecast revenue based on deal size trends.

- **Lagging indicators** reflect outcomes of past actions and help assess overall performance. Examples include:
  - **Revenue**: Total sales closed in a specific period.
  - **Customer Retention Rate**: Measures how well the business retains existing clients.
  - **Sales Cycle Length**: The average time to close deals.

4. Factor in Customer Engagement Metrics

- Metrics like client interaction frequency, engagement level during demonstrations, and response times can provide early signs of deal success or potential stalling. As B2B sales author and thought leader Brian Burns says, "what is not overtly positive is covertly negative."

5. Use Predictive Analytics

- Implement tools that utilize historical data and predictive analytics to forecast future sales. This could include AI-driven tools that analyze past performance to predict trends and patterns. We already discussed this in depth in the chapter on technology.

6. Regular Review and Adaptation

- Continuously monitor and revise KPIs to reflect changing market conditions or internal business changes. Regular reviews ensure that KPIs remain relevant and effective. Life and sales are dynamic, not static. Your KPIs should be too.

7. Incorporate External Factors

- Consider external factors such as market trends, economic indicators, and competitive landscape that could impact sales performance. We need to remember that we don't live in a vacuum and outside forces will impact us in ways we often can't predict.

8. Collaboration and Communication

- Ensure that KPIs are communicated clearly across the team and that there is a consensus on how they are defined and measured. Collaboration helps in maintaining a unified approach towards achieving sales targets.

Example of a KPI Dashboard for a Sales Leader:

- **Current Pipeline Value**: Total dollar value of all opportunities at various stages.

- **Win Rate**: Percentage of opportunities that are converted into sales.

- **Quota Attainment**: Percentage of salespeople achieving their sales quota.

- **Customer Acquisition Cost (CAC)**: The cost associated with acquiring a new customer.

- **Lifetime Value (LTV) to CAC Ratio**: A measure of the long-term value of a customer compared to the cost of acquiring them.

By focusing on these areas, sales leaders can create a more effective and dynamic approach to forecasting, which can adapt to the nuances of your sales process, leading to more predictable and consistent sales outcomes.

Now that you've assured yourself that you're working with the right KPIs, you can then put it all together ins a sales performance analysis using the following steps:

1. **Define Your Goals and KPIs**: Set clear sales goals and define KPIs that align with these goals.

2. **Collect and Analyze Data**: Collect data related to your KPIs and analyze it to assess your sales performance.

3. **Identify Trends and Patterns**: Look for trends or patterns in the data that can provide insights into your sales performance.

4. **Evaluate Performance**: Evaluate your performance against your goals and benchmarks.

5. **Identify Areas for Improvement**: Identify areas where performance is falling short and determine potential causes.

6. **Develop and Implement Action Plans**: Develop action plans to address areas of weakness and implement these plans.

Steps two through six are a never-ending loop. Get comfortable regularly going through that loop using a cadence that synchronizes up with your sales cycle.

A Warning on Becoming Obsessed with Data, Dashboards and Sales

While these tools are helpful, don't fall into the trap of depending too much on them. Nothing will ever replace you simply going out and meeting with clients face to face. Too many sales leaders become obsessed with their data driven dashboards and lose sight of what sales forecasting is: having a deep understanding of the structure of an opportunity, the client's pain, and their seriousness to solve that problem with the solutions you sell them. Staring at your dashboard all day and barking orders to your team isn't sales leadership.

Strategic Account Management

> "Bees do not go to the flowerless mango tree."
>
> —Chanakya

> "Given the same amount of intelligence, timidity will do a thousand times more damage than audacity."
>
> —Carl von Clausewitz

> "There are some routes not to follow, some armies not to assault, some cities not to attack, some grounds not to contest and some commands of the sovereign not to be obeyed."
>
> —Sun Tzu, The Art of War

We can't discuss strategic sales leadership without including Strategic Account Management. Strategic account management goes beyond traditional sales approaches, focusing on nurturing and growing key client relationships to maximize value and client satisfaction. Every sales organization strives to land large accounts that can change the future direction of your company. By prioritizing strategic accounts and developing comprehensive account plans, sales leaders can unlock significant growth opportunities and cultivate partnerships that endure in good times and bad. The 80/20 rule which we discussed earlier also applies to your accounts.

We will begin by discussing the process of identifying and prioritizing strategic accounts within your client base. By evaluating factors such as revenue potential, influence, and long-term value, sales leaders can allocate resources effectively and focus their efforts on accounts that offer the greatest opportunities for growth and success.

Once strategic accounts are identified, we will explore the creation of account plans that guide the sales team in maximizing client value. These account plans outline the goals, strategies, and tactics required to deepen relationships, expand business opportunities, and address client needs effectively. We will discuss the importance of conducting thorough account research, understanding client pain points, and developing tailored solutions that meet their specific requirements.

Building and nurturing relationships with key clients is a central aspect of strategic account management. We will delve into strategies for developing trust, providing exceptional client experiences, and positioning yourself as a strategic partner rather than just a vendor. By focusing on long-term relationship-building and understanding client goals, challenges, and aspirations, your sales team can foster loyalty and become invaluable to their strategic accounts.

Strategic account management is a client-centric approach that focuses on building long-term, mutually beneficial relationships with key clients. It is about much more than just sales – it's about creating value for both your organization and your key accounts. Let's delve into the components of strategic account management.[143]

Identifying Strategic Accounts

Strategic accounts are typically the key clients that contribute a massive portion of your revenue, have substantial growth potential, or hold strategic value in terms of market influence or partnerships. It's essential to identify and select these strategic accounts based on clearly defined criteria that align with your company's strategic goals.

The selection process may involve assessing the client's current and potential revenue contribution, profitability, strategic fit, and the strength of your relationship with them. Once identified, these strategic accounts should be the focus of your account management efforts.

Understanding Your Strategic Accounts

To manage strategic accounts effectively, you need a deep understanding of each account. This includes the client's business model, their goals and challenges, the industry they operate in, their competitors, and their clients. Granted, this

---

143   Sallie Sherman, Joseph Sperry, and Samuel Reese, The Seven Keys to Managing Strategic Accounts, 1st ed. (New York: McGraw-Hill Education, 2003).

takes more effort on your part, but it's well worth the time and energy you'll be investing.

Invest in research to understand the broader context in which your strategic accounts operate. This will give you insights into their strategic direction and help you identify how your products or services can add value to their business.

Building Strong Relationships

Strategic account management is all about relationships. This is not just limited to the relationship between the salesperson and the client but extends to relationships at multiple levels within each organization. The more points of contact your organization has with a strategic account, the stronger that relationship will be in the long term.

Establishing strong relationships with key decision-makers within the strategic account is crucial. This can help you gain deeper insights into the client's needs, secure their buy-in, and ensure a smooth sales process. Those relationships will also give you warnings when things aren't going as planned. If you and your team are forging real relationships, you will never be blind-sided by bad news such as the client dumping you and taking their business elsewhere.

Equally important is building internal relationships within your organization. The strategic account manager needs to coordinate with various departments like sales, marketing, product development, and client service to deliver a seamless experience to the strategic account.

Developing a Strategic Account Plan

A strategic account plan is a blueprint that guides your account management efforts. It outlines your understanding of the account, your objectives, your value proposition, and your action plan.

Start by outlining your understanding of the strategic account. This includes your analysis of their business, their needs, and their goals.

Next, define your objectives for the account. These should align with the client's goals as well as your company's strategic objectives. Objectives could range from increasing sales to the account, deepening your relationship, or becoming the client's preferred vendor.

Then, develop your value proposition. Your value proposition should clearly articulate how your product or service can help the client achieve their goals or solve their challenges better than any of your competitors can.

Lastly, create an action plan. This includes the specific steps you will take to achieve your objectives, the resources required, and the timeline. Your action plan should also outline how you will track and measure your progress.

Delivering Value

Strategic account management is about delivering value to your strategic accounts. This is not just about the value of your product or service, but also the value of the relationship and the overall experience you provide.

Delivering value involves understanding the client's needs

and expectations, aligning your offerings with those needs, and providing a seamless, personalized client experience.

In addition, it's essential to clearly communicate the value you are delivering. Regularly share updates with the client about the progress you are making towards your mutual goals and the benefits they are getting from your relationship. Just because you and your team may be doing an excellent job doesn't mean your client is aware of this. Make sure you regularly update your strategic clients on all the value you're bringing them.

Reviewing and Adapting

Strategic account management is a dynamic process that requires regular review and adaptation. Conduct periodic reviews to assess your progress towards your objectives, the value you are delivering, and the strength of your relationship with the account.

These reviews can provide valuable insights to help you improve your account management efforts. You may need to adapt your account plan based on the feedback from these reviews or changes in the client's needs or market conditions.

Final Thoughts

Strategic account management is a focused, client-centric approach to managing key clients. It involves identifying strategic accounts, understanding them deeply, building strong relationships, developing a strategic account plan, delivering value, and continuously reviewing and adapting.

While the process can be complex and demanding, effective strategic account management can lead to increased sales, stronger client relationships, and improved client retention. It can transform key clients into strategic partners, creating lasting value for both parties.

It's essential to note that strategic account management is not a standalone activity but an integral part of your broader sales and business strategy. It requires the support of senior leadership and coordination across multiple departments within your organization. With the right approach and commitment, strategic account management can become a powerful engine for your company's growth and success.

Keeping Your Team on Track

Once you've identified your strategic accounts and the metrics that align with your team's goals, maintaining focus and consistency is crucial. A practical approach is to schedule two one-on-one meetings each month with each member of your sales team. These bi-monthly check-ins are essential for gauging progress and steering towards success.

The Results-Objectives-Activities (ROA) Call

Each month, you'll conduct the first meeting to discuss four key areas:

1. **Results**: Review the most recent monthly sales numbers. If a team member has met or exceeded their quota, that's great news, and the call should be a short one. If not, it's time to dig deeper to understand the challenges.

2. **Objectives**: Discuss their primary goals for the month. Who are they targeting, and what specific outcomes, such as first meetings, proof of concepts, or other key actions, are they aiming to achieve?

3. **Pipeline**: Evaluate whether the top of their sales funnel is consistently being replenished with new opportunities and if existing prospects are progressing or stalling. A red flag should pop up if you see that a salesperson's pipeline is being depleted with closed opportunities and not being replenished at the top.

4. **Activities**: Analyze where they spent their time during the month. If a team member is meeting their targets, there's no need to ask how and where they're spending their time. However, if they're falling short, you'll need to examine their activities more closely to ensure they're aligned with achieving sales targets. Then have them commit to an activity plan for the following month. This is not a punitive action, it's a way to help them focus their efforts on what will help them get back on track and hit their quota.

Structure of the Meeting:

- **Setting**: The meeting can be held in person or virtually, with cameras on to capture nonverbal cues.

- **Duration**: Allocate about 30 minutes per meeting but adjust based on the team member's current performance. If they are performing well, a quick 10-minute check-in might suffice, giving them back valuable time.

■ **CRM Review**: Have them share their CRM screen to review details together, providing a clear and shared view of their progress and areas needing attention.

This monthly check-in serves as a pulse check on their alignment with yearly, quarterly, and monthly goals. It acts like course corrections like the trajectory-correction maneuvers made by NASA when the Perseverance was headed to Mars, minor but critical for staying on target. The objective is to keep each sales team member focused and prevent distractions from derailing their efforts.

Timing: Ideally, schedule this meeting within the first week after the month's sales results are available. This timing ensures the information is fresh and relevant, facilitating a more effective discussion about their achievements and areas for improvement.

By conducting these focused ROA calls, you help your team maintain clarity on their goals and the actions required to meet them, fostering a culture of accountability and continuous improvement.

Now we move on to the second important meeting you'll have with each member of your sales team.

The Strategic Coaching Call

The second critical meeting you should have each month is a strategic coaching call. This is a one-hour session where you and your salesperson discuss the top opportunities they're targeting.[144] It's advisable to focus on three opportunities,

---

144 Michelle Vazzana and Jason Jordan, Crushing Quota: Proven Sales Coaching Tactics for Breakthrough Performance (New York: McGraw-Hill Education, 2018)

allotting approximately 20 minutes to each. This ensures sufficient depth in your discussions, which is essential for effective coaching. During a sales coaching call, brevity is essential for maintaining focus and ensuring that key points are clearly understood and actionable.

Importance of Strategic Coaching

This call is crucial because, as we discussed earlier, according to research by the Sales Executive Council, improving the sales performance of the middle 60% of your team by just 5% can yield over 70% more revenue compared to the same improvement in your top performers. This insight highlights the significant impact of elevating your average performers to higher productivity levels.

Why Focus on the Middle Performers?

Most sales teams consist of a few top performers and many average (C-level) players. It's easier and more impactful for us to uplift the average performers than to recruit more top-tier salespeople. Great salespeople are like Unicorns.

The Strategy Call Framework

Objective: The goal is to help your salesperson develop a strategic plan for winning significant opportunities. You'll discuss:

- **Decision Makers and Influencers:** Identify who has the authority and influence over the purchasing decision.

- **Timeline:** Understand the timeline for decision-making and implementation.

- **Resources Alignment:** Ensure all necessary support, whether from engineering, sales engineering, or pre-sales, is available and aligned.

Methodology: Use the PACTT system, which stands for Pain, Authority, Consequences, Target profile, and Timing. This evolved from the older BANT (budget, authority, need, and timeline) method and better addresses modern sales challenges.[145]

1. **Pain:** Is the prospective organization experiencing enough pain that your solution is genuinely needed?

2. **Authority:** Are you engaging with individuals who have the authority to green light the deal?

3. **Consequences:** What are the implications for the prospective organization if they do not proceed with your solution? In other words, what's at stake if they don't move forward?

4. **Target Profile:** Does the prospective organization match the profile of clients you successfully serve?

5. **Timing:** Is there a critical time frame by which the solution must be implemented to avert the consequences?

---

145   Haensch, L. (2020, November 2). What is PACTT Framework and Why It Beats BANT. Pathmonk. https://pathmonk.com/what-is-pactt-framework-and-why-it-beats-bant/

Execution of the Call

- **Assessment:** During the call, evaluate each opportunities' aspects using the PACTT criteria to understand your sales professional's standing within the prospective organization.

- **Realism Check:** It's common for salespeople to overestimate deal viability. It's your role to discern whether a deal is substantial or just hopeful talk.

Results and Action

- **Resource Allocation:** If a deal aligns well with the PACTT criteria, ensure that your company's resources are strategically aligned to support closing the deal.

- **Honest Evaluation:** Address any discrepancies between what's reported and the actual situation. It's essential to prevent deals that look promising but are unlikely to close from inflating your pipeline and affecting your forecasts.

Timing for the Call

- Schedule the strategic call at the start of each month to review the previous month's results. This timing ensures that the information discussed is fresh and actionable.

By focusing on these strategic coaching calls, you ensure that your sales team prioritizes high-value targets effectively. This approach not only improves their success rate but also aligns with consistently winning larger opportunities which means a stable pipeline lacking the normal highs and lows resembling a roller coaster ride.

Part IV

COLLABORATION, OFFICE POLITICS, POWER, AND LEADERSHIP

"Nearly all men can stand adversity, but if you want to test a man's character, give him power."

- Abraham Lincoln

"Leaders must be close enough to relate to others, but far enough ahead to motivate them."

- John Maxwell

"Great things in business are never done by one person; they're done by a team of people."

- Steve Jobs

"Leadership is not about being in charge. It's about taking care of those in your charge."

- Simon Sinek

"When dealing with people, remember you are not dealing with creatures of logic, but with creatures of emotion."

- Dale Carnegie

In any workplace, the dynamics between colleagues play a crucial role in shaping the environment and the outcomes of projects. Part IV delves into the intricate world of collaboration, office politics, power, and leadership, exploring how these elements interact and influence each other in a professional setting. As a leader, understanding these concepts is essential for you, and it's also important to understand the concepts if you strive to navigate your career successfully.

Collaboration is the cornerstone of any successful team. It involves working together to achieve common goals, requiring communication, trust, and mutual respect among team members. However, the path to effective collaboration isn't always smooth. Office politics: the strategies individuals use to gain advantage in the workplace; often complicate interpersonal relations and team dynamics.

We rarely speak about power, who has it, who doesn't, and how best to use it. Power in the workplace can manifest in various forms, from the authority associated with one's position to the influence one gains through expertise or relationships. How power is acquired and used can significantly impact a team's morale and productivity. Understanding power is an essential leadership skill.

Lastly, leadership is about guiding and motivating a group to achieve their best. Great leaders understand how to harness the power and politics of an office environment to foster a culture of collaboration and achievement.

In this section, we will explore how these elements interact, offering strategies to manage office politics positively, utilize power effectively, and lead with integrity. By mastering these skills, you can create a more dynamic, fair, and productive workplace.

CHAPTER 12

Cross-Functional Collaboration and Leadership

"If you want to go fast, go alone. If you
want to go far, go together."

- African Proverb

"The role of a creative leader is not to have all
the ideas; it's to create a culture where everyone
can have ideas and feel that they're valued."

- Ken Robinson

"The strength of the team is each individual member.
The strength of each member is the team."

- Phil Jackson

More than ever, sales cannot operate in isolation.[146] The modern organization is a web of siloed departments, divisions, and business units. Close collaboration with other functions, especially marketing, is essential to aligning your

---

146   Roszak, C. (2021). The isolation of selling: Marketing researchers analyze social isolation and job performance. Kansas State University. https://www.k-state.edu/seek/fall-2021/marketing-researchers-analyze-social-isolation/

strategies, leveraging resources, and creating a unified client experience that drives growth and market success. Even if you and your sales team are doing all the right things, you're still going to be in for a painful journey if the other organizational departments aren't aligned with you and your sales strategy.

Collaboration extends beyond sales and marketing, encompassing other functions within the organization as well. We will explore the benefits of cross-functional collaboration, such as involving product development teams in understanding client needs or engaging client support teams in gathering valuable insights. By fostering collaboration with various functions, sales leaders can leverage diverse perspectives, drive innovation, and deliver holistic solutions that address client challenges.

Here are a few concepts and ideas you can use to get other company leaders on board:[147]

1. Communicate the Value and Vision:

The first step is to articulate the value of your sales strategy to the organization. How will it drive business growth? How does it align with the overall strategic goals of the company? Having a well-defined sales vision can help other leaders understand the importance of the strategy and why their contribution is essential. We addressed this at length in Part I.

---

147   Glenn M. Parker, Cross Functional Teams: Working with Allies, Enemies, and Other Strangers (San Francisco: Jossey-Bass, 1994)

2. Foster Cross-Departmental Collaboration:

It's important to create a culture of cross-departmental collaboration within the organization. This can be achieved by encouraging regular inter-departmental meetings, team building activities, or joint projects. Collaboration can lead to more comprehensive insights and strategies, as different departments bring unique perspectives and expertise to the table. Involve as many people as you can. This shows that you respect the input of the other departments and helps you get a feel for the egos of the individuals you're going to need to get on your side.

3. Involve Leaders in the Planning Process:

Involve other leaders early in the sales strategy planning process. This provides them with a sense of ownership and engagement in the strategy. Furthermore, their input can strengthen the strategy by integrating insights from different areas of the business. You might be surprised by some of the insight they give you. We all have cognitive blind spots that we need others to point out. In some cases, they may not wish to participate, which might happen, but at least you had the courtesy to ask. No one wants to be blindsided by a new initiative which no one bothered to discuss with them. Always keep in mind that you're dealing with humans who are emotional and irrational beings, many of whom are driven strictly by their egos.

4. Highlight Interdependencies:

Highlight how each department's success contributes to the success of the sales strategy. For instance, marketing efforts directly impact lead generation, product development can offer unique selling points, and client service can influence client retention. By emphasizing these interdependencies, other leaders can see how their work is crucial to the overall sales strategy's success. Appealing to self-interest will help you win over people.

5. Regular Reporting and Feedback:

Share regular updates on the sales strategy's progress, successes, and challenges. Transparent reporting can reinforce the importance of everyone's contribution and foster a culture of continuous improvement. Additionally, invite feedback and ideas to refine the strategy and processes.

6. Recognize and Reward Collaboration:

Recognize and reward departments or individuals who contribute significantly to the sales strategy's success. This could be through formal rewards or informal recognition. This not only motivates those rewarded but also signals to others the value the organization places on cross-functional collaboration.

A sales leader who effectively collaborates with other leaders can leverage the combined skills, perspectives, and resources of the entire organization. This can significantly enhance the implementation and success of their sales strategy.

Navigating Office Politics and Power Dynamics: A Strategic Framework for Effective Leadership

For some reason, most books on leadership and sales leadership rarely, if ever address office politics and the power dynamics within organizations. Understanding and managing power dynamics is crucial for steering teams toward success.[148] As a leader, you are at the heart of a network of alliances and allegiances, each woven intricately like a spider's web. These connections span across an array of motivations, competencies, and interests, continually evolving and reshaping. As Niccolò Machiavelli wrote in The Prince, "The wise prince ought to adopt such a course that his citizens will always in every sort and kind of circumstance have need of him, and then they will always be faithful to him." Recognizing that alliances formed out of mere convenience can often backfire is essential, as transparency and mutual benefits are key to their longevity and strength.

Strategic Positioning Within the Network

As a sales leader, positioning yourself at the center of this network (web) is vital. This central vantage point allows you to connect with the farthest reaches of your organization, aligning diverse thoughts, goals, and efforts toward a unified vision. This alignment is not just about directive leadership but about fostering a shared commitment to the collective goals. A failure to integrate these diverse elements can significantly hinder progress and diminish your chances of success.

---

148   Allison M. Vaillancourt, The Organizational Politics Playbook: 50 Strategies to Navigate Power Dynamics at Work (New York: McGraw-Hill Education, 2021)

Understanding the Human Element

Humans are inherently competitive, often vying for resources and status, a concept deeply embedded in our nature. James Madison highlighted this in 1787 in The Federalist No. 10, [149] noting the propensity of humans to fall into factions and conflicts over various opinions and loyalties.

As social animals, a battle for resources is hard wired into our DNA. Dominance hierarchy is a normal part of humanity. Ignore this at your own peril. Madison wrote, "The latent causes of faction are thus sown in the nature of man," He continues, "...and we see them everywhere brought into different degrees of activity, according to the different circumstances of civil society. A zeal for different opinions concerning religion, concerning government, and many other points, as well of speculation as of practice; an attachment to different leaders ambitiously contending for pre-eminence and power; or to persons of other descriptions whose fortunes have been interesting to the human passions, have, in turn, divided mankind into parties, inflamed them with mutual animosity, and rendered them much more disposed to vex and oppress each other than to cooperate for their common good. So strong is this propensity of mankind to fall into mutual animosities, that where no substantial occasion presents itself, the most frivolous and fanciful distinctions have been sufficient to kindle their unfriendly passions and excite their most violent conflicts," he concludes. In a corporate environment, this manifests as factions within

---

149   The Federalist Papers : No. 10 https://avalon.law.yale.edu/18th_century/fed10.asp

organizations, competition for promotions, budgets, and other forms of recognition.

Recognizing these dynamics is crucial as you climb the organizational ladder, where power plays and distrust can become more pronounced.[150]

Practical Steps for Leaders

1. Identify Your Allies and Adversaries

- Create a detailed list differentiating your supporters from your potential critics. This exercise is critical in understanding who can influence your strategic initiatives positively or negatively. Remember, neutrality is rare; individuals either propel or obstruct your efforts.

2. Assess and Analyze

- Next to each name, note the reasons for their support or opposition and assess the potential risks or disruptions they could cause to your leadership and strategic execution. This assessment helps in formulating strategies to either strengthen these relationships or mitigate their negative impacts.

3. Strategic Relationship Management

- For each adversary, contemplate actionable steps to

---

150   Marie G. McIntyre, Secrets to Winning at Office Politics (New York: St. Martin's Griffin, 2005)

transform them into allies, or at least neutralize their opposition. This might involve addressing their concerns, finding mutual benefits, or in some cases, implementing strategies to mitigate their negative impacts.

4. Continuous Engagement and Adjustment

- Develop and maintain strategies to ensure that your allies remain supportive, and continuously work to convert adversaries where possible. This proactive approach in managing relationships is vital in maintaining a conducive environment for executing your strategies. Less friction with your colleagues means less energy expended on internal battles.

George Washington's Application of These Principles

George Washington's leadership during the American Revolutionary War provides compelling examples of these principles in action. For instance, his handling of the Conway Cabal,[151] a conspiracy aimed at removing him from command, demonstrates his adeptness at neutralizing adversaries. Washington quietly gathered support from key figures such as Thomas Jefferson and Alexander Hamilton, using his connections and their loyalty to stifle the dissent quietly and effectively, displaying Machiavelli's advice: "Never was anything great achieved without danger."

---

151   Richard Brookhiser, *George Washington on Leadership* (New York: Basic Books, 2009)

However, not all was smooth sailing. Washington's decision to trust Benedict Arnold, which resulted in Arnold's infamous betrayal, highlights the risks involved in misjudging allegiances.[152] This incident underscores the importance of continually assessing and reassessing the loyalty and intentions of those within one's inner circle. Just because someone has your back one day doesn't necessarily mean they will the next.

Understanding Power Dynamics

How you use (or don't) use power will determine the level of success you achieve within any organization. Power dynamics refers to the ways in which power is distributed and exercised within an organization. This might be a distasteful topic to some, but it's one you can't afford to be ignorant of. These dynamics influence decision-making processes, resource allocation, and the ability to drive initiatives forward. Power can be derived from various sources, including positional authority, expertise, relationships, and control over resources. Whether you're aware of them or not, they are around you every day. To ignore them is to shorten your lifespan within an organization. If you understand who holds power, and how they use it, it also determines what you can accomplish. All sales leaders must understand the distinct types of power and how they will affect your efforts. You must also know how to wield power.

Recognize that power is not static, but fluid and

---

152   Dave Richard Palmer, George Washington and Benedict Arnold: A Tale of Two Patriots (Washington, D.C.: Regnery History, 2010)

context-dependent is essential. Power dynamics can shift based on changes in organizational structure, strategic priorities, and individual relationships. Hence why you must strive to keep your finger on the pulse within your organization.

Let's examine the most common types and sources of power you will either encounter or have.[153]

Positional Power

- **Definition:** Power that stems from an individual's formal position within the organizational hierarchy.

- **Example:** A project manager in a technology firm holds positional power that allows them to assign tasks, make pivotal project decisions, and represent their team's interests in executive meetings.

- **Utilization:** Positional power should be employed to set clear expectations, establish accountability, and drive alignment with organizational goals. It is important, however, to not overly rely on this authority as it can lead to resistance and decreased collaboration. Effective leaders use their positional power to inspire confidence and commitment, rather than compel compliance. For instance, a department head might use their role to champion cross-department initiatives, ensuring that each team's contributions are recognized and valued.

---

153   John Kenneth Galbraith, *The Anatomy of Power* (Boston: Houghton Mifflin Harcourt, 1983)

Expert Power

- **Definition:** Power derived from an individual's specific expertise, skills, or knowledge that is highly valued.

- **Example:** An IT security expert in a company possesses expert power, which becomes instrumental during cyber-security crisis management or system upgrades.

- **Utilization:** Use expert power to influence decisions and gain credibility within the team. It is beneficial to encourage team members to share their specialized knowledge, fostering a culture of mutual respect and continuous learning. An engineer with deep knowledge of a recent technology might lead a series of workshops to educate their peers, thereby enhancing the team's overall skill set and contributing to more informed decision-making processes.

Relational Power

- **Definition:** Power that arises from the ability to influence others through personal connections, networks, and people skills.

- **Example:** A sales director who has built strong relationships across the product development, marketing, and customer service teams can leverage these relationships to synchronize efforts across these functional areas effectively.

- **Utilization:** Develop strong, trust-based relationships across departments. Use relational power to facilitate collaboration, mediate conflicts, and align diverse stakeholders towards common goals. For example, a team leader might organize regular inter-departmental meetings to ensure open lines of communication and foster a cooperative environment.

Resource Power

- **Definition:** Power coming from control over essential resources, such as budgets, critical information, or technology.

- **Example:** A finance manager controls the budget allocations for project funding, which positions them as a key decision-maker in prioritizing which projects receive funding based on strategic value to the organization.

- **Utilization:** Ensure resources are distributed fairly to support cross-functional initiatives. Use resource power strategically to enable and accelerate collaborative projects. For instance, allocating extra budget to a team working on a high-priority project not only facilitates the project's success but also signals trust and support for the team's capabilities.

By understanding and effectively managing these various sources of power, you can enhance your influence and effectiveness in cross-functional collaboration. Be clear on the type of power you have, the kind you need and how to best apply it. Also be clear about the type of power others have so you can determine how best to work with them.

Strategies for Managing Power Dynamics[154] [155] [156]

Now let's look into the often-tricky world of power within organizations. Below are some practical tips and tools to help you figure out who holds the power, how to build strong alliances, and how to tap into the less obvious, informal power networks that can really make things happen.

1. Assessing Power Structures

- **Key Insight**: Conduct a power audit to map out the power structures within your organization. Identify key influencers, decision-makers, and gatekeepers across departments.

- **Action**: Use tools like social network analysis to visualize power relationships and understand how information and influence flow within your organization.

2. Building Alliances and Coalitions

- **Key Insight**: Form alliances with key stakeholders to build support for cross-functional initiatives. Coalitions can enhance your ability to drive change and secure necessary resources.

---

154   Robert Greene, The 48 Laws of Power (New York: Viking Press, 1998)

155   Jeffrey Pfeffer, Managing With Power: Politics and Influence in Organizations (Boston: Harvard Business School Press, 1992)

156   Jeffrey Pfeffer, Power: Why Some People Have It and Others Don't (New York: HarperBusiness, 2010)

- **Action**: Identify potential allies who share common goals or have complementary strengths. Engage them early in the planning process to build trust and commitment.

3. Leveraging Informal Power Networks

- **Key Insight**: Informal power networks, often based on personal relationships and social interactions, can be highly influential. Recognize and tap into these networks to gain support and disseminate information.

- **Action**: Cultivate relationships with informal leaders and influencers. Attend cross-departmental meetings and social events to build connections and enhance your visibility.

4. Balancing Power and Empowerment

- **Key Insight**: Effective leaders balance the use of their own power with empowering others. Empowered teams are more engaged, innovative, and committed to achieving shared goals.

- **Action**: Delegate authority and decision-making power to team members. Provide opportunities for professional growth and encourage autonomy in executing tasks.

5. Managing Conflict Constructively

- **Key Insight**: Power dynamics can lead to conflicts, especially in cross-functional settings. Managing conflicts constructively is essential for maintaining collaboration and trust.

- **Action**: Implement conflict resolution techniques such as active listening, mediation, and collaborative problem-solving. Address conflicts promptly and transparently to prevent escalation.

Final Thoughts on Power Dynamics

Managing and utilizing power dynamics is a sophisticated skill that can significantly enhance your effectiveness as a sales leader. By understanding the sources and influences of power within your organization, you can strategically navigate power dynamics to drive cross-functional collaboration, influence decision-making, achieve strategic goals, and avoid being sabotaged by internal adversaries. This comprehensive approach to power dynamics will help you build stronger alliances, foster a collaborative culture, and lead your organization towards sustained success. And remember, power is a game that is going to be played whether you choose to participate. You're already on the playing field. You might as well play to win.

Once you have a basic understanding of power, you can now focus your attention on collaboration.

The Evolving Role of Collaboration in Sales[157]

Collaboration extends beyond internal team dynamics to encompass interactions with other departments, partners, and even clients. Effective collaboration fosters a cohesive approach where all stakeholders work towards common goals, leveraging diverse skills and perspectives to solve problems and drive innovation. This section will explore advanced collaboration techniques and technologies that can help sales leaders enhance communication, streamline processes, and create a unified, high-performing team environment.

The Interplay Between Collaboration and Leadership

Collaboration and leadership are deeply interconnected. Effective leaders foster a culture of collaboration, empowering their teams to work together seamlessly and leverage collective strengths. Conversely, collaborative environments can enhance leadership effectiveness by promoting transparency, trust, and mutual support.[158] Understanding and harnessing this interplay can significantly enhance organizational performance and drive superior sales outcomes.

Key Themes in Collaboration and Leadership

To master collaboration and leadership, you must understand the five key elements.

---

157   KPMG. (2023). Drive revenue by rethinking marketing/sales collaboration. https://kpmg.com/us/en/articles/2023/driving-revenue-marketing-sales-collaboration.html

158   Dawna Markova and Angie McArthur, Collaborative Intelligence: Thinking with People Who Think Differently (New York: Spiegel & Grau, 2015)

1. **Cross-Functional Collaboration**: The importance of breaking down silos and fostering collaboration across different departments, such as marketing, product development, and customer support.

2. **Leadership Development**: Strategies for identifying and nurturing future leaders within the sales team, ensuring a pipeline of capable leaders ready to take on greater responsibilities.

3. **Building a Collaborative Culture**: Techniques for creating an organizational culture that values and promotes collaboration at all levels.

4. **Leveraging Technology for Collaboration**: Advanced tools and platforms that facilitate seamless collaboration and communication, both within sales teams and across the organization.

5. **Emotional Intelligence in Leadership**: The role of emotional intelligence in effective leadership and collaboration, including strategies for developing empathy, self-awareness, and people skills.

Enhancing Collaboration Across Departments

Effective collaboration across departments is essential for driving innovation, improving operational efficiency, and achieving strategic goals. However, fostering such collaboration can be challenging due to differences in departmental objectives, cultures, and communication styles. The various stakeholders in your organization are ruled primarily by self-interest. This section explores advanced strategies and best practices for enhancing cross-departmental collaboration, providing you with insights to create a more cohesive and high-performing organization.

The Importance of Cross-Departmental Collaboration

Cross-departmental collaboration involves the coordinated efforts of multiple departments working towards common goals. This is obvious and self-evident, but can easily be overlooked. This collaboration is crucial for:

- **Innovation**: Combining diverse perspectives and expertise to generate creative solutions and innovative ideas.

- **Efficiency**: Streamlining processes and reducing redundancies by leveraging the strengths of different departments.

- **Customer Experience**: Providing a seamless and consistent experience by aligning efforts across all customer touchpoints.

- **Strategic Alignment**: Ensuring that all departments are aligned with the organization's overall strategic objectives.

If you think of collaboration as a metaphorical minefield you're trying to successfully traverse, it becomes easier to avoid the mines that will blow up in your face.

Challenges to Cross-Departmental Collaboration

1. Siloed Departments

- **Insight**: Departments often operate in silos, focusing solely on their own goals and processes, which can lead to misalignment and inefficiencies.

- **Solution**: Break down silos by promoting transparency, communication, and shared goals.

2. Cultural Differences

- **Insight**: Different departments may have distinct cultures, values, and working styles, leading to misunderstandings and conflicts.

- **Solution**: Foster a unified organizational culture that values diversity and collaboration. Easier said than done, but critical just the same.

3. Communication Barriers

- **Insight**: Ineffective communication channels and lack of clarity can hinder collaboration efforts.

- **Solution**: Implement effective communication tools and practices to ensure clear, consistent, and open communication.

Cross-departmental can sometimes seem as daunting as orchestrating a military invasion. But much like a well-planned military operation, the success of such collaboration hinges on your leadership, your vision, understanding the psychological makeup of the key stakeholders in your organization, and your ability to launch a series of calculated actions.

Cross collaboration with other departments ties into collaboration within your sales team. Your team needs to smoothly collaborate with each other as well as they do other departments. They go together hand in hand.

Here's how you can apply broad strategic principles to foster exceptional cross-departmental collaboration within your sales team, enhancing effectiveness and driving success.

Establishing Winning Collaborative Strategies: Clear Goals and Objectives

Start with a clear-cut strategy session, much like a high-level military briefing, where every member of your sales team understands not just the "what" and the "how," but the "why" behind each objective. Facilitate workshops that include representatives from marketing, customer support, product development, and any other department you feel need to be involved. The goal is to align departmental goals with the organization's overarching objectives, ensuring everyone is rowing in the same direction towards the same finish line.

Forming Elite Units: Cross-Functional Teams

Think of forming cross-functional teams assembling specialized squads within your sales force, where members from different departments come together for specific projects. This strategy leverages diverse expertise, such as marketing insights or technical support, to empower your sales team in unique ways. These teams function as task forces aimed at cracking complex deals or exploring new market segments, equipped with the right tools and clear roles. People from different departments will see things that you may not see or have simply overlooked. A 360-degree perspective will make everyone better at their jobs.

Arming with the Best Tools: Collaborative Technologies

Just as modern soldiers are equipped with the best technology, equip your sales team with advanced collaborative tools. Platforms like Slack, Microsoft Teams, or Salesforce ensure seamless communication and integration of workflows across departments.[159] This tech stack makes your team more agile and better prepared to respond to real-time sales challenges and opportunities, enhancing overall efficiency.

Building a United Front: Fostering a Collaborative Culture

Create an environment where every sales call or client meeting is a joint mission. Foster a culture where open communication, mutual respect, and teamwork are paramount. Encourage your team leaders to exemplify collaborative behaviors.

---

159   Phil Simon, Reimagining Collaboration: Slack, Microsoft Teams, Zoom, and the Post-Covid-19 World of Work (Hoboken: Wiley, 2021)

Lead by example. Recognize and reward efforts that show-case exceptional teamwork, particularly those that leverage cross-departmental strengths, enhancing both morale and performance.

Strategic Huddles: Regular Cross-Departmental Meetings

Hold regular strategy huddles that not only align efforts but also serve as a forum for sharing insights and challenges from the sales front. These meetings are crucial for keeping every unit informed and engaged, ensuring that the sales team's strategies and immediate goals are understood and supported by the entire organization. Encourage your sales team to foster individual relationships with other departments. You'll be pleasantly surprised what these informal relationships will yield.

Streamlining Communications: Communication Protocols

Develop clear communication protocols that dictate how information should flow between sales, marketing, technical support, and other departments. This will ensure that every-one is on the same page, which is critical in fast-paced sales environments where timing and clarity are key.

Harnessing Data: Leveraging Analytics

Utilize data analytics to track sales performance and client engagement across different touchpoints. This data will help you understand where your strategies are succeeding and where they need refinement, allowing for data-driven decision making that continuously enhances sales effectiveness.

Leadership in Action: Encouraging Leadership Support and Involvement

As a sales leader, your active support and involvement in fostering cross-departmental collaboration are crucial. Set the tone by actively participating in collaborative initiatives, communicating the value of unified efforts, and allocating resources that support these endeavors. Your leadership is essential in driving home the importance of integrated teamwork and setting a precedent for the entire organization. Set the standard and live that standard that you expect your team to aspire to. There's no room for hypocrisy here.

By implementing these strategies, you transform your sales team into a more cohesive, powerful unit that can tackle complex sales landscapes effectively, much like a well-oiled military operation. Each step leads towards creating a force that is not only adept at meeting sales targets but also excellent at advancing the company's broader strategic goals.

The Genesis of Salesforce Einstein AI and Cross-Functional Collaboration Done Right

One of the best examples of cross-functional collaboration comes from Salesforce and their creation of Einstein AI[160]. The

---

160   Salesforce Launches Next Generation of Einstein, Bringing a Conversational AI Assistant to Every CRM Application and Customer Experience https://www.salesforce.com/news/press-releases/2023/09/12/ai-einstein-news-dreamforce/?bc=HA

journey began with a vision to embed artificial intelligence directly into the Salesforce platform, thereby empowering business users with predictive analytics and automation capabilities. To turn this vision into reality, Salesforce assembled a diverse team, each bringing a specialized skill set crucial for the project's success.

The Core Teams and Their Roles

- **Data Science and AI Research**: At the technical heart of Einstein AI were the AI researchers and data scientists. Their expertise in machine learning and AI algorithms formed the foundation upon which Einstein was built. They focused on developing sophisticated models that could seamlessly process vast amounts of data and offer insightful predictions.

- **Product Management**: This team was pivotal in defining the product vision for Einstein. They identified key use cases where AI could deliver significant value and ensured that the development aligned with the real and articulated needs of Salesforce customers across various industries.

- **Software Engineering**: The engineers were tasked with integrating these AI capabilities into Salesforce's existing products. Their challenge was not just in the technical integration but also in ensuring that the new features enhanced the overall functionality without disrupting the user experience.

- **User Experience Design**: With AI being a complex technology, the user experience (UX) team had a critical role in making these AI-powered insights accessible and actionable for business users. Their designs focused on creating interfaces that were intuitive and provided meaningful interactions for users, demystifying AI in the process.

- **Sales and Customer Success**: These teams brought in invaluable insights from the field, highlighting customer pain points and preferences. Their contributions helped prioritize features during the development phase, ensuring that the final product would meet market demands effectively.

- **Marketing**: Once the capabilities of Einstein AI were fleshed out, the marketing team developed key messaging and positioning strategies. Their campaigns were designed to communicate the unique benefits of Einstein AI to B2B customers, emphasizing how it could transform their business operations.

- **Legal and Compliance**: Given the sensitivities around AI and data usage, the legal and compliance team played a crucial role in ensuring that all of Einstein's functionalities adhered to industry regulations and standards. This was vital not only for customer trust but also for the broader adoption of the platform.

The Outcome

The collaborative efforts culminated in the launch of Einstein AI in 2016. This platform quickly became a key differentiator for Salesforce, enhancing its reputation as a leader in CRM innovation. Today, Einstein powers over 80 billion AI-driven predictions daily, across Salesforce's product suite. Its success is a testament to the effectiveness of combining diverse expertise to address complex challenges and deliver solutions that resonate deeply with customer needs.

Salesforce's development of Einstein AI serves as a compelling case study in cross-functional collaboration. It highlights how bringing together varied teams, each expert in their respective fields, can lead to the creation of innovative products that not only push technological boundaries but also provide tangible business value. This example highlights the strategic advantage of collaborative diversity in developing solutions that are comprehensive, compliant, and critically aligned with market demands in the B2B sphere. And when all is said and done, the sales team benefits from such a well-done collaboration.

Final Thoughts

As a seasoned sales leader, understanding the nuances of cross-functional collaboration and leadership can significantly enhance your ability to drive strategic success. By implementing the advanced strategies discussed, you can create a more integrated, agile, and high-performing organization. Embrace the complexity and fluidity of power dynamics, leverage innovative technologies, and foster a collaborative culture that values diversity and continuous improvement. These efforts will not only enhance your team's performance but also position your organization for sustained success in an increasingly complex and competitive business environment.

General Eisenhower, D-Day, and the Perfection of Vision, Strategy and Execution[161]

In the cool, pre-dawn light of June 6, 1944, a colossal armada, the likes of which the world had never seen, drifted quietly towards the French coast of Normandy. This was D-Day, the most ambitious military invasion in history, orchestrated under the code name Operation Overlord. At its helm was General Dwight D. Eisenhower, whose task was nothing less than to oversee the liberation of Nazi-occupied Europe. The operation was a masterclass in cross-functional collaboration and leadership, themes that resonate through the corridors of history, echoing even in today's corporate boardrooms.

Imagine the complexity: thousands of ships, aircraft, and over a million troops from different nations and branches of the military, each with their unique specialties, cultures, and command structures. Eisenhower, or Ike as he was known, wasn't just a military man; he was a principal conductor of a vast human orchestra. Each element of the Allied forces, whether on sea, air, or land, had to play in perfect harmony.

The naval forces had to ferry troops across the treacherous waters of the English Channel, a logistical feat of nightmarish

---

161   Michel Paradis, The Light of Battle: Eisenhower, D-Day, and the Birth of the American Superpower (New York: HarperCollins, 2024)

proportions. Meanwhile, the air forces, flying overhead, were not just there to provide cover but also to paint a picture of the battlefield below, a canvas constantly changing with every bomb dropped and every building reduced to rubble.

On the ground, young soldiers with an average age of 26 years old, many of whom had never set foot in combat before, had to execute the plans laid out for them with precision. The beaches of Normandy—Utah, Omaha, Gold, Juno, and Sword—were not just geographical locations but vast stages set for a drama of epic proportions.

What ties this vast, sprawling effort together is leadership, the Eisenhower kind. Leadership is less about commanding and more about orchestrating. Eisenhower's leadership style was not directive but rather inclusive. He knew the art of conversation and the power of listening. With each interaction, whether with a fellow general or a low-ranking officer, Eisenhower wasn't just giving orders but fostering a sense of shared mission. He understood that for collaboration to be effective, every unit, no matter how small, had to understand not just the 'what' and the 'how' but the 'why'.

His nightly visits to the troops just before the invasion were not merely to inspect; they were to connect, to embolden, and to reassure. Here was a leader who could distill complex strategies into a language that every soldier could understand and carry as a beacon as they stormed the beaches.

As the sun rose over Normandy, the chaos of battle took over, and yet the meticulous planning; the endless rehearsals, the detailed models of the French coast, the gathering of intelligence from every conceivable source, ensured that this colossal collaboration did not collapse under its own weight. The success of D-Day was a testament to the power of unity and the importance of diverse units working towards a common goal, driven by a leadership that knew the value of trust and the importance of clear, decisive communication.

In every story of great achievement, whether on the battlefield or in the boardroom, these themes emerge time and again: the vision to see the end from the beginning, the courage to trust your team, and the wisdom to lead not from the front, not from the back, but right alongside your people. D-Day, through the lens of Eisenhower's leadership, shows us exactly that.

Conclusion

As we reach the conclusion of this book, it is essential to reflect on the transformative journey we have undertaken through the realms of vision, strategy, execution, collaboration, and leadership. The modern sales landscape is complicated, ferociously competitive, dynamic, and increasingly demanding of ethical integrity and sustainable practices. The goal of this book has been to provide you with a comprehensive guide to navigating these challenges and seizing the opportunities they present.

Vision and Strategic Leadership

Our exploration began with the foundational concepts of vision and strategic leadership. We emphasized the importance of crafting a compelling vision that aligns with your organizational goals and inspires your sales team. Effective strategic leadership involves understanding the competitive landscape, setting ambitious yet achievable goals, and continuously adapting to market changes. These elements are crucial for steering your organization toward long-term success.

Executing with Precision

Execution bridges the gap between strategy and results. We delved into the critical components of effective sales planning and execution, highlighting the importance of aligning sales plans with strategic objectives, setting realistic targets, and leveraging data for informed decision-making. Continuous monitoring and coaching ensure that sales teams stay on track and are equipped to adapt to new challenges and opportunities.

Harnessing Technology

The role of technology in enhancing sales performance cannot be overstated. From CRM systems and sales automation tools to predictive analytics and AI, modern technology provides the tools needed to optimize every aspect of the sales process. Integrating these technologies effectively can streamline operations, improve customer interactions, and drive superior results.

Collaboration and Cross-Functional Teams

Cross-functional collaboration is vital for innovation and efficiency. By breaking down silos and fostering a collaborative culture, your organization can leverage diverse expertise to solve complex problems and drive strategic initiatives. Leading cross-functional teams requires a nuanced understanding of power dynamics, effective communication, and a commitment to shared goals.

Practical Tools and Frameworks

Throughout this book, we have provided practical tools, frameworks, and case studies to help you implement the concepts discussed. From developing your strategic sales vision to building high-performing teams and fostering ethical practices, these resources are designed to equip you with actionable insights and strategies.

The Path Forward

As you move forward, remember that the journey of a sales leader is one of continuous learning and adaptation. The principles and practices outlined in this book are not static; they must evolve in response to changing market conditions, technological advancements, and emerging ethical considerations. Embrace a mindset of agility and innovation, always seeking new ways to enhance your strategies and lead your team to success.

Parting Thoughts

The role of a sales leader is multifaceted and challenging, but it is also incredibly rewarding. By integrating vision, strategy, execution, collaboration, and great leadership, you can create a high-performing sales organization that not only meets its targets but also contributes to the broader goals of continued success despite the economic environment. Your leadership can inspire trust, drive innovation, and achieve lasting impact.

Thank you for embarking on this journey through the essential elements of strategic sales leadership. May the insights and strategies shared in this book empower you to lead with vision, integrity, and excellence, driving your organization towards a future of sustained success and positive impact.

If you have questions, or need help, feel free to reach me directly at: derek@derekwjohnson.com

About the Author

Derek Wellington Johnson's background brings a unique perspective to the subjects of great sales leadership, strategic thinking, and successful execution.

With over two decades of sales leadership experience in the high-tech world, Derek is recognized as an unparalleled strategist, technology expert and a trusted advisor to C-level decision makers. His expertise has led to him being repeatedly quoted in publications such as Inc. Magazine, Investor's Business Daily, Network World Magazine, CNet News, CIO Magazine, and PC World, to name a few. He has also appeared on radio and television programs.

Derek is a military veteran, a startup veteran and a lifelong student of human nature and history. He began his career working for Brian Tracy, the renown motivational public speaker and self-development author. Derek has led sales teams for both publicly traded companies and bleeding edge startups.

Derek was an original member on the board of directors of the Fiber Broadband Association, a consortium of companies dedicated to bringing Broadband Internet to Americans everywhere. The current ubiquity of broadband today is proof of the organization's success.

He may be reached at derek@derekwjohnson.com

Endnotes

1. Fairlie, R., & Fossen, F. M. (2021, March 31). The early impacts of the COVID-19 pandemic on business sales. National Center for Biotechnology Information. https://www.ncbi.nlm.nih.gov/pmc/articles/PMC8009687/

2. Elaine Biech, The ASTD Leadership Handbook (Alexandria, VA: Association for Talent Development, 2010)

3. Ettore, M. (2020, March 13). Why Most New Executives Fail -- And Four Things Companies Can Do About It. Forbes. https://www.forbes.com/councils/forbescoachescouncil/2020/03/13/why-most-new-executives-fail-and-four-things-companies-can-do-about-it/

4. Arruda, W. (2023, February 15). Why Most New Managers Fail And How To Prevent It. Forbes. https://www.forbes.com/sites/williamarruda/2023/02/15/why-most-new-managers-fail-and-how-to-prevent-it/

5. Feser, C., Nielsen, N., & Rennie, M. (2017, August). What's missing in leadership development? McKinsey Quarterly. https://www.mckinsey.com/~/media/mckinsey/featured%20insights/leadership/whats%20missing%20in%20leadership%20development/whats-missing-in-leadership-development.pdf

6. Gurdjian, P., Halbeisen, T., & Lane, K. (2014, January 1). Why leadership-development programs fail. McKinsey Quarterly. https://www.mckinsey.com/featured-insights/leadership/why-leadership-development-programs-fail

7. Xenophon. Memorabilia. Translated by Amy L. Bonnette. Agora Editions, 2001

8. Arrian. The Landmark Arrian: The Campaigns of Alexander. Edited by James Romm, translated by Pamela Mensch, series edited by Robert B. Strassler. (New York: Anchor, 2012)

9. Peter F. Drucker, The Practice of Management (New York: Harper Business, 2006)

10. U.S. Marine Corps. Command and Control (Washington, D.C.: Department of the Navy, 2018). https://www.marines.mil/Portals/1/Publications/MCDP%206.pdf

11. Patterson, J. S. (1995). COMMANDER'S INTENT: Its Evolution in the United States Army. Washington, D.C.: U.S. Department of the Army. https://apps.dtic.mil/sti/pdfs/ADA301158.pdf

12. Alan Axelrod, Patton on Leadership: Strategic Lessons for Corporate Warfare (Englewood Cliffs, NJ: Prentice Hall, 1999)

13. David Horsager, The Trust Edge: How Top Leaders Gain Faster Results, Deeper Relationships, and a Stronger Bottom Line (New York: Free Press, 2012)

14. Kennedy, J. F. (1963, June 28). Address Before the Irish Parliament. John F. Kennedy Presidential Library and Museum. https://www.jfklibrary.org/archives/other-resources/john-f-kennedy-speeches/irish-parliament-19630628

15. Peter Drucker: Father of Modern Management, November 17, 1988 https://billmoyers.com/content/peter-drucker/

16. John F. Kennedy moon landing speech, May 25, 1961 http://earthsky.org/human-world/this-date-in-science-kennedy-speech-ignites-dreams-of-moon-landing/

17. Jim Collins and Jerry I. Porras, Built to Last: Successful Habits of Visionary Companies (New York: HarperBusiness, 1994)

18. Andrew Chaikin, A Man on the Moon: The Voyages of the Apollo Astronauts, Illustrated ed. (New York: Penguin Books, 2007

19. George S. Patton, War As I Knew It, edited by Paul D. Harkins (New York: Houghton Mifflin Harcourt, 1995)

20. Bernie Smith, KPI Checklists (Practical guide to implementing KPIs and performance measurement, Metric Press, 2016).

21. Belinda Waldock, Being Agile in Business: Discover Faster, Smarter, Leaner Ways to Work (Pearson, 2015)

22. John Adair, Strategic Leadership: How to Think and Plan Strategically and Provide Direction. The John Adair Leadership Library (Philadelphia, PA: Kogan Page, 2010)

23. Tichy, N., & Charan, R. (1989, September-October). Speed, Simplicity, Self-Confidence: An Interview with Jack Welch. Harvard Business Review. Updated March 2, 2020. https://hbr.org/1989/09/speed-simplicity-self-confidence-an-interview-with-jack-welch

24. Chip Heath and Dan Heath, Made to Stick: Why Some Ideas Survive and Others Die (New York: Random House, 2007).

25. Cardenas, B. (2024, January 30). Transformative Leadership: Unveiling Satya Nadella's Three Revolutionary Strategies at Microsoft. Leadership Worth Following. https://worthyleadership.com/transformative-leadership-unveiling-satya-nadellas-three-revolutionary-strategies-at-microsoft/

26. Psico-smart Editorial Team. (2024, August 28). What role does employee feedback play in enhancing workplace satisfaction? Psico-smart. https://psico-smart.com/en/blogs/blog-what-role-does-employee-feedback-play-in-enhancing-workplace-satisfaction-151993

27. Joseph Grenny, Kerry Patterson, Ron McMillan, and Al Switzler, Crucial Conversations: Tools for Talking When Stakes are High, 3rd ed. (New York: McGraw-Hill Education, 2021)

28. Barb Grant, Change Management that Sticks: A Practical, People-centered Approach, for High Buy-in, and Meaningful Results (New Zealand: Barb Grant, 2023)

29. Jay Sullivan, Simply Said: Communicating Better at Work and Beyond (Hoboken, NJ: John Wiley & Sons, 2016)

30. Stephen R. Covey, The 7 Habits of Highly Effective People: Powerful Lessons in Personal Change (New York: Free Press, 1989)

31. James C. Humes, Speak Like Churchill, Stand Like Lincoln: 21 Powerful Secrets of History's Greatest Speakers (New York: Three Rivers Press, 2002)

32. Julius Caesar, The Gallic War: Seven Commentaries on The Gallic War with an Eighth Commentary by Aulus Hirtius, 1st ed., Oxford World's Classics (Oxford: Oxford University Press, 2008)

33. David H. Hackworth and Julie Sherman, About Face: The Odyssey of an American Warrior (New York: Simon & Schuster, 1989)

34. Willie Pietersen, Strategic Learning: How to Be Smarter Than Your Competition and Turn Key Insights into Competitive Advantage, Illustrated ed. (Hoboken, NJ: John Wiley & Sons, 2010

35. Sun Tzu, The Art of War, translated by Ralph D. Sawyer (New York: Barnes & Noble Books, 1994)

36. Nassim Nicholas Taleb, The Black Swan: The Impact of the Highly Improbable (New York: Random House, 2008

37. Marrs, S. (2023, March 14). Your Company's Quota Attainment Is Probably Around 50%, And That's Not A Bad Thing. Forrester Blog. https://www.forrester.com/blogs/your-companys-quota-attainment-is-probably-around-50-and-thats-not-a-bad-thing/

38. Glickel, H. (n.d.). 3 Reasons It May Just Be Harder Than Ever To Hire. Sales Recruiters Inc. Retrieved from https://www.salesrecruiters.com/blog-3-reasons-it-may-just-be-harder-than-ever-to-hire-9.php

39. Orlob, C. (2018, January 29). The average VP of Sales tenure has shrunk — here's why. Gong. io. https://www.gong.io/blog/vp-sales-average-tenure/

40. Michael E. Porter, "What Is Strategy?" Harvard Business Review 74, no. 6 (1996): 61-78.

41. Richard Rumelt, Good Strategy Bad Strategy: The Difference and Why It Matters (New York: Crown Business, 2011)

42. Brad Jeavons, Agile Sales: Delivering Customer Journeys of Value and Delight, 1st ed. (New York, Routledge, 2020)

43. Richardson, M. (2020, January 8). Sales Metrics: When Are You Measuring Too Much? https://brooksgroup.com/sales-training-blog/sales-metrics-are-you-measuring-too-much/

44. William J. Brown, Hays W. McCormick III, and Scott W. Thomas, AntiPatterns in Project Management (New York: Wiley, 2000)

45. Zuo Tradition / Zuozhuan: Commentary on the "Spring and Autumn Annals". Edited by Andrew Plaks, translated by Stephen Durrant, Wai-yee Li, and David Schaberg, University of Washington Press, 2016

46. Steve W. Martin, Sales Strategy Playbook: The Ultimate Reference Guide to Solve Your Toughest Sales Challenges (California: Tilis Publishers, 2018)

47. Bartolacci, G. (2018, December 11). HubSpot's Growth Story: Mastering SaaS Marketing Strategy. New Breed. https://www.newbreedrevenue.com/blog/the-evolution-of-hubspot-and-how-you-can-mimic-their-saas-marketing-strategy

48. Pereira, D. (2024, August 22). Cisco Business Model. Business Model Analyst. https://businessmodelanalyst.com/cisco-business-model/

49. Shah, H. (n.d.). How Salesforce Built a $13 Billion Empire from a CRM. Nira. Retrieved from https://nira.com/salesforce-history/

50. Patrick Hoverstadt and Lucy Loh, Patterns of Strategy, 1st ed. (Abingdon, UK: Routledge, 2017)

51. Gibson, K. (2024, May 8). Digital Platforms: What They Are & How They Create Value. Harvard Business School Online. https://online.hbs.edu/blog/post/what-is-a-digital-platform

52. Paul R. Howe, Leadership and Training for the Fight: Using Special Operations Principles to Succeed in Law Enforcement, Business, and War (New York: Skyhorse Publishing, 2011)

53. Robert B. Cialdini, Influence, New and Expanded: The Psychology of Persuasion (New York: Harper Business, 2021)

54. W. Chan Kim and Renée Mauborgne, Blue Ocean Strategy: How to Create Uncontested Market Space and Make the Competition Irrelevant (Boston: Harvard Business School Press, 2005)

55. Al Ries and Jack Trout, Positioning: The Battle for Your Mind, 20th Anniversary ed. (New York: McGraw Hill, 2003)

56. Andrew Roberts, Napoleon: A Life, Illustrated ed. (New York: Penguin Books, 2015)

57. Salesforce. (2022). New Research Reveals Sales Reps Need a Productivity Overhaul – Spend Less than 30% Of Their Time Actually Selling. https://www.salesforce.com/news/stories/sales-research-2023/

58. Chandler, A. D., Jr. (2023). Strategy and structure: Chapters in the history of the industrial enterprise. Sothis Press

59. Mintzberg, H. (1978). Patterns in Strategy Formation. Management Science, 24(9), 934-948

60. Jim Collins, Good to Great: Why Some Companies Make the Leap...And Others Don't (New York: Harper Business, 2001)

61. Ben Lamorte, The OKRs Field Book: A Step-by-Step Guide for Objectives and Key Results Coaches (Wiley, 2022)

62. Freshworks. (n.d.). Key Ingredient of Successful Companies: Sales Team Happiness. Retrieved from https://www.freshworks.com/crm/sales/sales-team-happiness/

63. Marcel Planellas and Anna Muni, Strategic Decisions: The 30 Most Useful Models (New York: Cambridge University Press, 2019)

64. Martin Reeves, Knut Haanaes, and Janmejaya Sinha, Your Strategy Needs a Strategy: How to Choose and Execute the Right Approach (Boston: Harvard Business Review Press, 2015)

65. Robert M. Grant, Contemporary Strategy Analysis, 11th ed. (Hoboken, NJ: Wiley, 2022)

66. Carucci, R. (2017, November 13). Executives Fail to Execute Strategy Because They're Too Internally Focused. Harvard Business Review. https://hbr.org/2017/11/executives-fail-to-execute-strategy-because-theyre-too-internally-focused

67. Richard A. Gabriel, Scipio Africanus: Rome's Greatest General, Illustrated ed. (Washington, D.C.: Potomac Books, 2008)

68. The Value of Keeping the Right Customers https://hbr.org/2014/10/the-value-of-keeping-the-right-customers

69. Customer Acquisition Vs.Retention Costs – Statistics And Trends https://www.invespcro.com/blog/customer-acquisition-retention/

70. Loyalty Rules https://www.bain.com/contentassets/29f74ec417fa4e36a1d7d7e7479badc5/loyalty_rules_chapter_one.pdf

71. Small Business Owners Shift Investment from Customer Acquisition to Customer Engagement https://www.bia.com/press-releases/small-business-owners-shift-investment-from-customer-acquisition-to-customer-engagement-new-report-by-manta-and-bia-kelsey/

72. Referral Rate https://www.madx.digital/glossary/referral-rate

73. Word of Mouth Marketing: Stats and Trends for 2023 https://www.lxahub.com/stories/word-of-mouth-marketing-stats-and-trends-for-2023

74. Bev Burgess and Dave Munn, A Practitioner's Guide to Account-Based Marketing: Accelerating Growth in Strategic Accounts (London: Kogan Page, 2021)

75. Hero: The Life and Legend of Lawrence of Arabia, Harper Perennial, November 1, 2011

76. It's January 7: Are You Sticking to Your New Year's Resolution? https://knowledge.wharton.upenn.edu/article/its-january-7-are-you-sticking-to-your-new-years-resolution/

77. Change or Die https://www.fastcompany.com/52717/change-or-die

78. The average VP of Sales tenure has shrunk — here's why https://www.gong.io/blog/vp-sales-average-tenure/

79. 4 Common Reasons Strategies Fail https://hbr.org/2022/06/4-common-reasons-strategies-fail#

80. Why 67 Percent of Strategic Plans Fail https://www.inc.com/tanya-prive/why-67-percent-of-strategic-plans-fail.html#:

81. Creating the Office of Strategy Management https://hbswk.hbs.edu/item/creating-the-office-of-strategy-management#

82. 70% of Strategies Fail https://www.linkedin.com/pulse/70-strategies-fail-set-up-strategic-management-office-david-tang/

83. 90 Percent of Organizations Fail to Execute Their Strategies Successfully https://www.intellibridge.us/90-percent-of-organizations-fail-to-execute-their-strategies-successfully/

84. Richard Koch, The 80/20 Principle: The Secret to Achieving More with Less (New York: Currency, 1999)

85. Buck, R. (n.d.). Improving your middle performers is the secret to improving your top & bottom line. Act!. Retrieved from https://www.act.com/blog/improving-your-middle-performers-is-the-secret-to-improving-your-top-bottom-line/

86. Cornerstone OnDemand. (n.d.). Employees Stuck in the Middle? How to Transform the Average Joe into an Everyday Superhero. Retrieved from https://www.dresserassociates.com/pdf/whitepapers/Employees-Stuck-in-the-Middle-How-to-Transform-the-Average-Joe-into-an-Everyday-Superhero.pdf

87. Sindell, T., & Sindell, M. (2013, September 1). Maximizing the Middle: Why Focusing Your Sales Talent Investment on Mid-Level Performers Will Exponentially Increase Sales Performance. Skyline Group. https://skylineg.com/resources/blog/maximizing-the-middle-why-focusing-your-sales-talent-investment-on-mid-level-performers-will-exponentially-increase-sales-performance

88. Phil Jackson and Hugh Delehanty, Eleven Rings: The Soul of Success, Illustrated ed. (New York: Penguin Books, 2014)

89. Xenophon, The Education of Cyrus, trans. Wayne Ambler (Ithaca, NY: Cornell University Press, 2001)

90. Marc Benioff and Carlye Adler, Behind the Cloud: The Untold Story of How Salesforce.com Went from Idea to Billion-Dollar Company—and Revolutionized an Industry, 1st ed. (San Francisco: Jossey-Bass, 2009)

91. Mike Weinberg, Sales Management. Simplified.: The Straight Truth About Getting Exceptional Results from Your Sales Team (New York: AMACOM, 2015)

92. Laszlo Bock, Work Rules!: Insights from Inside Google That Will Transform How You Live and Lead, Illustrated ed. (New York: Twelve, 2015)

93. Schmidt, F. L., & Hunter, J. E. (1998). The Validity and Utility of Selection Methods in Personnel Psychology: Practical and Theoretical Implications of 85 Years of Research Findings. Psychological Bulletin, 124(2), 262-274. https://www.researchgate.net/publication/283803351_The_Validity_and_Utility_of_Selection_Methods_in_Personnel_Psychology_Practical_and_Theoretical_Implications_of_85_Years_of_Research_Findings

94. Lucas, S. (2015, September 22). Ernst & Young Stopped Requiring Degrees. Should You? Inc. Magazine. https://www.inc.com/suzanne-lucas/ernst-amp-young-stopped-requiring-degrees-should-you.html

95. Trish Bertuzzi, The Sales Development Playbook: Build Repeatable Pipeline and Accelerate Growth with Inside Sales (Boston: The Bridge Group, 2016)

96. Daniel Coyle, The Culture Code: The Secrets of Highly Successful Groups (New York: Bantam Books, 2018)

97. The Alternative Board. (2016, November 2). How to Take an Ethical Approach to Poaching Employees. https://www.thealternativeboard.com/blog/taking-an-ethical-approach-to-poaching-employees

98. Ericsson, K. A., Prietula, M. J., & Cokely, E. T. (2007, July–August). The Making of an Expert. Harvard Business Review. https://hbr.org/2007/07/the-making-of-an-expert

99. 6sense. (2024, January 8). Don't Call Us, We'll Call You: What Research Says About When B2B Buyers Reach Out to Sellers. https://6sense.com/blog/dont-call-us-well-call-you-what-research-says-about-when-b2b-buyers-reach-out-to-sellers/

100. Steve W. Martin, Sales Strategy Playbook: The Ultimate Reference Guide to Solve Your Toughest Sales Challenges (Laguna Hills, CA: Tilis Publishers, 2018)

101. Robert S. Kaplan and David P. Norton, The Execution Premium: Linking Strategy to Operations for Competitive Advantage (Boston: Harvard Business Press, 2008)

102. Jason Jordan and Michelle Vazzana, Cracking the Sales Management Code: The Secrets to Measuring and Managing Sales Performance (New York: McGraw-Hill, 2011)

103. Eric Ries, The Lean Startup: How Today's Entrepreneurs Use Continuous Innovation to Create Radically Successful Businesses (New York: Crown Business, 2011)

104. Trent Hone, Mastering the Art of Command: Admiral Chester W. Nimitz and Victory in the Pacific (Annapolis, MD: Naval Institute Press, 2022)

105. Horatio Alger Association. (2023). Frederic B. Luddy: Horatio Alger Award Recipient, Class of 2023. Retrieved from https://horatioalger.org/members/detail/frederic-b-luddy/

106. Gordon, J. (2024, March 3). Fred Luddy's Remarkable Comeback. Just Go Grind. https://www.justgogrind.com/p/fred-luddy

107. GuideVision. (n.d.). What is ServiceNow's strategy for 2021? Retrieved from https://www.guidevision.eu/insights/what-is-servicenow%27s-strategy-for-2021

108. Willem. (2023, December 29). ServiceNow Gen AI: An Introduction. ServiceNow. https://www.servicenow.com/community/intelligence-ml-articles/servicenow-gen-ai-an-introduction/ta-p/2776240

109. Fugere, T. (2023, November 13). Navigating the Path to ServiceNow Excellence in 2024. Thirdera. https://www.thirdera.com/insights/navigating-the-path-to-servicenow-excellence-in-2024

110. Thomas, S. (2023, April 6). Inside ServiceNow's Award Winning Employee Culture. ERP Today. https://erp.today/inside-servicenows-award-winning-employee-culture/

111. Barker, L. (2020, August 17). Driving culture and motivating our people in challenging times. ServiceNow. https://www.servicenow.com/blogs/2020/corporate-culture

112. ServiceNow. (n.d.). Baseline and track performance, usage KPIs, and metrics. Retrieved from https://www.servicenow.com/content/dam/servicenow-assets/public/en-us/doc-type/success/playbook/performance-kpi-metrics-guide.pdf

113. Petrone, P. (2023, May 2). How B2B Sales Has Changed Over the Last 20 Years – And How to Best Respond. LinkedIn. https://www.linkedin.com/business/sales/blog/strategy/how-b2b-sales-has-changed-in-the-past-20-years

114. The Dock Team. (2023, August 29). The B2B buyer journey has changed. Have you? Updated June 26, 2024. Dock. https://www.dock.us/library/b2b-buyer-journey

115. Contentserv. (n.d.). How B2B commerce has changed in the last 20 years. Retrieved from https://www.contentserv.com/infographics/infographic-how-b2b-commerce-has-changed-in-the-last-20-years

116. Lofthouse, G. (n.d.). The customer journey: How has B2B buying changed? Financial Times. Retrieved from https://longitude.ft.com/the-customer-journey-how-has-b2b-buying-changed-gareth-lofthouse/

117. Davidson, M. (2023, July 10). 3 Ways B2B Buying Behavior Has Changed—Forever. Allego. https://www.allego.com/blog/how-b2b-buying-behavior-has-changed-forever/

118. Tobias, G., Riley, C., Giblin, C., & Gregory-Hosler, B. (2023, August 22). Sellers Are Overwhelmed by New Technology. Harvard Business Review. https://hbr.org/2023/08/new-technology-is-overwhelming-sales-teams

119. Connaughton, B. (2023, October 15). 12 Best Sales Productivity Tools to Empower Your Sales Team. Qwilr. https://qwilr.com/blog/sales-productivity-tools/

120. UserGems. (n.d.). 13 of the best sales tools we recommend for sales reps in 2022. Retrieved from https://www.usergems.com/blog/sales-tools

121. Korn Ferry. (n.d.). How does sales technology improve sales productivity? Retrieved from https://www.kornferry.com/insights/featured-topics/sales-transformation/how-does-sales-technology-improve-sales-productivity

122. Ross, K. (2024, August 24). The future of sales: How technology is revolutionizing sales performance management. AZ Big Media. https://azbigmedia.com/business/the-future-of-sales-how-technology-is-revolutionizing-sales-performance-management/

123. Impact. (2022, August 25). 5 Innovative Technologies That Can Actually Improve Sales Performance. https://www.impactmybiz.com/blog/how-to-improve-sales-performance-with-technology/

124. Swenson, D. (2024, January 25). Professor's research explores the impact of technology on sales team interactions with clients. Elon University News. https://www.elon.edu/u/news/2024/01/25/professors-research-explores-the-impact-of-technology-on-sales-team-interactions-with-clients/

125. Sasson, M. (2024, May 22). How to Build the Perfect Sales Tech Stack for 2024. Walnut. https://www.walnut.io/blog/sales-tips/sales-tech-stack/

126. Gervet, E. (n.d.). The Future of B2B Sales. Kearney. Retrieved from https://www.kearney.com/documents/291362523/291368496/The%2Bfuture%2Bof%2BB2B%2Bsales%2B%281%29.pdf/90f77854-6899-dedb-84d1-12b4aa7c8147

127. Draup. (2023, November 14). Future of B2B Sales: 8 High-Impact Trends to Watch For in 2024. https://draup.com/sales/blog/future-of-b2b-sales-8-high-impact-trends-to-watch-for-in-2024/

128. McKevitt, J., & Burt, A. (2017, March 29). Salesforce's Einstein AI wants to count your bottles of Coca-Cola. Supply Chain Dive. https://www.supplychaindive.com/news/einstein-artificial-intelligence-salesforce-ibm-watson-coca-cola-inventory-management/439201/

129. Siemens. (2024, June 10). 5 ways industrial AR transforms work. Siemens Blog. https://blogs.sw.siemens.com/teamcenter/industrial-ar-transforms-work/

130. Cat Simulators https://catsimulators.com/

131. Jenkinson, G. (2022, May 6). Blockchain technology to power De Beers' diamond production. Cointelegraph. https://cointelegraph.com/news/blockchain-technology-to-power-de-beers-diamond-production

132. RTInsights Team. (2016, October 11). How Rolls-Royce Maintains Jet Engines With the IoT. RTInsights. https://www.rtinsights.com/rolls-royce-jet-engine-maintenance-iot/

133. Avaus. (n.d.). Sales in 2025 – The Future of B2B Sales is all About Data and Hyper Automation. Retrieved from https://www.avaus.com/blog/sales-in-2025-the-future-of-b2b-sales-is-all-about-data-and-hyperautomation/

134. Shkurina, E. (2023, April 20). 27 Top HubSpot Integrations for Marketing, Sales, and RevOps. New Breed. https://www.newbreedrevenue.com/blog/5-hubspot-integrations-you-should-be-using

135. Accenture. (2023, July 26). Strategy at the Pace of Technology: Reinventing Business Strategy to Harness Technology Acceleration. https://www.accenture.com/us-en/insights/strategy/strategy-pace-technology

136. Nasstar. (n.d.). The Benefits Of A Defined Technology Strategy. Retrieved from https://www.nasstar.com/hub/blog/benefits-defined-technology-strategy

137. OSIbeyond. (2023, June 8). Technology Strategy 101. https://www.osibeyond.com/blog/technology-strategy-101/

138. Sinclair McKay, The Secret Life of Bletchley Park: The WWII Codebreaking Centre and the Men and Women Who Worked There (London: Aurum Press, 2011)

139. John T. Mentzer, Sales Forecasting Management: A Demand Management Approach, 2nd ed. (Thousand Oaks, CA: Sage Publications, 2001)

140. Cameron, C. (2024, March 21). Sales Forecasting Process - Step-by-Step Guide. BoostUp. https://www.boostup.ai/blog/sales-forecasting-process

141. Frost, A. (n.d.). The Ultimate Guide to Sales Forecasting From HubSpot's Senior Director of Global Growth. HubSpot. Retrieved from https://blog.hubspot.com/sales/sales-forecasting

142. Bernard Marr, Key Performance Indicators (KPI): The 75 Measures Every Manager Needs to Know, 1st ed. (Harlow, England: Financial Times/Prentice Hall, 2012)

143. Sallie Sherman, Joseph Sperry, and Samuel Reese, The Seven Keys to Managing Strategic Accounts, 1st ed. (New York: McGraw-Hill Education, 2003).

144. Michelle Vazzana and Jason Jordan, Crushing Quota: Proven Sales Coaching Tactics for Breakthrough Performance (New York: McGraw-Hill Education, 2018)

145. Haensch, L. (2020, November 2). What is PACTT Framework and Why It Beats BANT. Pathmonk. https://pathmonk.com/what-is-pactt-framework-and-why-it-beats-bant/

146. Roszak, C. (2021). The isolation of selling: Marketing researchers analyze social isolation and job performance. Kansas State University. https://www.k-state.edu/seek/fall-2021/marketing-researchers-analyze-social-isolation/

147. Glenn M. Parker, Cross Functional Teams: Working with Allies, Enemies, and Other Strangers (San Francisco: Jossey-Bass, 1994)

148. Allison M. Vaillancourt, The Organizational Politics Playbook: 50 Strategies to Navigate Power Dynamics at Work (New York: McGraw-Hill Education, 2021)

149. The Federalist Papers : No. 10 https://avalon.law.yale.edu/18th_century/fed10.asp

150. Marie G. McIntyre, Secrets to Winning at Office Politics (New York: St. Martin's Griffin, 2005)

151. Richard Brookhiser, *George Washington on Leadership* (New York: Basic Books, 2009)

152. Dave Richard Palmer, George Washington and Benedict Arnold: A Tale of Two Patriots (Washington, D.C.: Regnery History, 2010)

153. John Kenneth Galbraith, *The Anatomy of Power* (Boston: Houghton Mifflin Harcourt, 1983)

154. Robert Greene, The 48 Laws of Power (New York: Viking Press, 1998)

155. Jeffrey Pfeffer, Managing With Power: Politics and Influence in Organizations (Boston: Harvard Business School Press, 1992)

156. Jeffrey Pfeffer, Power: Why Some People Have It and Others Don't (New York: HarperBusiness, 2010)

157. KPMG. (2023). Drive revenue by rethinking marketing/sales collaboration. https://kpmg.com/us/en/articles/2023/driving-revenue-marketing-sales-collaboration.html

158. Dawna Markova and Angie McArthur, Collaborative Intelligence: Thinking with People Who Think Differently (New York: Spiegel & Grau, 2015)

159. Phil Simon, Reimagining Collaboration: Slack, Microsoft Teams, Zoom, and the Post-Covid-19 World of Work (Hoboken: Wiley, 2021)

160. Salesforce Launches Next Generation of Einstein, Bringing a Conversational AI Assistant to Every CRM Application and Customer Experience https://www.salesforce.com/news/press-releases/2023/09/12/ai-einstein-news-dreamforce/?bc=HA

161. Michel Paradis, The Light of Battle: Eisenhower, D-Day, and the Birth of the American Superpower (New York: HarperCollins, 2024)

Index

www.ingramcontent.com/pod-product-compliance
Lightning Source LLC
Chambersburg PA
CBHW060113200326
41518CB00008B/818